40⁰⁰

Black Prisoner of War

Black Prisoner of War

A Conscientious Objector's Vietnam Memoir

James A. Daly and Lee Bergman

Introduction by Jeff Loeb

University Press of Kansas

Originally published in 1975 by The Bobbs-Merrill Company as *A Hero's Welcome*.

Published by the University Press of Kansas (Lawrence, Kansas 66049), which was organized by the Kansas Board of Regents and is operated and funded by Emporia State University, Fort Hays State University, Kansas State University, Pittsburg State University, the University of Kansas, and Wichita State University

Library of Congress Cataloging-in-Publication Data

Daly, James A.
    Black prisoner of war : a conscientious objector's Vietnam memoir / James A. Daly and Lee Bergman.
        p. cm. — (Modern war studies)
    Originally published: A hero's welcome. Indianapolis : Bobbs-Merrill, 1975.
        ISBN 0-7006-1059-6 (cloth : alk. paper)—ISBN 0-7006-1060-X (pbk. : alk. paper)
    1. Vietnamese Conflict, 1961–1975—Conscientious objectors.
    2. Vietnamese Conflict, 1961–1975—Prisoners and prisons, North Vietnamese.   3. Vietnamese Conflict, 1961–1975—Afro-Americans.
    4. Vietnamese Conflict, 1961–1975—Personal narratives, American.
    5. Daly, James A.   I. Bergman, Lee.   II. Daly, James A. Hero's welcome.
    III. Title.   IV. Series.
    DS559.8.C63 D34 2000
    959.704'31—dc21   00-040414

British Library Cataloguing in Publication Data is available.

Printed in the United States of America

10 9 8 7 6 5 4 3 2 1

The paper used in this publication meets the minimum requirements of the American National Standard for Permanence of Paper for Printed Library Materials Z39.48–1984.

Contents

Introduction
Jeff Loeb

James Daly's POW memoir was first published (as *A Hero's Welcome: The Conscience of Sergeant James Daly versus the United States Army*) in 1975, the very bottom of a grim, gray decade, when the culturally encapsulated idea of the Vietnam War was already being transmuted into the term "post-Vietnam."[1] With gas lines and Nixon *agonistes* in our past, albeit a very recent one, as a country we were beginning our slow stagger through burgeoning unemployment, double-digit inflation, the Iran hostage crisis, and disco. By the time this desperate decade ended, America would be forever changed. Ronald Reagan would have occurred, for better or worse, things would hereafter be identified by the term "postmodern," and people would be using phrases like "Greed Is Good" and "Just Say No" and expect to be taken seriously.

In the decade and a half between the publication of this memoir and the point where Reagan's protégé, George Bush, sat behind his desk in the White House and crowed, "We've kicked the Vietnam syndrome," the prevailing story of this war went through several versions. The most vicious and unremittingly paranoid were the *Rambo* series and their spawn, which saw a few brave souls returning to Southeast Asia to rescue POWs supposedly left there to molder until eternity, for no apparent reason. The common thread, beginning with the mid-seventies spate of POW narratives that stressed courage and self-sacrifice in the face of overwhelming odds (of which *Black Prisoner of War* was *not* one) and continuing through Oliver Stone's *Platoon* and *Born on the Fourth of July,* was an uneasy mixture of veteran victimization and cultural conspiracy best expressed as something like, We failed because of [pick one]: (a) poor leadership, (b) cowardly politics, (c) a hostile liberal press, (d) all of the above.

It was thus overwhelmingly likely, from these versions, for people to see the war as having been something of a noble cause gone wrong (that is, if one ignored Gustav Hasford's and Stanley Kubrick's view of the war as absurd travesty in *The Short-Timers* and *Full Metal Jacket,* respectively, and most audiences did).[2] In very few places—perhaps only in certain novels, like Tim O'Brien's *Going after Cacciato,* for instance—was it possible in the stories received and accepted into popular culture to find the version in which there was anything other than cowardice and self-interest in opposing the war.[3]

The heroes in this emerging, post-Reagan master narrative of Vietnam were ones who could in some way ideologically affirm the rearmament of America that has so far seen its fullest flowering in the Gulf War. These heroes were, of course, the POWs—at once, in the view that came to prevail, the practitioners of untold acts of courage and, at the same time, the consummate victims of the failure of American will. This was a mold into which James Daly's story most decidedly did not fit; the emerging national narrative, fueled by a newly ascendant right flexing its ideological muscles, simply had no room for a black religious conscientious objector who nevertheless went to Vietnam, was captured and spent five years as a POW, and then renounced the U.S. position in various ways. In the transition from Rambo to *Platoon* to John McCain, the story of James Daly dropped through the cracks, and the book failed.

Yet this memoir is, in my estimation, one of the most significant books to have come out of what we now euphemistically call the Vietnam experience. Not only is it one of the very few texts to have been published by an African American participant in the war but it manages to position itself clearly astride many of the important cultural and ideological fault lines that divided this country then and now, including those of race, resistance to the war, collaboration with the enemy, the POW/MIA question, and the relationship between personal belief and public duty. In addition—and this is as important as the thematic matters—it is simply a great story, heroic in its way, though Daly had certainly meant that word to be viewed ironically in his title, and one that enriches our understanding of one of America's most divisive periods. Most importantly, it demands our attention not as a reductive or simplified story—a la the "works" of the culture mongers who would sum up our knowledge of an entire era into a two-and-a-half hour film—but as one that adds complexity and fosters more questions rather than fewer.

The importance of Daly's story resides in part in the fact that it is a unique social, cultural, and political document of the war. No other piece of literature—and I think the book needs to be regarded as literature along with other significant memoirs such as Tim O'Brien's *If I Die in a Combat Zone* (New York: Delacorte, 1973), Philip Caputo's *A Rumor of War* (New York: Ballantine, 1978), Michael Herr's *Dispatches* (New York: Avon, 1978), and Lewis Puller's *Fortunate Son* (New York: Bantam, 1991)—visits the theme of individual conscience quite so tellingly; nor do any, save memoirs like John Balaban's *Remembering Heaven's Face* (New York: Touchstone, 1991) and Tobias Wolff's *In Pharaoh's Army* (New York: Knopf, 1992) or the novels and stories of Robert Olen Butler, so effectively put human faces on the Vietnamese.[4] In addition, though unique and somewhat idiosyncratic, it is an integral component of the total black experience in Vietnam. In many ways it calls into question some beliefs about African American roles in the war and in America. I further feel that the book clamors for a niche in the pantheon of significant African American texts of this century, first, because it has attributes of the spiritual autobiography that black literature is rich with, and, second, because it explores the limits of both accommodation and resistance in a racially volatile era. In addition, *Black Prisoner of War* reveals an otherwise untold story about conditions for prisoners in South Vietnam, in the process shedding light on accounts by Daly's fellow prisoners such as Frank Anton and Robert Garwood. Finally, the book demonstrates how the definition of collaboration has been altered: Behavior that was previously defined in rigid terms as traitorous no longer was, not because the nature of captivity had changed—Andersonville and Bataan were far worse than Plantation Gardens or the Hanoi Hilton—but because we had changed, and Vietnam had caused this change in us.

Before continuing, I need to say a word about James Daly himself. It should be noted that *Black Prisoner of War,* for many of the reasons mentioned in the previous section, is a controversial book, as Daly was a controversial figure, both among his fellow captives and in the United States he returned to in 1973. Though later I will discuss him and the circumstances in which he wrote the book, as well as how I found him, readers need to know that he died at age 52 on December 13, 1998, at his home in Willingboro, New Jersey. He remained committed until the end to the dictates of his conscience and was enthusiastic about the possibility of his story's being reintroduced to a new generation of readers, not only because it had personal meaning for him but also because he felt his stance had in many ways been vindicated by events.

As might be discerned from the information above, this is the story of a religious conscientious objector, one who, despite being reared in one of America's worst ghettos, enjoys a warm and nurturing family life and aspires to a ministerial position in the Jehovah's Witnesses. Despite his views, when he gets his draft notice he is told that he does not qualify for a religious exemption. When he naively seeks counsel from, of all people, an Army recruiter (who, though black himself, proves to be unscrupulous), Daly finds himself duped into volunteering in order, he is led to believe, to select a cook's billet instead of being routed directly into the infantry, as were the majority of African American draftees.

With the help of his mother, Daly sees his mistake even before he reports for service. Once in, he attempts right away to seek separation on religious grounds. He fails, repeatedly, and eventually is sent to Vietnam. There, he first refuses to carry a weapon and, when finally forced to, will not load it. Incredibly, his commander still sends him on patrols, even though Daly has made clear his vow never to load or, of course, fire his rifle. Eventually, during a fire fight in the northern highlands, told in harrowing detail, he is wounded and captured by units of the North Vietnamese Army. Along with other prisoners, he is turned over to the local Viet Cong and spends the next three years in the South, being shunted from camp to camp as a prisoner, in incredibly deprived circumstances.

While a prisoner in the South, despite constant political indoctrination, he refuses to sign any documents stating his opposition to the war. Later, when he and the other prisoners, those who remain alive, are taken to the North via the Ho Chi Minh Trail, he relents and does so, even going so far as to join the so-called Peace

Committee, a group of POW "antiwar activists," as their detractors call them. As a result, when the POWs are released and returned to the United States in 1973, Daly is inexplicably charged with treason by the ranking member of the POW contingent, Air Force Colonel Ted Guy. The charges are found to be without merit, but they sting Daly, who has, throughout his ordeal, considered himself a loyal American simply being true to the dictates of his individual conscience.

Such a thumbnail sketch does not, however, do justice to the intricacies of the story, its style, or, most especially, the issues raised by it. Throughout, Daly shows himself to be a person who acts within the framework of a moral code, although not one so rigid that he does not subject it to intense scrutiny, nor one exclusively formed by the dogma of the Jehovah's Witnesses, although their belief in nonviolence is one of its bases. Unlike his fellow black captive Norman McDaniel, who also has written a memoir, *Yet Another Voice,* he rarely calls on God to sustain him; faith in some sort of divine providence, while certainly integral to Daly's morale throughout his ordeal, is nevertheless secondary to more human-centered ethics such as how one treats other people.[5] Ultimately, Daly's is a personal code, somewhat pragmatic and with tenets taken from a variety of sources, but one against which he tests his every decision. It is one capable of sustaining him in the harshest of circumstances, whether the challenges to it are posed by his Vietnamese captors or the U.S. Army (which in some ways provides the more severe test). In fact, *Black Prisoner of War* is in many ways as much the story of Daly's code as that of the captivity he endures. Read this way, the book may thus be seen as a moral history of his life and times, as well as a Vietnam survivor narrative.

From his opening chapters, in which he reveals his incredible naiveté at consulting an Army recruiter about the intricacies of the draft, through his persistent though fruitless assertions of conscientious objection while in the military, to his weighing of the teachings of his captors against the beliefs of the Jehovah's Witnesses, Daly presents himself as a person operating within an ethical universe against outside authorities of questionable moral character. It is important to note that Daly at no point contemplates actively resisting lawfully constituted U.S. authority. It is clear that such activities as draft evasion are not within the acceptable bounds of his code. Throughout his ordeal of trying to gain separation from the Army, Daly shows himself as patient and longsuffering, following the proper channels and never disobeying orders. Although he clearly sees the connection between his being African American and the failure of his conscientious objector status requests, he never publicly asserts this linkage. Nor does he condemn in print those officers and NCOs (all white) who have deceived and manipulated him in the military, even though it is some nine years later when he writes his narrative, well after the point when any retaliation would have been possible.

When Daly eventually relents and signs letters condemning the U.S. position, he does so on the basis of personal convictions, not due to the political indoctrination he has received. He is keenly aware, however, of the irony of his position (pp. 124–25):

> But I considered even then how all this [the defense of democracy] was a way of thinking I'd seriously have to question sooner or later. Here I was, truly against the war and everything it represented, probably with stronger convictions than any other POW at the camp—yet I was refusing to sign a letter protesting it. And what really bothered me was that somewhere along the line I had allowed the system to intimidate me. Somehow, I had been made to act contrary to what I believed in—just like when I joined the army and came to Vietnam in the first place.

It is only after witnessing or hearing about a number of American atrocities—including the poison spraying of North Vietnamese rice paddies and Henry Kissinger's public pronouncements of sincerity and piety while Richard Nixon secretly authorizes the bombing of civilians—as well as undergoing a great deal of self-searching that Daly begins to reexamine his position. His doubts extend not just to whether to sign the letters but also to his affiliation with the Jehovah's Witnesses, heretofore a sustaining element for him. Ultimately, while in Vietnam, Daly decides that the human supersedes the divine, and he signs the letters. When he does so, he also "converts," as it were, to the communist ideology, at least insofar as it calls for an activism grounded in a desire for human betterment, whereas the Jehovah's Witnesses counsel noninvolvement in contemplation of rewards in the hereafter.

Even facing charges for treason, he continues to rely on his ideals rather than taking the pragmatic course. The attorney assigned to him advises Daly to seek an immediate discharge, as other members of the Peace Committee were doing, so that the military would have no jurisdiction over him. He refuses because he is convinced that his actions in signing the letters have been completely ethical and thus completely defensible. As he closes the book, he continues to wrestle with the sorts of uncertainties that cause some critics to find him inconsistent but which really only identify him as human—i.e., he changes his mind again. While still professing to adhere to certain communist tenets, "more and more, I found myself looking toward religion again," he says (p. 265). His dilemma, which he has first formulated in Hanoi, remains whether to be of the world, and attempt to change it as well as better himself, or to seek only to spread the word of personal salvation in a distant hereafter. Thus the spiritual autobiography ends, not with answers but with the resistance to closure that marks it as being among the first stirrings of the postmodern consciousness.

Daly's memoir is also among the important African American books about the war. As I mentioned above, there are very few autobiographical works about Vietnam by black authors. Basically, there are but ten memoirs, not all of them fully integrated texts—i.e., some, like Eddie Wright's *Thoughts about the Vietnam War: Based on My Personal Experiences, Books I Have Read, and Conversations with Other Veterans* (New York: Carlton Press, 1984) and Fenton Williams's *Just before the Dawn: A Doctor's Experiences in Vietnam* (New York: Exposition Press, 1971), have aspects of a linear story about them but ultimately become as much essay as autobiography, and one of the better known, David Parks's *G. I. Diary* (1968) (Washington, D.C.: Howard University Press, 1984), is exactly that, a diary. Norman A. McDaniel's *Yet Another Voice* (New York: Hawthorn, 1975), mentioned above, is, like Daly's, something of a spiritual autobiography, but McDaniel's faith is set at the beginning of the book and never wavers or changes. Further, the book is so deracialized that one would never know McDaniel is black if it weren't for his picture on the cover. Samuel Vance's *The Courageous and the Proud* (New York: Norton, 1970), by contrast, is a narrative of testing in which he, as decorated hero and career military man, overcomes systemic prejudice and proves himself not just equal, but in most cases superior, to the whites who oppress him. In addition, there is one Internet memoir, Phillip Coleman's *Cannon Fodder,* which is lengthy and detailed but lacks any sense of the tension or introspection we associate with effective memoirs.[6]

Journalist Phillipa Schuyler's *Good Men Die* (New York: Twin Circle Publishing, 1969), published a year after her death in a helicopter crash in Vietnam, is a fascinating text from the point of view of race in that she successfully disguises herself as a Vietnamese woman in order to collect stories, despite the U.S. command's attempts to limit her access. It is, however, extremely hard to get a copy of, because it had only a limited printing by a very small house that soon went out of business. Terry Whitmore's *Memphis Nam Sweden: The Autobiography of a Black American Exile* (1971) (Jackson: University Press of Mississippi, 1997), a story of resistance and desertion, emphasizes racial injustice from the very beginning and essentially says that America is an inherently flawed place for a black person to live. The most recent memoir, noted novelist Albert French's *Patches of Fire: A Story of War and Redemption* (New York: Anchor Books, 1997), is a sensitive consideration of the dual trauma of combat and racial oppression. Only these latter three works equal the literary quality of *Black Prisoner of War,* and in terms of internal linkage of story and theme, Daly's book exceeds them in certain ways.

Primarily, this memoir is valuable as a work exploring racial difference because Daly consciously sets out to undermine what were then ironclad stereotypes of black life in America and of African Americans in general. At the same time, his representations of the problems resulting from his religious beliefs are inextricably bound up with his perceptions of racial difference, and in many cases they compound each other. Thus, the book moderates its solutions to internal racial tension, saying essentially that the resultant problems can be solved. Daly counsels a strategy of integration rather than resistance, despite his spending a good portion of his book showing how he himself has been victimized by racial oppression. As a result, he—unlike Whitmore, the classic romantic outsider who ends in exile in Sweden—in effect transcends his own turbulent times to provide a model for racial harmony through community, however problematic the practicalities of reaching such a state. Finally, like Schuyler, Daly probes the inherent link between African Americans and the Vietnamese—in Daly's case the North Vietnamese—in order to show that American racism is truly an international phenomenon, one indeed responsible in large part for the war.

As if to counter the stereotype, dating to Richard Wright, of life in the black community as being somehow deficient, Daly represents himself as coming from a warm, nurturing family and community, despite growing up in Bedford-Stuyvesant. His mother is highly supportive of his achievements in school, his religious beliefs, and his aspirations toward a career as a chef. He carefully constructs a picture of himself as an industrious, caring, and responsible individual possessed of strongly instilled values: "I spent almost all my spare time at odd jobs . . . for families in the neighborhood—cleaning houses, washing windows or cars, and even baking cakes and pies on the weekends" (p. 13). In fact, because the demands of helping to support his family will not permit the investment of time necessary to become a minister in the Jehovah's Witnesses, Daly, in postponing this training, ironically makes himself vulnerable to the draft.

Another operative truism of race in America that Daly seeks to explode is that there is some sort of natural bond between African Americans, a sort of essentialism. For instance, he suggests through his experience with the black recruiter that bonds of race alone are not always sufficient for trust—that community values and ethical behavior are, in fact, the correct bases for responsible human relationships. In addition, when the Viet Cong attempt to win over the black soldiers by capitalizing on American racial stereotypes, separating them from whites and affording them easier treatment, Daly wryly notes that segregation is still segregation, whatever its purposes. In this same circumstance, Daly is also at pains to show that the individual differences among these soldiers transcend their racial bonds, and, once separated, they get along with each no better than they had with the whites they had previously been sequestered with.

In fact, it is only when Daly reaches the North and finds the Peace Committee, primarily consisting of white members, that he finds any true sense of community. Contrary to the operative picture that has evolved over the past generation of POW life as being close-knit and built on trust and mutual reliance, Daly shows it as largely divisive, whether along racial lines or not. When the prisoners from the South first encounter those from the North, mainly

Air Force personnel who have never seen ground combat, they are not welcomed but rather told by one of the ranking officers not to participate in any "antiwar activities." By contrast, Daly shows members of the Peace Committee carrying on actual conversations about social and philosophical matters, suggesting that the American command structure from Colonel Guy on down is so rigid in its attitudes that any possibility of community is eliminated.

In addition, as his captivity lengthens, and particularly in the North, Daly begins to develop various relationships with his Vietnamese captors. Knowing that the public exploitation of Daly's race would prove to be an especially effective propaganda coup for them, they put pressure on him to sign the antiwar letters, some of this pressure through other members of the Peace Committee. However, he resists, largely on moral grounds, and even when the Vietnamese again segregate him with other black prisoners, lecturing the group on the racial inequities in the United States, he remains unconvinced, though he weighs his captors' arguments carefully. When he ultimately makes his decision to sign, it is based not only on his reactions to the facts of racial and social difference in America, a point toward which the argument with himself has been building, but also his perception that American racism has affected the Vietnamese as well in terrible ways (pp. 180–81):

> I could understand why [the whites] were down on communism. Everything in their backgrounds and upbringing acted to make them resist what Cheese and Roly-Poly [guards] taught. And, of course, the North Vietnamese were not able to appeal to them on the basis of [their] being both poor and black. That was a tough combination to beat when it came to hard times and hard living in the United States. And the funny part of it was, as much as our backgrounds, as Negroes, might have made it easier to be sympathetic to the Vietnamese at times, I sensed, as I often had, an understanding and sympathy for us on their part. Maybe that awareness helped play a role in my going like I did.

This passage not only illustrates the affinity between the Vietnamese and black Americans based on their mutual perception of being classified as racially other by white Americans—an observation made, incidentally, by every single African American memoirist except McDaniel—but its tone, one of understanding rather than venom, exemplifies what I believe to be Daly's ultimate purpose in the narrative: a self-reconstruction as one committed to overcoming boundaries through interracial cooperation and assimilation. For instance, while Daly seems to pattern his prison conversion on that of Malcolm X, whose autobiography his captors provide him with (p. 211), his attitude toward whites following this conversion is far different from that of Malcolm, who, of course, spends a good deal of the latter half of his book castigating white people. Rather, forgiveness and forbearance are themes that Daly develops, although subtly, throughout his narrative, and they are only amplified, by weight of their repetition, after his conversion. For example, never once does he before his conversion speak an ill word against the several whites who either failed to process his conscientious objector application, in effect condemning him to five years of captivity, or harassed and threatened him for not firing his weapon. Nor does he, later in the book, criticize the actions of those white ex-POWs who bring charges against him. This underscores the ethical dimension of Daly's character, thereby lending more emphasis to the sincerity of his claims that he is truly opposed to violence, the fact that produces the central conflict and raison d'être of the autobiography.

It is difficult to separate the controversies that swirl around *Black Prisoner of War* from Daly as a person, and I won't attempt to do so; rather I intend to discuss both together in the remaining section. The path to getting the book back into print has been rocky at best, and one that has taken several years to traverse. Ultimately, with its twists and turns and blind alleys, the journey constitutes something of a quest, and as with all quests, what is revealed says much more about the process of seeking than the thing sought. In this case, I set out to find James Daly, and while clearly accomplishing this task, in many ways I also located the mind of America on the subject of Vietnam a generation after our part in the war there ended, complete with the many deep fault lines that still exist. Tension over which war stories get told, as well as the shape of their telling, continues unabated, not just among men and women growing old with tragic visions of their own truncated youth, but also by others who would like to see a particular ideological position prevail within American culture. This discovery is in part why I dwell at some length in the following pages on the process of locating Daly and getting his important story back before the public. To paraphrase Captain Willard in *Apocalypse Now,* I cannot tell his story without telling ours.

My interest in the book dates to 1994 when I first read it in the course of working on my dissertation.[7] The African American literature of the Vietnam War represented an intersection of interests for me: Having been a marine in Vietnam myself in 1968 and 1969, I was, some twenty-five years later, using my study of the war's literature as a self-recovery process; at the same time, I was fostering a long-term interest in African American literature by studying its first-person narratives with William L. Andrews, then a professor at the University of Kansas. This intersection of subjects caused me to add a chapter on the black-authored texts of the war, discovering in the process that very few had ever found their way into print and that none had remained there long. Much digging, and a liberal use of interlibrary loan, was necessary to get a look at these increasingly hard-to-find books. Once I was able to read them all, two, Daly's and Whitmore's *Memphis-Nam-Sweden,* stood out, both for their writing and for the stories they told.

Eventually my interest in this subject produced articles for *VVA Veteran* (1996) and *African American Review* (1997) on the subject of the African American autobiography of the Vietnam War.[8] Both articles featured *Black Prisoner of War.* During the same period, I also gave several conference presentations that were in part dedicated to analyzing the book. It was at one of these, the 1995 Modern Language Association Convention, that I had occasion to meet Kali Tal, founder and editor of *Vietnam Generation,* the publication which was for several years the major meeting point of those interested in the war's writing and cultural reception. I not only admired her achievements with this journal but also her critical work on the literature of trauma and had reviewed her book *Worlds of Hurt* (New York: Cambridge University Press, 1996). After hearing me describe Daly's and Whitmore's books, she shared my excitement about their quality and urged me to try to get them reissued.

This was a new idea to me, but I immediately saw its merit. Having observed how Andrews had systematically resurrected scores of nineteenth-century autobiographies and written introductions for them, I began what I thought would be a slam-dunk process (not thinking, at least initially, about small matters like copyright, which, of course, prove no impediment to reprinting books a century old). On his advice, I first attempted to gauge any interest the publishers, Bobbs-Merrill and Random House, respectively, might have in such projects but got no replies to my inquiries (not realizing that Bobbs-Merrill no longer existed as such). I was thus faced with trying to find the authors themselves, a daunting task at best and one that I had no idea how to carry out since neither book, of course, gave any clue as to the writers' whereabouts following publication. In addition, since literally nothing had been written about either book beyond contemporary reviews, there was no one to contact about what had become of the authors.

That same winter, at the 1996 Meeting of the Popular Culture Association, I found myself on a panel with noted Vietnam War poet Gerald McCarthy. Both of us, completely independently of one another, were giving papers on Daly and Whitmore, a fact that confirmed my judgment of the value of the two works and spurred my desire to seek republication for them. McCarthy was also interested in seeing them back in print, in part so that he could use them in his course on the literature of the war at St. Thomas Aquinas College. He suggested attempting to write to family members through use of the local phone books.

I chose Whitmore first, largely because there were far fewer people of that surname in the Memphis phone book than there were Dalys in the Brooklyn one. I wrote to all, and fortunately one of them turned out to be Whitmore's mother, with the ultimate result being the republication of *Memphis Nam Sweden* in 1997.[9] I had been, as it turns out, extremely lucky in my search for Whitmore. Finding Daly presented far greater problems. For one, the Afterword to his book has him opening a laundromat in Englewood, New Jersey, not far in distance from his native Brooklyn but a world away when trying to locate a person, since there is, of course, no single phone book for all the cities in northern New Jersey. In addition, the Brooklyn Dalys numbered in the hundreds (as opposed to forty or so Whitmores in the Memphis book), and I had no clear way of narrowing them down by address inasmuch as I could not distinguish which were in Bedford-Stuyvesant and which were not.

By this time, 1997, I had the Internet to use, and indeed I called all of the Brooklyn and northern New Jersey James Dalys that I found in Yahoo's white pages, but none was the right one. I was, however, able to locate the phone number of Lee Bergman, Daly's coauthor. I had guessed that he was from New York and was proven correct. Bergman, however, had had no word from

Daly for several years and was thus not able to get me any closer. This, however, was an important find for me since he was co-holder of the copyright, and certainly he blessed my efforts. In addition, he later proved extremely helpful in describing the nature and circumstances of their collaboration, which began while Daly was still under charges and consisted of a good many taped sessions that Bergman then transcribed and helped assemble into the book.

The Internet also took me down one of the strangest paths that I was to follow in my quest for Daly. I had been for some time monitoring Vietnam War list-serves and newsgroups and, seeing the amount of interest being generated there, felt their subscribers might provide some information. I dutifully posted messages to *soc.history.vietnam, alt.war.vietnam,* and *Sixties-L* but received no useful replies. I then reasoned—correctly as it turned out—that there were probably web pages dedicated to POW/MIA matters and, if so, that I might obtain information through them, however antithetical the politics of their probable sponsors to Daly's conscientious objector beliefs and his so-called collaboration.

I was indeed able to make one productive contact, with former Marine Gunnery Sergeant George Fallon, who maintains a very interesting web page, replete with music and pictures, in which he, in a persona he calls "The Old Gunny," takes visitors on a nostalgic tour of the sixties.[10] Fallon proved to be very interested in helping me, Daly's politics notwithstanding, and he provided me with the e-mail address of former-POW Frank Anton, whose own book *Why Didn't You Get Me Out?* had just been published. I e-mailed Anton about Daly right away but received no reply, not becoming aware until later, when I had found Daly and spoken to him on the subject, that there was a certain animus between the two men as a result of their experiences while POWs in South Vietnam.[11]

Fallon also provided me with the e-mail address of another of the major players in Daly's story, ex-colonel Ted Guy himself, the ranking officer among the POWs in the North and Daly's chief antagonist when they returned to the States. Fallon suggested that Guy was essentially uncompromising in his attitudes about the POW experience and warned me that he might well prove hostile to my requests about Daly. He also asked me not to reveal the source of the address, and I only do so now because Guy died in 1998 at almost the same time as Daly.[12]

When, at about 11:00 one night, I e-mailed a suitably apologetic letter to Guy, I received an almost-immediate but extremely puzzling response—the message section was blank. I sat in half darkness, staring at the blank screen for a while. Finally, thinking that there had been some error in transmission, I sent the message again, and again received the same reply, or rather non-reply. It was eerie; clearly there was someone on the other end, late as it was, and I was being sent some sort of no-text messages. However, I resisted the most obvious interpretation and called Fallon the next day to see if perhaps there weren't some mistake in the address. He very kindly suggested the explanation I had been resisting: Guy had indeed received the message, but, in merely clicking on the "Reply to Author" icon without appending any text, he was giving me the electronic finger while avoiding having to soil himself by the actual contact that words would have implied.

The Internet having proven interesting but ultimately less than useful, I returned to my tried-and-true method of mailing to potential relatives—i.e., anyone with the last name of Daly living in Brooklyn or Queens. I printed up some two hundred letters, dutifully signed them, and set about addressing and stamping envelopes. Within a few days of mailing them, I began receiving replies, all very nice and with avid wishes for my success, but none from anyone who knew the James Daly I was seeking. Finally, after about a month, when the volume of replies had dwindled to zero, I put the project aside, resigned that there was no way to find Daly but consoling myself with the rather hollow feeling that I had done everything I could.

Once again, however, a mother proved to be her son's biggest supporter. One of the letters had indeed found a home, Daly's mother's to be exact, and about a month after I had given up, in December of 1997, I got a call one evening from Daly himself. His mother had delayed giving him the letter because he had been in the hospital with some serious medical complications. Daly was very excited about the possibility of the book's being reissued, and he seemed genuinely flattered that someone would take an interest in his story after all these years. He was in extremely good spirits, and it was therefore with a sort of shock that I received the news that his medical problems entailed having both legs amputated as a result of severe diabetes. His positive attitude seemed to belie the reality of the situation. Yet, I remember noting to myself, the

sentiments I was hearing and the voice in which they were expressed were precisely those he presents to us in the book when
he was in the worst of straits in Vietnam—hopeful and focused on
the job at hand, with very little time to worry about pain. He was
clearly, as the book presents him (and for lack of a better term), a
glass-half-full person.

It turned out that Daly had been residing in southern New Jersey, not northern, and thus my Internet address searches had been
too limited. He and his wife, Jean, had run the laundromat for slightly
over two years before competition (and, as Bergman later told me,
the failure of the Small Business Administration fully to live up to its
promises) had compelled them to close it. At that point, Daly had
gone to work as a mail carrier for the Postal Service, moving first to
Teaneck and then to Willingboro. He had done this for sixteen years,
until 1993 when the diabetes had forced him to retire.

We talked for over an hour, and he filled me in on what he had
done following his discharge from the Army (the point where the
book proper, minus its Afterword, ends). His situation had been
highly publicized; the *New York Times,* among other papers, had
run stories that featured his trials with Guy and the Army and that
emphasized his conscientious objection. Many people in the now-
splintered antiwar movement saw him as a symbol—Cora Weiss,
for example, who in turn put him in touch with Gloria Emerson,
an association that lasted for several years. Immediately following
his discharge, Jane Fonda had asked him to accompany her, along
with her husband Tom Hayden and several others, on a speaking
tour designed to raise money to rebuild hospitals destroyed by the
Christmas bombing. He was interviewed for the nightly news by
Walter Cronkite himself, though, according to Jean Daly, Daly
broke down and could not complete the taping, so only part of it
was ever broadcast.

By the time the book was released, however, his brief fame had
passed, and it sold poorly. Bergman, through his contacts as a pub-
licist, was able to get him an appearance on the *Today Show,* and
the reviews of the book were, with very few exceptions (and these
ideological), very positive. Zalin Grant's 1975 POW book *Survivors*
(New York: W. W. Norton) featured Daly as one of its primary
interviewees, and there was an occasional story done about him by
one or another of the New York area papers. The grim realities of
post-Vietnam America had set in: Stagflation, malaise, and unem-

ployment dominated the news and people's concerns. No one was particularly interested in reading about the trials of a black conscientious objector POW.

Although Daly had been somewhat reluctant during this first conversation to talk about life in the camps, when I spoke to him again about a month later, he was more than ready to open up. This time, I heard the voice of a different James Daly, the one that had made him controversial and sometimes unpopular among his fellow prisoners. Assertive and deeply opinionated, he was still angry about certain things and with certain people. He reiterated what he had said in the book, that he felt the two officers he had been with as a captive in the South, Anton, a warrant officer, and Captain Floyd Kushner, a doctor, had both been shirkers, causing him and other prisoners to have to shoulder more of the load than necessary (p. 102). Kushner, he still felt, had essentially been motivated by hatred of blacks, and it was only the sensitivity of his Vietnamese captors to American racism that had helped ease the resultant burden on Daly and the other African American prisoners (pp. 107, 133, 148).

Most of his anger he reserved for Anton, whose book Daly had not yet read (and never was to, it turns out). He had, however, seen a review a short time before and had apparently spoken with fellow ex-POW and Peace Committee member Bob Chenoweth about it. Daly (easily forgetting his own confusion over similar matters in his own book) was incensed that Anton would stay in the Army for twenty years and then write a book critical of the military. He also recounted what he felt were Anton's derelictions, essentially recapitulations of those in *Black Prisoner of War*—hoarding salt to eat all at once so his feet would swell and thus excuse him from work detail, defecating in the water supply because he was "too lazy to go any further," and publicly denying the existence of God only to cry out for divine help during American bombing raids (see note 11 for more discussion of the relationship between Daly and Anton).[13]

Robert Garwood, by comparison, was beneath Daly's contempt, or at least Daly couldn't work up the same anger for him that he did for Anton, though what he told me (along with what the book says) about Garwood's activities should dispel any confusion about what constitutes collaboration and what does not. The book clearly shows Garwood acting in complicity with his captors, whatever his later pieties about being forced to do so. And in our conversation, Daly emphatically stated his belief that

Garwood's story about being a POW for several years—the one seized upon as "proof" of continued American captivity well into the nineties by the POW/MIA organizations—was "a lie, totally invented to protect himself." Garwood had "always collaborated with the North Vietnamese," Daly stated. "Willie Watkins [a fellow black POW] and me were both told we were going to meet an American officer who carried an AK-47. He wasn't considered a prisoner; he even wore their uniform."[14] In fact, Daly was emphatic about the subject of MIAs following the 1973 cease fire agreement—there weren't any, he stated. The whole idea defied logic in his estimation, because had Vietnam kept any, they would have used them to their advantage when the United States had violated the peace agreement.

I spoke with Daly two more times over the course of the next several months while I was attempting to secure a publisher, and each time he seemed more affected by his health problems. He really added very little to the information gleaned from the first two conversations. The last time I talked to him, in October, he told me that he was about to undergo another surgery, this one on his eyes, and he was clearly very depressed, sounding totally unlike the person I had first spoken with some ten months before. When I called him again at Christmas, Jean, obviously very upset, told me he had died twelve days earlier. He was never to know that I had positive news about the book—an editor at the University Press of Kansas was very interested in the book and had agreed to send it out for peer review, the first step in securing reissue.

Yet, as I set about the process of trying to accomplish this reissue in the year following his death, I discovered that Daly proved to be as controversial dead as he had been alive. As I found out during the review process over the next several months, his story does not go down any more easily with some people in 1999 America than it did in 1975. Attitudes about the war are, if anything, more hardened than ever, especially those having to do with conscientious objection, collaboration with the enemy, and which stories will define the war for future generations. Ultimately, six people, including the editor and the series editor, read the book. Though four liked it and thought it worthy of being in print, two did not. Their major objections are interesting and should be aired.

The most strident comments fell along the same lines as those of the POW/MIA contingent who had always been critical of Daly. One representative comment went as follows:

> [He] was one of the antiwar POWs in Hanoi, and thus broke the Code of Conduct and, by necessity, faith with the other prisoners there and to . . . reprint *A Hero's Welcome* gives legitimacy to what that group of men did in Hanoi. . . . That the author became a Jehovah's Witness in captivity approaches the ridiculous simply because it became an excuse not to hang tough, remain a soldier, or to resist the captors.

In another missive, this same respondent states that "Daly should have been charged with aiding and comforting the enemy and collaboration." Factual errors about when Daly became a Jehovah's Witness aside, the two major assertions here—that he was both a traitor and a coward—deserve an answer because, in my estimation, they show a rather profound misunderstanding of how American attitudes about these matters have changed in the last three decades, largely because of Vietnam.

The nature of collaboration is at the heart of all such comments. This is a concept that is bound to be controversial, though the whole experience in Vietnam, in addition to the Pueblo and Mayaguez incidents, the Iranian hostage situation (though by and large nonmilitary), and the Gulf War, have all moved our understanding of and feelings about what constitutes collaboration a large distance. For instance, there was, in my memory at least, absolutely no outcry by the public or the military about the statements made, clearly as a result of duress, by the captives in the Gulf War. In fact, the military, though maintaining in their training manuals the old name, rank, and serial number stance (at least according to the relatively recent USMC manual in my possession), has remained fairly silent on the issue, at least publicly, for several years, indicating that they at least have some feeling that this old standard probably will not stand up to public scrutiny.

Even by the standards of the day, the whole concept of collaboration seems problematic. In fact, *Black Prisoner of War* chronicles instances of Guy himself signing letters condemning the war. And, of course, there is the well-known feigned collaboration by some of the more stalwart POWs on North Vietnamese propaganda films that used semiotic twists (i.e., "secret" signals within their "text" that the Vietnamese captors wouldn't and didn't catch). The growing opinion—here and there—that the war was clearly wrong would have provided a moral basis for finding ways of alleviating extreme physical discomfort being endured for unprecedentedly long times (e.g., Daly had been badly wounded and was a captive for five years). Ultimately, when charges were brought against Daly and others for collaboration and treason, the military itself twice hastened to throw these out as being unfounded. Moreover, I can find no trace of any civilian opinion that supported the idea that whatever Daly and the other members of the Peace Committee did was wrong. Indeed, the temper of the times was "let's put it behind us," as we can see from the collective sigh of relief from the majority of the country when Jimmy Carter finally dealt with the draft avoidance issue after Richard Nixon's and Gerald Ford's inept fumbling with it.

Another subject implied by this discussion is that of torture, which is, of course, a very touchy issue and one Daly curiously avoids. One factor in this avoidance is that about half of his time as a captive was spent in the South, where none of the prisoners was, strictly speaking, tortured, although all were certainly deprived. Another has to do with the minimal contact prisoners from the South were allowed to have with those from the North. Also, there was a high degree of sequestration, and information among the prisoners was sketchy and often distorted as a result of the rudimentary communications (and, of course, memory itself). This is even more the case with, first, black prisoners, who were given preferential treatment for propaganda reasons, and, second, with members and potential members of the Peace Committee, for the same reasons.

Another problem, though also a sensitive one, is, what is torture? There is POW testimony that firmly denies that torture in the truest sense of the word took place; rather, severe physical deprivation, spontaneous beatings, and psychological pressure were translated by other POWs into the term torture. In other words, torture is a loaded word, and even some of those who were subjected to it would rather call it mistreatment—i.e., it seems to break down along the same political lines that mark the rest of the POW situation. So, in sum, these charges of collaboration and cowardice, and those like them, whether directed at Daly or any other POW, seem to be ideologically motivated rather than objective in nature, as do essentially all of the objections that I encountered to the reissue of the book. In my estimation, however, the possibility of controversy and the attempt to tell a story that challenges the received narrative is not a reason for repression of the dissenting voice.

Given its uniqueness in the American literature of the Vietnam War in general, and certainly within POW testimony, one question remains about Daly's story: Why should we believe him? His critics certainly claim that what he says is distorted and self-serving. My answer relies, first, on the observation that, however confused Daly is when facing decisions, he is absolutely consistent in his ethical strategy of testing these decisions against a code. His problem is that the world is a constantly changing place that seldom allows for unchanging codes, and thus some of the things he does end up looking silly or ill-advised. This brings up the second reason why readers should believe Daly: Unlike many of his critics, he is not afraid to show his warts. Nowhere does he try to excuse or apologize for his actions in Vietnam. In fact, he insists on attending the White House POW dinner just to show everyone that he is not ashamed of signing antiwar documents. Rather, the strength of Daly's approach is his insistence on showing his uncertainties—and his consequent soul-searching—as opposed to covering them up. Thus, this admission of confusion opens up the discussion of what's right versus what's smart that each of us faces at one time or another. Finally, never once does Daly ask us to feel sorry for him, or to view anything that he has done as particularly heroic for that matter, as certainly someone in his position might have done as a sort of apology.

In summary, *Black Prisoner of War* provides much-needed illumination of the many areas of American culture that the Vietnam War touched, which is to say, nearly all areas. As a consideration of ethical and moral values, it provides a valuable road map for us still. As a history, it provides a fresh view of key events of that tumultuous time. As African American literature, it fills a large gap, telling a story not found elsewhere, certainly not in white testimony. As trauma literature, it exemplifies the violence seen or done during that ignominious war. In all respects, it is a book that deserves to live. Like all great testimonial works, its author, speaking through its pages and for us, says, "I mattered, what I did—what I saw—mattered." And though James Daly's words are often simply chosen, the complex dilemma they pose for us is not, because his story challenges us to put ourselves in his place to see whether what we would have done and felt would have been any different. "Who knows," he finally seems to say, along with the narrator of *Invisible Man*, "but that, on the lower frequencies, I speak for you?"

NOTES

1. James A. Daly and Lee Bergman, *A Hero's Welcome: The Conscience of Sergeant James Daly versus the United States Army* (Indianapolis: Bobbs-Merrill, 1975).

2. Gustav Hasford, *The Short-Timers* (1979) (New York: Bantam, 1980).

3. Tim O'Brien, *Going after Cacciato* (New York: Delacorte, 1978).

4. Robert Olen Butler, *A Good Scent from a Strange Mountain* (New York: Henry Holt, 1992) and *The Deep Green Sea* (New York: Henry Holt, 1997).

5. Norman A. McDaniel, *Yet Another Voice* (New York: Hawthorn, 1975).

6. Phillip Coleman, *Cannon Fodder* (December 1999) *http://members.aol.com/warlib/cf.html*. The narrative has had its authenticity questioned by various Internet readers who posted messages on *alt.war.vietnam* from 1997 on. More particularly, the credentials of Coleman himself as a Vietnam veteran have been challenged, although since he includes a picture of himself clearly taken in Vietnam, these charges of personal inauthenticity do not seem warranted. Coleman also runs a whole enterprise dealing with the war, including stories, a forum for comments, and a veterans' locator service. The site, which he calls "The American War Library," is at *http://members. aol.com/veterans.index.html*.

7. "After the Flood: Survivor Literature of the Vietnam War" (Ph.D. diss., University of Kansas, 1995).

8. The two articles are "MIA: African American Autobiography of the Vietnam War," *African American Review* 31 (1) (1997): 105–24; and "Among the Missing: Black Memories of the Vietnam War," *VVA Veteran* (February 1996): 13–16.

9. For a more complete description of the circumstances of the reissue, see Jeff Loeb, "Afterword" to Terry Whitmore's *Memphis Nam Sweden: The Story of a Black Deserter* (Jackson: University Press of Mississippi, 1997), 191–202.

10. The site may be found at *http://whitetail.nji.com/~gfallon/frame.htm*.

11. Frank Anton, with Tommy Denton, *Why Didn't You Get Me Out? Betrayal in the Viet Cong Death Camps: The Truth about Heroes, Traitors, and Those Left Behind* (Arlington, Tex.: Summit Publishing Group,

1997). Specifically, Daly felt—and expresses in his book—that Anton failed to carry his share of the burden while the prisoners were shuttled between various temporary camps in the South. Daly also told me, with some acrimony in his voice, that while he was the cook at one of these camps, he caught Anton defecating in the stream just above where Daly was drawing water for cooking purposes because Anton was too lazy to walk further. Anton essentially verifies this fact in his book, though he claims it was because of weakness caused by a vitamin deficiency (pp. 85–86). I should say that while Daly in our conversations was very critical of Anton, Anton, for his part, at least in his book, is kind to Daly and makes no excuses, save weakness, for any of his own behavior. Further, in his testimony in Zalin Grant's *Survivors* (New York: W. W. Norton, 1975), Anton speaks well of Daly, saying in reference to the charges brought against him by Guy, "I considered Daly a friend and didn't want to see anything happen to him" (p. 340). This difference suggests a certain magnanimity in Anton that Daly lacked and indeed underscores Daly's inflexibility that is both a strength and a weakness.

12. Though Guy is himself gone, one may visit his web page at *http://www.ojc.org/tedguy/index.html* or read about him at *http://www.ojc.org/hawk.html* ("ojc," incidentally, stands for Operation Just Cause, the major organization fueling the POW/MIA effort).

13. Most of this is mentioned in the book at pp. 102 and 148, among other places.

14. Daly's remains the most complete written testimony against Garwood, even though some thirty prosecution witnesses were called during Garwood's trial for treason, at which he was convicted. Some of these witnesses reported seeing him with an AK-47, either guarding or accompanying prisoners. Interestingly, Daly was not called to testify, presumably because the prosecution felt his testimony could be discredited on the basis of Guy's accusations of collaboration. Interestingly, in a strained bit of logic, Monika Jensen-Stevenson, in *Spite House: The Last Secret of the Vietnam War* (New York: W. W. Norton, 1997), an arch apologist for the POW/MIA cause, opines that Garwood's defense was hurt by the fact that Guy's charges had been dismissed because, had they not been, "witnesses might have been robbed of credibility." This, of course, misses the fact that Daly was not called to testify. Garwood's apologists, who came largely from the ranks of the POW/MIA organizations, retort that no one could actually testify that Garwood had a loaded weapon or that it had a firing pin in it (*Spite House,* pp. 305–6). In addition to the trial, there is other testimony as to Garwood's traitorous behavior as well. Zalin Grant includes an American military operations report in *Survivors,* published four years before Garwood surfaced, in which several witnesses identify Garwood from pictures as being involved in a fire fight on the

xxx **Black Prisoner of War**

Viet Cong side (pp. 111–16). Anton, in *Why Didn't You Get Me Out?*, says that "Garwood commanded the Viet Cong guard detail that brought Watkins and Daly to our camp," and that he had "taken up arms against his country in 1967," two years after he was captured (p. 110). Therefore, Daly's statement that Garwood had been a traitor "from the first" probably refers to when he first saw him in 1967 rather than in 1965, when Garwood was captured.

CHAPTER 1

Bedford-Stuyvesant, Brooklyn, 1966

In my senior year in high school, I was still completely convinced I'd never have to serve in the armed forces. That was back in 1966. Of course, I realized that my student classification was certain to be changed after I graduated. Yet, because of my religious beliefs—because I was totally against killing, in any war—I was confident that I would be given conscientious objector status and would not be drafted.

When I graduated from Franklin K. Lane High School that June, I was reclassified 1-A. Still certain I'd be exempted from the draft, I started job hunting and made plans to enroll in night classes at Community College in September. I had decided to take Hotel Technology, a course in which I could eventually specialize in pastry baking. I'd always believed that if you ever go to school to study something special, it should be something you really like. And for me, cooking and baking were the greatest. I had been into both at home since the age of eight, could cook up just about anything, and especially liked baking pies and cakes.

During the months following graduation, I'd found out that many prospective employers just weren't about to hire someone with a 1-A classification. So, though I'd managed to land a clerical job at B. Altman's department store, I decided to make it over to the Selective Service office in Brooklyn and submit an application for conscientious objector status. After all, I figured, why shouldn't I qualify? Though I was officially a Baptist, I'd been studying with

Jehovah's Witnesses since the age of eleven and planned, one day, to become a full-time minister.

I clearly remember the afternoon I went to the Selective Service office. It was a few weeks before Christmas, and the store windows were all bright with holiday displays. Never in my wildest thoughts would I have imagined that many years might pass before I'd see Christmas in New York again.

The lady at Selective Service listened carefully to my reasons for requesting conscientious objector status. She then explained that although I had studied many years with Jehovah's Witnesses, this would not qualify me for draft exemption. Only full-time ministers were considered, she explained. I was not even allowed an application.

For the first time, I began to realize that I might have to serve in the armed forces. Rather than accept the word of the Selective Service interviewer, however, I decided to see an army recruiter. Maybe he would know more. The next day I took off from work, went to the army recruiting office, and once again explained my situation—this time to a young black recruiting sergeant.

"Well, I'm afraid Selective Service gave it to you straight," the sergeant said. "As things are, you just don't qualify for exemption."

"Maybe I don't qualify," I said, "but the truth is, I don't believe in war and I don't believe in killing. No way would I ever shoot a man."

"That's no problem for the army," the sergeant said. "We have a special program for conscientious objectors."

"How's that?"

"Well, for one thing, we make certain you get noncombat status. That way, you're never put into a position where you have to use a weapon."

"I see. And how does a guy get into this program?" I asked.

"He enlists in the Regular Army and asks for it, that's all. You see, when you enlist in the RA, you can get anything you want. Not so when you're drafted. Then, you're a cinch to end up in the infantry. You can almost bet on it."

The sergeant gave me a booklet on the Regular Army. "You go home and read this over," he said. "Meanwhile, if you'd like me to, I can check out where you stand with the draft. I'll be over at Fort Hamilton in the morning and can look up the files."

"And you can find out when I'm going to be drafted?"

"Sure thing. If you're up for an early draft, it'll be right there in black and white. Come back and see me tomorrow afternoon and I'll let you know."

I read the booklet on the way home. It made the Regular Army sound pretty good—a choice of careers and all that. Yet, even if it was like the sergeant explained and I could be given noncombat status, it would still be going against my religious beliefs. Jehovah's Witnesses teach that to join any army is wrong—because a man cannot serve two masters at the same time and be faithful to both. In other words, you can't be part of God's army and serve in the military, too. That thought stayed in my head, bothering me, and I realized that I was going to have to make a really important decision before very long.

As I walked along the familiar blocks of Bedford-Stuyvesant and turned down Madison Street toward the old house we lived in, I kept wondering whether I should discuss the interview with my mother, or maybe with my older sister, Phyllis. When something needed working out, I'd often get with one of them about it. When I was a kid, my mother always encouraged me to talk problems over. Then, Phyllis—just two years older than me—was only a youngster herself. As for my father, we never had been able to talk, or do things together. It had been like that right up till the day he'd left us four years before. It hadn't taken him long to forget about us, either. About a year after he'd gone, just by chance I came to sit right across from him in the subway one day. He looked right into my face—and never even knew it was me.

When I arrived home, everyone was there except my brother James. My mother and Phyllis were making dinner in the kitchen; my younger sister Pamela, setting the table; my brothers Dennis and Ralph, busy with homework; and Elaine, the youngest, then eleven, listening to records on our old turntable.

"Hi, Bubby," Phyllis called out. "What's new with you?"

I hesitated. "Oh, nothing," I said.

Everyone in the family, and a few friends, always called me "Bubby." Phyllis had been responsible for the nickname when we were very little. She could never manage to say "brother"—it came out "bubby" instead. And the name had stuck ever since.

I think they must have realized that something was on my mind that night. Especially my mother. Several times, she asked, "Something troubling you? Something bothering you?"

I decided it was best not to discuss the situation just yet. Who could tell, maybe the sergeant wouldn't find me listed for the next draft. With luck, maybe I wouldn't even be drafted until the spring, or even the summer. Then there'd be time to get some proper advice and work things out.

I returned to the army recruiting office the following afternoon. "Well, Jim," the recruiting sergeant said, "there's a big draft coming up after the first of the year—and you're part of it. If you don't make a move now, you can count on being in the infantry before the end of January."

"You're sure about it?" I asked.

"Absolutely."

I just sat there, not knowing what to say.

"Let me give you some advice," the sergeant said finally. "If you want to be safe and see the world at the same time, the best place to be is on land. Forget the air force, or navy, or marines. In the Regular Army, you only have to put in two years, then you're out. As a conscientious objector you can pick the kind of noncombat job you want. After basic training, the choice is yours."

"Well, maybe I ought to think it over," I said.

"That's up to you. But, man, you're really under the gun. The draft is breathing down your neck. If I was you, I'd sign up right here and now."

I tried to think it through. Even if I was to officially become a regular member of Jehovah's Witnesses (I had never joined), it wouldn't make any difference as far as the draft was concerned, since I still wouldn't be a full-time minister. But if I joined the army and served for two years, I'd never have to worry about being drafted again. And I'd be young when I got out. If I still believed the same way, I could join Jehovah's Witnesses then. And even though I'd be acting against my beliefs by going into the army, at least I'd continue to live according to one of God's most important commandments, "Thou shalt not kill." In my way, I'd still be a member of God's army. And I'd make it understood right from the start—in no way was I to take part in any killing.

"Well, what do you say?" the sergeant asked.

I nodded. "Okay," I said.

He put the forms in his typewriter and began to fill them in. "Now, then, what noncombat field would you like?"

"Well, I'm studying Hotel Technology at Community College," I said. "I like cooking a lot."

"That's good. We'll put you down for cooking school. How about a second choice in case that doesn't work out?"

"My only other experience is in clerical work," I said. "I've got a job doing that now."

"Fine," he said. "It's guaranteed—either you'll go to cooking school or be a clerk."

He pulled the forms out of the typewriter and marked where I was to sign them. I didn't bother reading all those different papers. Instead, I just wrote my signature everywhere he had put an X.

This time when I arrived home, I told my mother and sister what had happened. That's when the trouble exploded. They were both really upset and went on about it for a long time. "It was a stupid thing to do, Bubby, really stupid," Phyllis kept saying.

"Don't worry," I told them. "I'll be okay. I've been guaranteed that if I don't go to cooking school, then I'll be a clerk. With noncombat status, I won't even be going out of the country."

"I just don't believe it," my sister said.

"But that's exactly what he told me," I insisted. "Otherwise I'd never have joined up."

"Well, you mustn't go around telling everyone in the army how you're a conscientious objector," my mother said. "They just won't understand, and you're certain to be in for a real bad time. You're to tell only those you have to tell, understand?"

"After basic, it will all happen automatically," I explained. "There'll be no need to talk about it even."

My reassurances didn't seem to convince anyone at home, and during the following days, when I told my friends how I had enlisted, they acted very doubtful, as well.

From then on, it was just a matter of waiting. The next move was up to the army, and it could happen any time. Despite knowing how limited my time at home was, we all managed a good Christmas.

Then, one afternoon during the second week in January, I received a phone call at work. I was to report to Fort Hamilton for induction on January 17.

On the Saturday night before I left, the family gave me a party. Aside from relatives and my brothers and sisters, a number of my better friends had been invited. William Smith was there— a buddy ever since the day he'd taken away the money my mother had given me for buying groceries, and my sister had made him give it back. I was five at the time. The twins, Alonso and Alfonso, came, two of my closest friends, a pair who would never miss a swinging party. And even my old girl friend Renee turned up, though we'd broken off a long time before. In my mind, though, I'd always kept thinking that one day Renee and I would be getting together again.

We'd first met when I was fifteen, and we'd walk home from school every day with a group of kids. One of my friends kept saying how he could tell Renee really liked me. "Why don't you ask her to go with you?" he'd be after me all the time.

I really wanted to, but I was just too shy to say anything.

Finally, one day as we walked home, I turned to her and said, "There's something I've been wanting to ask you, Renee."

"Oh? What is it?" And she sounded like she was really anxious to hear.

Then I said, "Aw, never mind, forget it. I'll tell you tomorrow."

"Why not tell me now?" she insisted.

"No, I'll tell you tomorrow," I said.

The next day, when we met after school, the very first thing Renee asked was, "What did you want to tell me yesterday, James?" I just shrugged and put her off again.

Almost a week passed before the question came up again. Then, one afternoon, Renee simply asked me straight out. She said, "James, do you want to go with me?"

I said, "That's what I'd been wanting to ask you all the time, but I didn't know how."

So she invited me to her house for dinner, and I met her mother, who smiled at me and said, "So this is the James I've been hearing so much about!"

So then I started going to Renee's house seven days a week —from the time I'd leave school until I got ready to go to my part-time job at the corner grocery—and then again at night till all hours. And the thing of it was that my mother always knew when I got home really late, because I could never manage to keep the keys to the house for very long without losing them. So when my mother let me in, she'd always fuss, "What kind of a mother can that be to let you visit her daughter so late, knowing you've got school in the morning? What do you two be doing all that time around there, anyway?"

So I'd explain how we'd just sit up playing cards, the three of us, and I'd forget about the time.

A couple of nights, on the weekend, I fell asleep and didn't get home until lunch the following day. My mother, not remembering that she hadn't let me in the night before, would ask, "How come you got up so early this morning and even cleaned your room?" Of course she never realized that my room was clean because I'd never slept in it. And I'd just shrug, change the subject, and let it go at that.

The reason Renee and I finally split was over her wanting to join the Spearhead's Drum and Bugle Corps. I was against it. The Corps was a group of fellows and girls who seemed to be partying all the time. The truth was, I found the whole bunch just too fast for me, and besides, I really didn't like any of them very much.

Well, when Renee joined the Corps, we had it out. Then she started making other dates. And even though I still visited her house every couple of weeks, it never did get back to where it had been.

But still, I figured when the time was right maybe we'd pick it all up again. The plain truth was, I liked her a lot. She was really the first girl friend I'd had, and as far as I was concerned she was different from most girls. She was nice. She was quiet. She liked to go out but she knew how to act.

So at the party, I kept thinking how I'd soon be gone in the army—and that maybe I ought to tell Renee just how I felt. But it seemed we were never alone. Every time I'd try to get her off away from everyone, sure enough a group of friends would crowd around.

Next thing I knew, Renee was ready to go. We never did get a chance to talk.

But it was a really great party. On my way to Fort Hamilton a few days later, I kept thinking back to it. Somehow, it made going into the army just a little bit easier.

CHAPTER 2

Basic Training

The morning I was to report to Fort Hamilton, I was up at five o'clock. It was only a subway ride away, and I wasn't due there until nine, but it had been impossible to sleep. Even then, knowing that now there was no turning back, I still kept wondering if I'd made the right decision.

I pulled on my bathrobe and slippers and shuffled along the chilly hallway to the bathroom, the only one in the house. The door was closed. Though the sounds coming from inside were muffled, I could hear my mother crying.

A few minutes later she came out, eyes red and puffy. I didn't say anything, and a short while later the two of us had coffee together. As we sat talking quietly across the kitchen table, I tried to reassure her that there was nothing to worry about, that everything would turn out fine.

She stood at the door, watching, as I left. "See you later when I return for my things," I said, smiling. The recruiter had told me on the phone that before taking off for basic, we would be able to stop home briefly.

At Fort Hamilton, a short while after arriving, we were sworn in. The fellow next to me was from Brooklyn also. His name was Arnold Webster.

"Well, I guess that makes it official," he said with a grin. "Funny, I don't feel any different."

"Maybe it takes a while to sink in," I said.

We spent a good part of the day waiting for our orders. Webster and I were hoping we'd be assigned to Fort Dix, New Jersey, for basic. Instead, we both ended up on the list for Fort Jackson, South Carolina. And now we were told that there'd be no time for stopping off at home. Our train was to leave Pennsylvania Station at seven that evening.

I called my mother and asked if she could meet me at the station with the suitcase of things I had packed.

At five o'clock, after roll call, we took army buses into Manhattan. When we arrived at the station, my mother was not at the information booth where we'd made up to meet. Arnold and I covered the entire area and continued to look for her until our train was called. Then, just as we were about to go through the gate to the platform, I spotted them—my mother, my sister Phyllis, my sister Pam, and my brother Dennis.

"Hey, is that girl in the front your sister?" Arnold asked. "She really is pretty!"

"They both are. That one is Pam."

"Will you introduce me? I'd really like to meet her," he said.

The family crowded around us and I introduced Arnold to everyone. When it came to Pam, I said, "By the way, Arnold wanted to meet you the first he saw of you." Arnold grinned, a little embarrassed, I think, and Pam smiled back.

They walked down to the train with us. I hugged and kissed everybody good-by, climbed aboard, and walked back to the last car, where I could see them all through the window. As the train pulled away, we all started waving. I continued to watch until the train was out of the station.

At my last glimpse, all of them were still waving to me.

That night, as I lay in bed listening to the steady click of the train wheels, I kept thinking how my mother had advised me to discuss my beliefs in the army only when it was absolutely necessary—how the guys wouldn't understand. It seemed like she was right, especially when I thought back and remembered how being different had always made things a lot rougher.

A long time before, I had come to learn that it's not easy going your own way and sticking to what you believe—even less so when your way is not the accepted one.

When I was in school, if I would mention that I was studying with Jehovah's Witnesses, I was laughed at and called many kinds of names. Sometimes, it seemed, I was the most hated guy around.

Before I started studying with Jehovah's Witnesses, though, I found life very easy to live as a Baptist. At the age of twelve, I hardly ever missed going to church on Sunday. As a matter of fact, I just about lived in church on Sunday. I really enjoyed it, especially things like joining the different clubs and going on trips.

But as far as the Bible went, I didn't learn much as a Baptist. In fact, I was never even taught God's name.

It all changed that day in June, 1959, when Phyllis came home and told us how she had met this lady selling magazines in the street, and that she wanted to come to our house to give us Bible studies. My mother agreed to allow the lady to visit us, or at least to see what it was all about. And that was the start. She'd been coming to see us ever since, one hour every Friday. And so we came to learn and understand the beliefs of the Jehovah's Witnesses.

By the time we reached Columbia, South Carolina, almost a full day after we left New York, all the guys on the train had become very friendly. We arrived at about three in the afternoon, then waited almost four hours for the buses from the post to pick us up.

The first seven days were called Zero Week because they were't part of the eight weeks of basic training. At the Fort Jackson reception center we were kept on the go every day, running from one place to the other, filling out forms, being issued gear, taking medicals, getting shots, learning to jump when one of the cadre yelled out.

Finally, on the morning we were to move to the area of Fort Jackson used for basic training, a long line of trucks came in for us. Each man's name was called out, followed by the company to which he had been assigned. Arnold and I were both to report to Company F—Fox Trot Company. As we climbed onto the trucks, the Pfcs and corporals who had been chasing us up and down for the past week crowded around in a group and shouted about what a rough time we were in for. "Just wait till you guys get up on the hill—you'll find out what hell really is!" "So you all thought this week was bad, huh!" "So long, pussies!"

By the time the trucks started to roll, every guy on them was nervous as hell. We just didn't know what to expect, and whatever it was, it wouldn't have surprised us.

It was a short ride. When the trucks pulled to a stop, all we could hear was shouting and screaming from all sides. A bunch of sergeants and corporals swarmed around, waiting, and everyone of them yelled out at us at the top of his voice, "Okay, you guys, move your asses!" "Shake it, you fuckers—climb down and line up!" "I want every swinging dick out here in one minute flat!" And all of us started scrambling out as fast as was humanly possible, practically climbing over one another to get down.

As I started off, I fell flat on my face in the company street. Immediately, a sergeant stood over me and shouted, "Don't move, soldier—just lie right where you are. And the rest of you, keep coming. Nobody goes around him!"

So all the guys charging in my direction continued right on. One by one, their feet stomped into my back as they ran over me. Finally, when the very last man was in line, I was allowed to get up.

We were then divided up into five platoons, with about forty men in each. I was in the first platoon and, my luck, I had Sergeant Joiner—the very same sergeant who had made me lie where I'd fallen getting off the truck. However, I soon found out that, as mean as Sergeant Joiner was, most of the other sergeants were even worse. We were always being shouted at, cursed at, called every kind of name imaginable. They were hard-core dudes, all right, and there was nothing for us trainees to do but take whatever they dished out.

Two days after we arrived, Sergeant Joiner interviewed each man, one by one. There were only two blacks in the platoon, me and another guy. I found out fast that the sergeant already had us categorized in his mind.

When it came time for my interview, Joiner started right off by asking how come I hadn't volunteered to be a squad leader. Then, before I could answer, he shot another question at me.

"Where you from, Daly?"

"New York," I answered.

"Where in New York?"

"Brooklyn."

"Where do you live in Brooklyn?"

"I'm from Bedford-Stuyvesant."

He stared at me for a minute, then asked, "Do you know where I'm from?"

I said no, and then he told me, "I'm from Brooklyn too. Do you know where Crown Heights is?"

I nodded and he said, "Do you know what gets me so damned mad? It seems I have two or three black guys from Brooklyn every damn cycle. Never once has any of them ever come to me and asked to be a squad leader or a platoon leader. With the white guys, it's different. From the minute they get here they're buggin' me to be a squad leader. So why the fuck is it that you colored guys never ask for a leadership position?"

"I can only answer for myself," I said. "Being a leader calls for certain qualifications, and the truth is, I've always been poor in physical education. Because of that, I don't think I'd make a very good squad leader."

"Well, that's too damn bad, Daly. Too bad for you—'cause you know what? From now on, every time I see you, you'd better drop into a thinking position just as fast as you can move your ass. Do you know what a thinking position is?"

I shook my head.

"Do you know how to do push-ups, Daly?"

"Yes, I do."

"Well, that's the thinking position. And by God, when you see me comin', that's just what you're gonna start doing. Understand?"

"I understand," I said.

So for the next two weeks, whenever I saw Sergeant Joiner, I had to start doing push-ups, and he'd stand over me and watch. Then, when I thought I'd done enough, I'd ask for permission to get up.

Actually, what I'd told Sergeant Joiner about being poor in physical education was the truth. When I was small, I'd never gotten any encouragement at home to take part in sports or to learn them. With my father being the way he was—very strict and seldom around very much—he never took me to the park or played ball with me like the other fathers in the neighborhood did with their kids. Then, whenever I tried to play games with the guys and they'd choose up sides, I'd always be the last one to be picked. Nobody really wanted me on his team, and I can't say I blamed them.

By the time I was eleven or twelve, it got so I never played at all. That was better, I figured, than being yelled at during the game and ending up angry myself and yelling back. So, I'd mostly just stand around and watch, or else not even bother—just stay in the house and help out with the cooking and cleaning.

When I got a little older, I had even less time for sports than before, because now I spent almost all of my spare time at odd jobs. My mother had mentioned to friends how good I was at doing things around the house, and before I knew it I had plenty of job offers from families in the neighborhood—cleaning houses, washing windows or cars, and even baking cakes and pies on the holidays.

Most weeks I'd end up making only five dollars or so, but that money made it possible for me to get the things I knew I had no right asking my mother for, things she just couldn't afford. Besides, I knew my mother would never do for one what she couldn't do for all.

I'd buy most of my own clothes, too, paying a few dollars a week on installments. And regardless of what I bought, I always managed to give at least two dollars a week to my mother. I wanted to help, no matter how little. I felt it just wasn't right that she should have to raise the family all by herself—and with my father never around, that's about what it amounted to.

I never imagined then that not developing any athletic skills might be a problem for me one day, as it was in the army. During my time in the service, being clumsy sure took its toll. Like my falling head-first off the army truck. And all during basic, my physical ineptitude made passing PT—Physical Training—damn near impossible.

PT tests were scored by points, 500 the maximum and 300 needed to pass. The company commander of F Company was determined that we would be the outstanding company in the battalion when it came to PT. He was out to win the Commander's Trophy.

The orders were out that every man had to score at least 450 on the PT test, and anyone who didn't measure up was to be put into the extra-PT platoon. If you ended up there, it meant doing extra PT just about any free minute you had—exercises first thing every morning, running in place whenever there was a short break during the day, and an extra hour of PT in the afternoon when everyone else got off.

The first PT test was held about the end of our second week.

I scored 320. So, from then on, right through the eight-week cycle, I was assigned to the extra-PT platoon.

As I struggled with PT, I couldn't help but envy some of the GIs from the South who had lived in the country and were used to hard work. PT was a snap for them. Not so, I found, for the average guy from the North. Luckily, I became quite friendly with Francis, the other black fellow in the platoon. He was from Charlotte, North Carolina, the biggest and strongest guy in the company. Francis really helped me get through the rougher physical parts of basic. Many a time when I needed a boost, literally needed one, he was right there to give it to me.

Surprisingly, as much of a drag as it was, the weeks moved fast. Each day, it seemed, I was running like crazy from one training class to the other—the firing range, hand-to-hand combat, marching, all the rest. Most of the time I managed to keep my attitudes to myself. Sometimes, though, I guess they showed.

I just couldn't take part in the marching to songs, for instance. Every morning when it came time to line up and go out into the field, we'd always march to a song to keep in step. I thought the words were really stupid. Actually insulting. Like, "Jody's got your girl and gone—Jody's got your mama, too." Or your sister. Or somebody. While everybody else shouted out the marching cadence, I kept my mouth shut tight.

Or during bayonet practice, when the sergeant would yell out at us, "What's the spirit of the bayonet?" And everyone hollered back, "To kill!" And then, the sergeant always shouted, "I can't hear you! Now this time let me hear it—what's the spirit of the bayonet?" And then, shouting as loudly as possible, everybody answered, "To kill!"

One day the sergeant noticed that I wasn't shouting back. He came over to me. "What's wrong with you, pussy?" he asked. "How come you can't holler like everybody else?"

And it was impossible not to tell him. "Because I don't believe in killing, that's why!"

He started to say something, then turned and walked away.

Competition played a big part in basic training. Just as the company commander was set on winning the Commander's Trophy, each platoon sergeant was out to win the platoon plaque which was awarded to the top-rated platoon each week.

Sergeant Joiner had made a big thing about the plaque on the very first week. He had lined up the platoon one morning. "Do you see that plaque up there?" he asked. "That's been up there for twelve weeks running—'cause for that period of time, this has been the best damn platoon in the company. Now I want you all to understand this. I never intend to lose that plaque. It's right there on that door—and that's where it's gonna stay!"

Unfortunately for Sergeant Joiner, it didn't work out that way. The very next week, he lost his plaque.

Joiner was angry—but he found a way to justify what had happened. "It's all right," he told us, "because I'm still satisfied that this platoon is the best damn platoon in the company. I think the only reason they took it from us is because they're jealous of me."

The further along into the eight weeks of basic I went, the more I came to realize that the way the trainees were treated was completely wrong—that it could never accomplish the goal of building disciplined soldiers who respected the military and the leaders. How can a man coming into the army have any respect for the first noncommissioned officers he meets when he's constantly cursed and insulted, when he marches in cadence to words that call his mother and his sister a whore, when he's put down time and time again?

The theory, I guess, is that you're supposed to stand up there and take it—be ready to obey any order without getting mad. Like when a drill instructor curses you out, calls you "pussy," or "asshole," or "fuck-up." And, of course, most of us did just that—we took it. But it wasn't out of respect or because we were well disciplined. It was only out of fear of what would happen if we didn't.

I was raised to believe that the best way to have a man learn respect for you is by showing respect to him. And that never happened in basic training. They never seemed to understand that if the military wanted a soldier to be disciplined, then it was up to those in authority to show respect for the men under them, in order for it to be returned. Then, when a leader has the respect of his men, discipline will be no problem. It will follow automatically.

So, week by week, I made it through. Even though Arnold Webster was in another platoon, we remained good friends. He had started corresponding with my sister Pamela. And most nights we'd visit together, either at his barracks or mine.

Francis was always around to give me—or anyone else who needed it—a helping hand. Sometimes during running in PT, when I was so tired I could have just about fallen out, Francis would come up beside me, grab an arm, and practically carry me along for a while.

Actually, Francis was great at just about everything. He made 500, the top score for PT, and got excellent scores on the rifle range and on all the other tests. We all thought it really unfair that he didn't win "soldier of the cycle"—an award given to the outstanding all-around trainee. The guy who won it was related to our company commander. I'd like to think that that was the reason, rather than because he was white and Francis was black.

Many things used to bug me during those eight weeks, but I tried not to let them get to me too much. Like smart-ass remarks from sergeants or others when they'd spot me praying or saying grace. Or the way some of the guys would make cracks because I didn't curse up a storm like the others. Or the stupid approach to cleanliness at basic—just a means of harassment, really. Making you spit-shine a floor on your hands and knees, then running everybody over it to mess it up. Or shining your boots till every mark was off, then charging you through every mud hole they could find so you'd have to do them over again.

But all in all, I found it wasn't too bad. The food was okay, and I never really minded pulling KP. Sometimes, in fact, I offered to take someone else's. Not that I liked it *that* much—but for fifteen or twenty bucks for half a day on a weekend, it was hard to turn down. The extra money helped a lot, because I never received more than ten dollars a month from my pay. Out of the ninety dollars we got, I sent an allotment of fifty-five home. Then, with insurance and savings bonds, only ten bucks remained.

All the time, right up until the night before graduation, I continued to believe that I was guaranteed a noncombat assignment at the completion of basic training—that I'd either be sent to cooking school or given a clerical job. What I didn't know then —what the recruiting sergeant in Brooklyn had never told me— was that such guarantees are only given when a man enlists for three years, not for two. When you join the RA for two years, you're unassigned, and that means the army can assign you whenever and to whatever it likes.

We were to graduate on a Friday. On Thursday afternoon, we lined up to hear our orders—to learn what our future assignment was to be.

First, it was announced that all men assigned to A.I.T.—Advanced Infantry Training—were to receive no leave and must report directly to their next duty. A few minutes later, when they called out my name, I learned that that directive applied to me. No cooking school. No clerical job. Instead, Advanced Infantry Training at Fort Polk, Louisiana!

As soon as the formation broke, I asked to see the company commander, a young lieutenant right out of OCS. He had always seemed friendly enough and often encouraged me in the field. I hoped that now he'd be able to help.

I was admitted to his office without waiting. "Yes, Daly, what can I do for you?" he asked, smiling.

"Sir, I have something to tell you," I said.

I told him the whole story. Why I had enlisted in the army and what I had been told by the recruiter. How I hadn't believed it necessary to state that I was a conscientious objector, since I thought I was guaranteed to be assigned a noncombat job.

He explained how I would have had to enlist for three years in order to be guaranteed the assignment I wanted. Then he said, "Unfortunately, you have your orders now, and there's nothing I can do to change them. But as soon as you arrive at Fort Polk, ask to see your company commander. Tell him you're a conscientious objector and that you want to submit an application for that status."

The commander got up and placed a hand on my shoulder. "I'm really sorry I didn't know about this earlier," he said.

The following morning, I was told not to report for the graduation ceremony. I was to be given the opportunity of taking the PT test again, since I had failed it the last time. Actually I should have passed, but, by mistake, I had not been given any credit for the running test. When I considered the consequences of failing PT, it put me in a cold sweat.

Before it was time to report for the test, Sergeant Joiner called me over.

"Well, Daly," he said, "this is it. As you know, if you fail the PT test this time, you'll be recycled for another eight weeks. And before that, you'll spend two weeks right here with me, helping to get the area in shape for the next batch of trainees. Now let me tell you something. If you don't pass that damn PT test, I'm really gonna fix your ass when you get back over here. If you think it's been hell up till now, that won't be nothin' compared to the hell I'm gonna give you for two damn weeks."

"No sweat, Sergeant," I said. "I'm gonna pass all right."

It was a really cold morning. I took off for the test area with Cachoian and A.B., two other guys in the platoon who still hadn't passed PT either. A.B.'s name was actually Abramowitz, but the sergeant had had trouble pronouncing it right from the start. He decided to give up on it and call him A.B. instead.

No matter how many times A.B. took the PT test, he never came close to passing. The story about him was that the only reason he enlisted was on a bet with his girl friend, and now he was determined to get himself out. Actually, he was a very bright guy, had his master's in English. But all during basic he acted as stupid as possible, and he did such a good job of it that he could get away with practically anything. He'd turn the wrong way during drill, walk slow when the order to double-time was given, sometimes show up an hour late for class. The CO had already agreed he should be out of the service—only the doctor refused to sign the papers that stated he couldn't adjust.

Cachoian should never have been in the army in the first place. He was very good at everything except PT, and the reason was that about a year before, he had been in a bad car accident. After being hospitalized for many months in a coma, he had suddenly snapped out of it. But he was left with one leg shorter than the other. With two of the five PT tests based on running, Cachoian never had a chance of passing.

On this last attempt at PT, I made it. Not that I whizzed through. But I came off with a score of 320 again, and that was twenty points more than I needed to pass. It was good enough for me.

When I returned to the platoon, Sergeant Joiner was waiting. I handed him the PT report. "Well, you sure are a lucky son of a bitch," he said.

Cachoian and A.B. weren't so lucky. Both had failed again.

The following morning, Saturday, we were up at three o'clock. I said good-by to Webster, who was to report for A.I.T. at San Antonio. The only guys going to Fort Polk from my company were Francis and one other fellow, Hatmaker. After chow, the three of us took a bus to Atlanta. From there, we flew to New Orleans, where we boarded buses for Lake Charles.

The bus ride to Fort Polk was a little over an hour. The closer we came to the camp, the more anxious I was to get there. I couldn't wait to see my company commander and get things straightened out once and for all.

CHAPTER 3

Fort Polk, Louisiana, Spring 1967

When we pulled into Fort Polk, it was raining steadily, and the entire camp was one mess of mud. It was nothing like Fort Jackson—the buildings were old and worn-looking. With the first glimpse of my company area—Company E, 4th Battalion, 3rd Training Brigade—I knew I wasn't going to like it. And to make matters worse, it was the day before Easter Sunday. I kept thinking how festive New York would be the following day, everyone dressed up, all the ladies out in new dresses and hats.

The very first thing on Monday morning, I went to the platoon sergeant and asked for permission to see the company commander.

"Why?" he asked. "In only one day the problem can't be all that serious?"

"It's a personal matter, Sergeant,"

"I don't buy that, Daly. Let's just forget it!"

Early the following morning, I approached the platoon sergeant again. "It's really important that I see the company commander," I said.

"I still don't know the reason," he said.

"Well, like I said, it's personal."

"Nothing's personal in the army, Daly. Why do you want to see him?"

"Because I'm a conscientious objector and I want to apply for conscientious objector status," I said.

He stared at me. "And just when did you decide you were a conscientious objector?"

"That's part of what I want to talk to the company commander about."

Again the sergeant refused to set in motion the chain of command that would get me a hearing with the CO. If he had wanted to arrange the meeting, he would have gone to the first sergeant, who would have taken my request to the company commander.

On the following day, I tried once more. This time he spun around angrily and said, "Daly, just get off my fucking back, hear? I don't give a shit what you are. As far as I'm concerned, you're no different than any other guy in this platoon."

I was tempted, right then, to refuse to go out into the field. I decided to hold off and think it through.

Meanwhile, if I'd had any doubts about how much I disliked Fort Polk and A.I.T., after only three days, none remained. Some things about the training were okay. For example, it wasn't nearly as rough as basic, and we weren't constantly harassed by the sergeants. We even got from one place to another on trucks, instead of marching or running like at Fort Jackson. And there was very little PT. But the entire atmosphere of the post, and the training itself, made it clearer than ever that it just wasn't my bag—that I really belonged out of the army completely.

The old teaching of the Jehovah's Witnesses seemed truer than ever: a Christian belongs in only one army, the army of God.

At Fort Polk, everything you did, heard or saw was geared to the war and to killing. Areas had signs up—"Tigerland"—and we had to run and growl because, they kept telling us, we were tigers. It was hard sometimes to believe what you were seeing—all these grown men running and growling, many of them wearing T-shirts they had bought in the PX with "I'm A Tiger!" on the front, or "To Kill A Cong!" It was like they were really all just a bunch of kids, and you almost expected to see their T-shirts read "Grandma Loves Me!" or something like that.

Right from the start, all the instructors kept telling us how horrible the enemy was in Vietnam, barbarians who tortured all prisoners. Gruesome-looking drawings representing "The Cong" were hanging all over the post and in the classrooms. Even one of the chapels had a big sign up on its outside fence—"To Kill A Cong!"

The army's fighting technique in Vietnam at this time was called the "search and destroy" method, and they made it clear what that meant right at the start of A.I.T. "When you come into an enemy village," we were told, "you come in opening fire. You kill everything that's living—women, children and animals! You destroy everything that is a means of survival—food, houses, even tools!" And when we asked how to tell an enemy village from a friendly one, we were instructed that an enemy village was any village from which you were fired upon. Even if only one round was shot by only one person—that village was an enemy village as far as the army was concerned. And that meant you killed everyone. You destroyed everything.

Many times I almost walked right out during this instruction, or yelled out how wrong I thought it was. And I thought how I really had no right to be taking it in the first place, how it was against everything I'd been taught and everything I believed. Then I decided I wasn't going to apply for a noncombat job as a conscientious objector. Instead, I was going to ask for separation from the armed forces.

On one thing, though, I made a bargain with myself. Even if I did go along with the training, I'd remember everything only long enough to pass the tests—and I'd have to pass them just to make sure I'd never have to take the entire nine weeks of training all over again. Once I was out of A.I.T., I told myself, I could forget every bit of it. As far as I was concerned, one thing was certain—I'd never be putting any of it to use.

Finally, on the fourth day at Fort Polk, while pulling KP, I decided I wouldn't be put off any longer about getting to see the company commander. On the first break, I went to a phone booth and called the office of the post commander. An officer on his staff asked what the call was about. I explained how I had been refused permission to see my company commander on an important personal matter ever since I arrived.

"Your platoon sergeant had no right to do that," I was told. "What is your name and company?"

Within minutes after I returned to KP, a Pfc from the company commander's office came to the mess hall and said the CO, Captain Riley, wanted to see me.

The first sergeant waved me in without a word, and the first thing Captain Riley asked was, "Daly, have you ever heard of the chain of command?"

"Yes, sir," I said.

"Then why didn't you follow it?"

"I tried, Captain. I asked the platoon sergeant for permission to see you every day for four days. He refused."

"Well, okay this time, Daly. But in the future you come straight to me, understand? Forget about phoning the post commander. Well then, what's the problem?"

I told him everything from the beginning. He seemed really sympathetic. "You'll have to submit a detailed application to request separation as a conscientious objector," he said. "If you'd like, I'll help you with it."

For the following two weeks, I worked on that application. It ran fifteen written pages and was typed up by the company clerk, who bitched all the time he was doing it. I covered everything. I explained my religious training with the Jehovah's Witnesses. One of the many questions on the application asked: "Describe the nature of your belief that is the basis of your claim, and state whether or not your belief in a Supreme Being involves duties that to you are superior to those arising from any human relation." I answered this by explaining that I believed in a Supreme Being, Jehovah God. And then, I wrote: "I believe in God the Father and Jesus Christ, His son. I believe, as a Christian, that I should be like Christ and should follow the path which Christ walked. I believe the Holy Bible to be my guide in all matters of life. Whenever human laws conflict with divine law, I choose to obey God rather than man."

Throughout the fifteen pages, I quoted from the Bible, citing the basis of my beliefs. I even explained why I did not believe in saluting the flag, how the Bible tells in the Book of Daniel, Chapter 3, how early Christians, with God's approval, refused to render homage to a state emblem.

And I put down what it says in the Ten Commandments in the Book of Exodus: "You must not make for yourself a carved image or a form like anything that is in the heavens above, or that is on the earth underneath, or that is in the waters under the earth. You must not bow down to them nor be induced to serve them, because I Jehovah your God am a God enacting exclusive devotion." And this commandment, I explained, could well relate to the flag, which is considered sacred—its stars a symbol of the heavens, and the stripes symbolic of the rays of light emanating from the sun.

I went on to explain why I didn't believe in the use of force.

I described my religious training as a youngster. And I told in detail the circumstances of my interview at the local Selective Service board.

I provided references—the Presiding Minister of the Jehovah's Witnesses Madison Congregation in Brooklyn, the President of the Cornerstone Baptist Church, seven friends and relatives.

Finally, I stated that I would be willing to perform work under the Selective Service Conscientious Objectors' work program. This would be a noncombat job, as a civilian.

A few days after I had started writing the application, Captain Riley suggested that I visit the assistant brigade chaplain, Captain Elmer G. Horn. The chaplain didn't have much to offer in the way of advice, but he was encouraging and agreed to do all he could.

During this time, I continued with the training. The word was out that I was a conscientious objector, and quite a few of the forty guys in the barracks questioned me about it. Some wanted to talk religion, and I always enjoyed doing this, even when it turned into a debate instead of a discussion. A few of the guys, though, who seemed friendly enough when they were sober, turned openly hostile after a few drinks. Then, I'd just refuse to argue, at least until they were sober again.

One fellow I really enjoyed talking to was Dickie Siegler from Indianapolis. We became good friends. Many nights we'd sit around trading ideas and beliefs—and it was a good kind of talk, even though we didn't think very much alike. Dickie struck me as the kind of guy who had led a very sheltered life before the army and now was trying to make up for it as best he could, running around in town, looking for girls, hitting the local bars.

I liked shooting the bull and drinking with the guys, and did a better job at both than most of them. Once I'd get started talking about something, it was almost impossible to shut me up. And liquor never bothered me much. I could put away quite a lot before I even felt it. I learned that about myself when I was sixteen and Renee's mother gave me my first drink.

Whenever they had the chance, the fellows would make it into Leesville, the nearby town everyone called "the home of Fort Polk," or sometimes "Diseaseville," which was closer to the truth. Without the GIs of Fort Polk, Leesville would be nothing at all. And with them, it was nothing more than a bunch of bars and whorehouses, mainly. One night I agreed to go in with three of the guys, all white. It was my first time in town.

None of us really knew our way around. We picked out, at random, one of the many bars, a small place packed with GIs. Once inside, we pushed our way up to the bar and ordered beer. The bartender leaned over to me and said in a low voice, "I'm sorry, we don't serve Negroes here."

With all the noise, I wasn't sure I'd heard him right. I just stood there.

A few minutes later, he came back. Now his manner had changed. "I thought I told you," he said sharply, "we don't serve niggers here!" Before I could answer, he turned and walked away.

When I told the guys what had happened, they were really upset. The four of us stormed out of the place.

After that, I didn't make it back to the bars in town very often. There wasn't much point. All the nicer places were for whites only. There were just no decent places for a black GI to go.

As for that incident at the bar, it was one of the few times while in the service that I faced open racial discrimination. And surprisingly, it hadn't come from the army at all, the one place where I might have expected to find it.

The only parts of Leesville where color didn't matter were the black districts. In these areas, the bars and whorehouses were open to all—and, in fact, brought in more white patrons than black. One night, I agreed to go to one of the black parts of town with Dickie Siegler and Red, one of the guys in my barracks.

Siegler and a few of the others were always kidding me about my attitude on sex, which was, simply, that I thought it ought to be left for married couples. "Hell, Daly," Siegler joked, "it's time we put an end to all this preachin' of yours. Red and I have decided to take you into town, fill you up with booze, and then see to it that you get a good piece of ass."

I laughed. "Why are you two so interested in taking care of me, anyway?"

"Oh, I don't know. Maybe it would just be fun to get you drunk one time."

"That's not too easy to do," I said. "I drink pretty good."

"Yeah—we'll see about that," Siegler said.

So the three of us took off for the one place in Leesville that every GI at Fort Polk knew about—The Casino. You went there for only two things, liquor and girls.

The Casino was in a black district that was just one whore-house after the other, and the streets even had trailers lined up, ready for business. Girls stood around the houses, smiled as you went by, and motioned for you to come inside. Some hung out the windows.

In front of the entrance to each house, a man or woman sat at a table with two cigar boxes. One box was for making change. The other was filled with rubbers.

Police cars cruised up and down but business went on as usual.

As soon as we walked into The Casino, the man at the entrance asked, "Do you fellows want a good time?"

We said we were just going to do some drinking for a while, and took a table away from the crowd. Siegler and Red lined up the whiskey drinks on the table, and every time I finished one, another replaced it. I kept up with them, drink for drink. By the time I began to feel them, both of them were really drunk.

"Well, what do you say, Daly, let's find the action around here," Siegler said. "And remember, no chickening out, now."

I followed them to an outside doorway where an old woman sat with her cigar boxes, like she was selling tickets to a movie. I considered turning back but Siegler and Red were right there behind me. If I did, I knew I'd never hear the end of it.

The woman took my money and told me what room to go to. I walked down a long hall, dark and smelly. I found the room and went inside.

The girl was sitting on the edge of the bed. She was dark-skinned, pretty, a little on the skinny side. Her robe hung open and she wasn't wearing anything underneath.

I looked over at her and didn't say anything. She stared back at me. Then finally she asked, "What you gonna do—just stand there and look?"

I had always been shy around girls, even to talk to them, sometimes. Now I was really shy, and I couldn't do anything but gape.

She stood up. "Well?"

I really didn't know what to say. "You know, I never did this before," I blurted out.

"Honey, don't you have a girl friend?" she asked.

"Sort of. But she believes the same as me."

"An' how's that?"

I told her.

"Aw, c'mon, honey," she said. "What's marriage got to do with it? Listen here, I've seen plenty of guys who've never had sex before. You just leave everything to me."

"Well, the thing is—" I began, and then explained about Siegler and Red, and how I'd come to be there.

Just as I finished talking, there was a knock at the door. Our five minutes were up.

"Gee, I'm sorry, honey," she said. "But I tell you what, you come back this week on your own and I'll show you everything. Unless you got some more money on you now."

"No, I ain't got no more money," I told her.

"Let me see your wallet," she said.

And just like a fool, I pulled out my wallet and let her look through it. She found a dollar bill and change. "I thought you had no more money," she said.

"That's my fare to get back to the post."

"Well, okay," she said, handing me back the wallet, like she was giving me a break by not taking my last dollar.

So I left and walked back down that dreary street to the bus station, passing all those broken-down houses, the whores beckoning to me from the stoops.

A little while later, Siegler and Red showed up. They were still so drunk they never even asked me what happened. And I just kept tight-lipped about the whole thing.

In no time, back at the post, they spread the word all over the company. Then, everybody kept saying, "Well, Daly, I guess now you can't be preachin' to us all the time."

And I just let it go at that. None of the guys ever did find out. I'd learned that when you're sitting around and shooting the bull, it's really an embarrassing thing to come out and admit you're a virgin. I figured that what they didn't know couldn't hurt.

It was after the third week of not hearing a word about my conscientious-objector application that I decided to refuse any more training. I sent the word along the chain of command—from my squad leader, to the platoon leader, to the platoon sergeant, to the first sergeant, to the CO. Captain Riley called me in.

"Now you know, Daly, these things take time," he said, "and you've got to be patient. Your application has been sent to the post commander. Now it must go to the Department of the Army for approval or disapproval."

"Yes sir, I understand," I said. "But it's been bugging me, and I really think the right thing for me to do is to stop taking the training."

"That would be a big mistake, Daly." He considered for a moment, then suggested that we visit Captain Horn, the chaplain, once more.

Horn was quick to agree with Riley. "The captain is absolutely right," he told me. "You could do yourself a lot of harm. First of all, you'll probably end up in the stockade. If that happens, chances are your application will not be considered for approval."

"But I believe that what I'm doing is wrong," I said. "What about that?"

Horn shook his head. "That's nonsense, Daly. You're not doing anything wrong at all. You're not out there killing anyone on the firing range—you're only shooting at targets, not human beings. It's training, that's all, and there's nothing wrong with that. Now if you're to stand any chance of getting conscientious-objector status, you'd better get back into the field and keep yourself out of the stockade. That's the best advice I can give you."

The two captains waited for my decision. Finally, I agreed. It seemed like I had no choice, really.

Still, it bothered me. I was compromising what I believed in. In fact, just by being in the army at all, I was doing that. The longer I stayed at Fort Polk, the more I realized how true that was—like at night when I'd be lying down, thinking about religion. At times like that, I'd understand why the Jehovah's Witnesses were so against the military, where, instead of accepting the commandment "Thou shalt not kill," a man in training is out in the field all day long shouting, "To kill! To kill! To kill!"

And I questioned that I should be going along with even the less important things, like saluting the pay officer, for instance. In order to get paid, I had to salute him. But even saluting only one officer was wrong if you believed that the principle of saluting was wrong. It was no different, really, than going to Vietnam and killing only one soldier. Killing one was the same as killing one hundred. Killing was killing. Saluting one officer was the same as saluting them all.

So the weeks of A.I.T. moved along with no word of my application. I was told that if nothing came through by the end of the cycle, I'd be held at Fort Polk to wait. But at least if I passed the tests, I wouldn't have to repeat the training. And so far, I was doing okay—even without a helping hand from Francis this time.

Soon it was May. And then, graduation day.

For me, that turned out to be a terribly sad occasion.

CHAPTER 4

Fort Polk, Louisiana, Summer 1967

Graduation was held on a beautiful day in May—but I was miserable. I was pulling KP. Everyone returned from the ceremonies all smiles, happy as anything. They were all going someplace. Not me. I was to stay right there at Fort Polk for at least two or three more months as a holdover. If nothing happened on my conscientious-objector application before July, I'd get a fifteen-day pass. But right then, that seemed like a hundred years away.

All the buses were lined up, the destination of each posted in the front window—Chicago, Houston, Detroit, Cleveland, New York City. I looked at those buses and told myself, golly, just think, if you'd wanted to, you could be going too. Finally, it got to me so bad, I was on the verge of crying. I went to a phone booth and called home. When I heard my mother's voice, it was just impossible to keep back the tears.

"What's wrong, Bubby?" she asked.

"Well, everybody's leaving," I said. "I guess it's just that I'd like to be going home too, like all the rest."

"Sure, I understand—but you mustn't let yourself get upset like that."

"I know it. But sometimes things just get to me. I'll be fine."

"At least you can be happy about one thing," my mother said, "you're not on your way to Vietnam. And when the army comes to understand about your being a conscientious objector, maybe you never will have to go—at least not to do any fighting."

After we talked for a few minutes, I felt a lot better. I

guess I still didn't look all that great, though. Soon as I returned to the company area, all the guys kept coming over, trying to cheer me up, saying how they hoped I'd have good luck with my conscientious-objector application.

Then, a short time later, I stood watching the buses take off, wishing like crazy I was on one of them, bound for home. Still, I had to know it was much better for me this way.

The next weeks really dragged. I stayed in the old company area and was assigned different details every day—cleaning barracks, painting, fixing broken windows, doing just about anything that would help shape up the area for the IG inspection.

Then, during the second week in June, I was assigned to Headquarters Company. Now, every morning during formation, a bunch of sergeants from different offices turned up to request men for various details. I could end up almost anywhere—the finance office, mail room, mess hall. And all the time, not a word from anybody about my application.

It was while pulling KP that I met Kingsberry—and that helped brighten things up. He was a big black guy with a mind all his own. Nobody dared mess with him.

After his brother returned from Vietnam, Kingsberry had put in for conscientious-objector status, too—so we had plenty to talk about.

One week, we both pulled KP together and were assigned to three different places over a few days period—KP for our own company, for the officers' mess hall, and for the reserves in the camp. No way was Kingsberry about to go along with that. He'd made up his mind that he was only going to do KP once a week —and he stuck to it.

Seems that somewhere along the way, Kingsberry had become very friendly with the company commander of Headquarters Company, who just happened to be black. And when anybody tried to give Kingsberry a hard time, forget it. He always came out on top. Like that time when he was taken off the extra KP.

We had a hi-fi in the back of the mess hall, and Kingsberry always spent a good part of his KP day dancing his behind off. One day, the first cook, a Frenchman who had joined the army to get his citizenship, blew his top at Kingsberry, screaming at him to get out of the mess hall.

"Hell, man," Kingsberry told him, still dancing, "I ain't goin' no place. I ain't goin' to do no work jus' now—but I ain't gettin' out of the mess hall, either."

The cook went charging outside to report Kingsberry to the first sergeant, who restricted him to the company area. But not for long.

Kingsberry went off to see the company commander, and before you knew it, the restriction was lifted. Not only that, he ended up with a three-day pass besides.

All conscientious objectors are required to have what the army calls a mental hygiene consultation. On June 19, I was told to report to the post psychiatrist, Captain Sidney J. Dupuy. Even though I had a good idea of what to expect—Kingsberry, who'd already had the interview, had filled me in—some of his questions still caught me by surprise.

"I see you'd be willing to accept a noncombat job under the Selective Service work program," he said. "You indicated that on your c.o. application."

"Yes, that's true."

"Well, how about a noncombat job in the army?"

"At first, I was going to go along with that," I said. "That had been my idea when I came into the army, to be a cook or a clerk."

He studied me for a minute. "I see. Well, Daly, if you'd have taken a job as a cook or a clerk, how would you have justified that? Just by being in the army, you'd still be helping to kill in a way. Isn't that so?"

It was really hard for me to answer that, because, deep down, I believed that what he had said was right. It was what the Jehovah's Witnesses had always taught—that it makes no difference what you do in the army. You're part of it, and it's wrong. I related this to the captain and then explained that that was exactly why I had decided to put in for separation.

Captain Dupuy asked a few more questions on my religious beliefs, then changed the subject. To sex.

"Have you ever masturbated?" he asked.

At that time, I didn't even know what the word meant. It just wasn't the way the guys on the block ever spoke.

When I told the captain I didn't understand, at first he didn't believe me. Then he explained and asked me again. I told him no.

He looked a little doubtful. "Do you have a girl friend?"

"I used to," I said. "But we broke up some time ago."

"Have you ever had intercourse?"

I told him no.

He looked up quickly. "Why's that? It's not normal for a man nineteen years old to—"

I interrupted him. "Wait a minute—what do you call normal? I don't call a thing normal just because everybody does it. To me, normal is when a thing is right. As far as I believe, sex is only for the married, and its purpose is for reproduction."

Today, I might have answered that question differently. But then, it was exactly how I believed.

Then he asked, "What do you think of homosexuals?"

"I look at it that some people can't help being that way," I said. "It depends a lot on how someone is brought up, I think. I knew a little boy from my block whose parents wanted to have a little girl so bad they raised him playing with doll babies all the time. It's things like that that can make a difference."

He asked questions about other things, my family, growing up, then he had me explain all the circumstances that led up to my enlisting.

"In other words," he said, "you completed your infantry training because you were told it would not in any way affect your application to be a conscientious objector. Is that so?"

I told him yes, it was.

He stood up and thanked me. When I left, he gave me no idea how his report was going to read.

After a few weeks of pulling details at Headquarters Company, I decided to volunteer to be a cook, and from then on I worked regularly in the mess hall. I liked that. At least, it was better than pulling details. Then, before I knew it, it was July and time for going home.

Even Bed-Stuy looked good. And being with the family was great. The fifteen days just flew by.

I got to see my friend William Smith and spent time with the twins, Alonso and Alfonso. While I was away they'd started drinking, and since I now considered myself a real veteran with the booze, we'd go to local bars together and spend hours talking. We went to a few parties, too. But, like always, the twins were still a heck of a lot faster-living than I was—and I always knew when to pull out.

I met Renee a few times during the fifteen days but she always seemed to have someplace to go or someone to see. Again, we never did have that talk.

The only disturbing part of being home was seeing how my younger brothers, seventeen and fourteen then, had started giving my mother a hard time and seemed to be getting caught up in the neighborhood wildness. I knew how easy it could be to get into trouble in a ghetto area like Bedford-Stuyvesant, and I was sorry I wouldn't be around to keep an eye on them.

And then the leave was over, and once again it was time for good-bys. During the trip back to Fort Polk, I kept hoping that maybe I'd be surprised and find good news on my conscientious-objector application waiting for me.

No good news back at the post. Instead, I returned to find half my clothes missing—my fatigue uniform, two pairs of pants, my overcoat and even my bedding.

No word of any kind on my application.

So it was back to cooking and the mess hall. August in Louisiana can be plenty hot no matter what you're doing. In the kitchen, it's even hotter.

A few days after returning to Fort Polk, I wrote home and told everyone how glad I was to have gotten back for a while. I asked my mother to tell my brothers that I said they'd better change their ways and take the studying of the Bible seriously. If they wanted to live together in a new world, I wrote, they'd better start preparing for it right now.

Meanwhile, for me, in the world of the army, I just couldn't understand why no action had been taken on my conscientious-objector application. Actually, it had. But I didn't know that then. And I didn't find out until the morning of September 4 when the first sergeant of my old company called me into his office.

"Well, Daly, you're moving on at last," he said. "You're on orders for Vietnam and will process out tomorrow. After a twenty-five day leave, you report to Oakland Army Terminal."

I couldn't believe it. "But what happened to my conscientious-objector application?" I asked.

"Why, that came back in June. Didn't anyone over in Headquarters tell you?"

"Nobody told me anything," I said.

"Well, I'm afraid it's too late now, Daly. You should have

been notified when the application was rejected so you could have resubmitted it. Once you're up on orders, it's too late for that."

"But that's not right," I said. "How was I supposed to know the application was turned down if nobody told me?"

The sergeant shook his head. "It's a tough break, Daly. There was plenty of time for you to resubmit had you known." He held up a folder. "It's all right here. You were turned down all along the way."

"Can I see that?" I asked.

He hesitated, then handed over the folder.

Just like the first sergeant said, it was all there. And it went like this:

Captain James M. Riley, the commanding officer of Company E, had found my conduct and efficiency "excellent." However, he had recommended disapproval and stated, "In view of his voluntary enlistment and failure to declare his convictions regarding military service, the sincerity of this application is questionable."

Major William T. Hayden, the commanding officer of the 4th Battalion, 3rd Training Brigade, had recommended disapproval.

The adjutant for the commanding officer of the 3rd Training Brigade had recommended disapproval on the CO's behalf, without comment.

The adjutant for the commanding general of the post had recommended disapproval for the general in a memo to the Chief of Personnel Operations, Department of the Army, Washington, D.C.

A memo from Headquarters, Department of the Army, Washington, D.C., to the commanding general at Fort Polk agreed to the recommendation for disapproval but asked for additional information—statements from the post chaplain and the post psychiatrist.

All of this correspondence had taken place in May.

Then, dated June 19, 1967, two statements had been submitted —one from Captain Sidney J. Dupuy, post psychiatrist, and one from Captain Elmer Horn, the assistant brigade chaplain.

Captain Dupuy reviewed my background and related the events leading up to my enlistment as I had described them. He then stated that he found no evidence of mental illness, that I could distinguish right from wrong, that he had found no mental or physical defects. In his final recommendation, Captain Dupuy stated: "This Enlisted Man is cleared psychiatrically for action as deemed appropriate by command. It is the examiner's opinion that the EM is sincere in his belief."

Captain Horn, the chaplain who had led me to believe he would do all he could to help, stated: "Pvt. Daly is affiliated with the Jehovah's Witnesses religion through personal study. EM isn't a member of this sect. I personally feel that Pvt. Daly is using this effort to get assigned somewhere other than Vietnam. Had his sincerity been affirmative, he would probably have made a more positive approach in basic training for a change of MOS."

I returned the folder and the first sergeant said, "My only advice to you at this point, Daly, is to go and see the chaplain."

No way was I about to return to Captain Horn. Instead, I went to see the Catholic chaplain. He listened attentively to the entire story. Then he said, "I think you should go personally and see the brigade commander. I'll be glad to set up the appointment for you."

My interview with the commander of the 3rd Training Brigade didn't take long. Without getting up from his desk, he shouted across the room, "Soldier, I won't lift a finger to help any conscientious objector. Now get out of my office!"

I returned to the chaplain.'When I told him what had happened, he shook his head sadly and said, "Look, I'm not telling you to do this, Daly, but it seems like the only action left for you now. Go home on leave—and stay home! Let the MPs pick you up. You'll be charged with AWOL, but you'll get attention and be able to plead your case."

The following day, I was on my way back to New York City. The thought of getting home again, this time for twenty-five days, lifted my spirits. Only now I was really confused, uncertain of what to do. All kinds of questions kept going through my mind. Should I take the chaplain's advice, should I turn to the Jehovah's Witnesses for help—or maybe would it make more sense to just desert? Take off for Sweden or someplace?

Something else that really bothered me was Renee. This time I was determined to have a talk with her. As crazy as it seemed,

I kept thinking how I'd like to ask her to marry me. Right then and there.

As the plane came nearer to home, I tried my best to stay cool and relaxed—and, for a little while, anyway, to stop thinking about the hard decisions I'd soon be making, for better or for worse.

CHAPTER 5

Exploring Options

Who knows if I ever really meant to follow through with it—but one of the first things I did after returning home was to check the cost of a one-way flight to Stockholm. Since I'd kept little money for myself during my eight months in the army, I had no way of coming up with the $289 for a ticket except by working during my leave, and even a while after if necessary.

B. Altman's department store agreed to take me back on a temporary basis as a clerk in the credit office. I also went back to my old job at the corner grocery store during spare time.

I really hated the very idea of deserting. But I knew that once I ended up in Vietnam, getting conscientious-objector status would then be just about impossible. Taking off for Sweden, I figured, just might be the only way out. And the Jehovah's Witnesses listings in the back of my Bible showed many congregations in Stockholm. Maybe, I thought, I could live there and become a minister.

Of course, I realized, if I did desert, I could probably forget about ever coming home again. The only way I'd ever get to see the family was when they came to visit me. Considering this, I knew going to Sweden would be a really tough decision to make. Still, I had to leave that door open.

On my first Sunday home, I went to see the head overseer of the Madison Congregation of Jehovah's Witnesses. I'd known him ever since I first started studying, and he'd often visited at our house to explain some of the more involved questions about the religion. I knew it would be great just to talk everything over with him, even though I had a very good idea what he thought about my enlisting in the army. Yet, talking it through might help me straighten out my thoughts.

And then, I'd greatly value his opinion of the suggestion the Catholic chaplain had given me. Staying home and waiting for the MPs to pick me up just didn't seem like the greatest idea in the world. Also, I thought, maybe with a letter from the head overseer it would be possible to resubmit my conscientious-objector application at Fort Hamilton in Brooklyn while I was home.

I arrived at Kingdom Hall on Madison Street in time for the Sunday morning public lecture. I knew the head overseer would be free following it since the Watchtower study period wasn't until the afternoon.

He gave me a warm greeting and asked me into his office where we could talk. I explained how I was to report to Oakland for assignment to Vietnam and then told him what the Catholic chaplain had advised.

"Well, James, we've talked about most of this before," he said. "You know what Jehovah's Witnesses teach. As a believer, you should not be in the military under any conditions, even if you were guaranteed a noncombat job. It's truly unfortunate that you could never have become a Pioneer so that you'd have been able to qualify for exemption as a minister."

As he spoke, I remembered my conflict after getting out of high school, how I'd then considered becoming a Pioneer and a Jehovah's Witness. But that would have meant putting in one hundred hours every month in the field, teaching and visiting homes. At the time, getting a job was more important, I'd decided. Without any financial help, it was just about impossible for my mother to manage taking care of seven kids.

"Even as a conscientious objector," the head overseer went on, "you could have refused to go into the military. You could have elected to go to prison, instead. There you could have taken part in the special programs for conscientious objectors—Bible studies and ministry school. And even though you might have been given a five-year sentence, with good behavior you probably could have been out in two."

At one time, I had thought about the idea of going to prison and even discussed it with my mother. As much as she didn't want to see me in Vietnam, she had been totally against it. She'd felt so strongly, in fact, I had just given up the idea right then.

"Well, it's all too late for that now," I said to the head overseer. "Tell me what you think about my staying home and waiting for the MPs."

"No, you can't do anything like that, James. Remember, you are in the service now and you must go by the rules and regulations of the military. Not to report would be breaking the law. And you would be charged with being AWOL—not simply as a conscientious objector who has refused to go to Vietnam and kill."

When I asked if he would write a letter that I could take to Fort Hamilton, he agreed immediately.

As we said good-by and he went off to tend to other chores before the afternoon Watchtower study, I thought how great it was for someone to truly believe in something and to devote himself to it. As all ministers in Jehovah's Witnesses, he served without pay. He lived on his income as an attorney. Jehovah's Witnesses believed that no minister should preach for pay but should earn his money doing something else—just as Christ had made his living as a carpenter.

At Fort Hamilton, when I explained my purpose, I was taken in to see a captain in the main administration building. He read the head overseer's letter, which requested that my application as a conscientious objector be given every consideration. Then I explained what had happened at Fort Polk and asked if I could resubmit my application at Fort Hamilton.

"I'm sorry," the captain said, "but you will have to wait until you get to Oakland Army Terminal—nothing can be done from here. I'd suggest you report there at least one day early and get your application in immediately."

I thanked him.

Working two jobs didn't leave much time for anything else—the family, friends, or going out. But I did manage an evening with Renee.

We'd gone out for a couple of hours in the neighborhood. In a way, it was almost like it used to be when we were going together. The talk didn't turn serious, though, until we were back at her house, alone in the living room.

I asked her straight out. "Renee, I thought maybe we should get married."

She was really surprised. "Gee, I never expected you to say that."

"Well, it's been on my mind a long time."

"But James, we've hardly seen one another for months and months. And in one week's time you'll be off again. You could even end up in Vietnam for a whole year, right?"

"I'm hoping it won't—but it could happen that way," I said. "Maybe that's one reason I'd like for us to get married now."

"I just couldn't, James. Not now. But look, why don't you ask me again when you're out of the army?"

And so that took care of my problem about Renee.

Two days before I was to report to Oakland, I was still considering the idea of Sweden. Not too seriously, though. The more I thought about it, and the more I pictured myself away from home and the family—maybe forever—the more I realized I just couldn't do it.

What seemed to make the most sense was to take the advice of the captain at Fort Hamilton and arrive at Oakland early, then to submit my application again and hope for the best. If it wasn't acted on, and I was shipped to Vietnam, I could always keep on trying there. And the truth was, deep down, I somehow figured on just that happening.

At least, I told myself, I'd stick to my beliefs no matter how it worked out. I'd never kill a man. And if I did stay in Vietnam for one year, it would give me the chance to really help at home. I figured I'd be able to save a good ninety-five percent of my pay.

Also, I'd be acting legally. I kept remembering what the head overseer had often said: "A Christian's obligation is to obey the law, as long as it doesn't conflict with the law of God."

September 27, 1967, was the day I left for Oakland, California. I worked at the store right through that afternoon. Then, that evening, my mother and my sisters Phyllis and Pam drove me to the airport.

At the boarding area, it seemed that there was just nothing left for any of us to say. We kissed good-by.

Just before going through the door, I looked back. All three of them were crying, and it brought tears to my own eyes. As embarrassed as I felt, I just couldn't hold them back.

When we got up into the air was when it really got to me. I looked down and thought how beautiful New York was, and that it was the last time I'd ever see it. I just had the feeling I wouldn't ever be coming back.

So I prayed. I prayed to be punished if what I was doing was really wrong. I *asked* God to punish me, even severely. Let me lose my arms or legs. Anything, rather than being killed in Vietnam and never coming back again to see my family.

And with that prayer in my mind, I fell off into a deep sleep. Next thing I knew, we were ready to land in Oakland.

CHAPTER 6

In Country

Two days later, September 29, I was on my way to Vietnam. Arriving at Oakland one day early hadn't helped one bit as far as resubmitting the conscientious-objector application was concerned. Like I expected, I was told I'd have to hold off until I reported to my company.

At Oakland, when the sergeant called my name for Vietnam, I wasn't sure I'd heard him right. He had gone down the list, and when he failed to get an answer from one man, he added one more name. Mine.

"Did you just say 'Daly'?" I asked in a shaky voice.

"You bet your ass I did!" the sergeant shouted back, grinning.

Then all the guys started to laugh and yell out. "Yeah, man, he called your name, all right!" "Yeah, man, you're goin' to Nam, too!"

Early the next morning we took trucks to Travis Air Force Base, and at nine o'clock we were in the air. By six, Vietnamese time, on October 1, we had touched down at Ben Hoa Airfield. When we finished checking through customs and changing our currency, we still had almost two hours to kill before the arrival of the buses to take us to LBJ Camp—the 199th Replacement Center.

As I walked around, my first impression of the airfield wasn't too great. It was really dingy—dirt everywhere. The bathroom was so filthy that, as bad as I had to go, I decided to wait until we reached the camp.

Finally, the convoy of buses pulled in to pick us up. We crowded around—all hundred and two of us—and you could tell by the look on the guys' faces that most were plenty shook up. Every bus had a jeep in front of it with a mounted machine gun. It was the first time any of us had come face to face with anything that even looked like a combat situation. What we didn't realize was that since we were in a combat zone, there was nothing unusual about the jeeps or the machine guns. Not knowing this, everyone figured that things must be sort of bad to take such precautions.

Once the buses started moving toward LBJ, I got my first real look at Vietnam. I don't know what village we went through first, but I just couldn't believe how horrible it was. The narrow streets were packed with people, dirty and raggedy. It reminded me of movies I'd seen of Hong Kong—crowds all over, people eating and sleeping in the streets, little tables set up to sell all kinds of things, and the terrible smell of it all sweeping up at you, filling the air.

We drove through a number of towns like that, one as bad as the other. And it really surprised me to see the awful conditions in which the Vietnamese people lived—houses made of tin cans or straw, cardboard shacks, roofs put together from tin or beer cans, anything that could be used for shelter.

After an hour, we pulled into LBJ, and it started to pour down rain. As the buses edged through the mud and puddles into the camp area, the smell wasn't much better than before. Even now, in the heavy rain, you could tell it was a busy, crowded camp. As I was soon to learn, it was a place of many different activities. It was the home of the Long Binh Jail, from which it got the name LBJ. It took in many GIs, all moving in different directions—some coming in, like us, others going back to the States, many passing through on their way to R & R. And in the middle of it all was the stink of garbage and filth we smelled through the open windows of the bus. A stink so bad I was sorry I hadn't gone to the bathroom back at the airfield when I'd wanted to.

We pulled in to a stop. Mud was everywhere, and we filed along on walking boards to get from one spot to the other. Considering the heavy rain, it would have made good sense to bunk us down anywhere for the night and to put off checking in until morning. But like you'd expect from the military, we were lined up outside the administration building to process in—and we stood in the downpour and mud for forty-five minutes.

That's when I made friends with Fones. I liked him right off —he was a warm, quiet-speaking guy who never used foul language, really much different from the average GI. We ended up in the same barracks, and during the next few days we kicked around many things. He especially liked to talk about his home and family. Fones had married just before coming into the army, and the top layer of his wedding cake had been frozen and was being saved to help celebrate his return.

We spent a lot of time trying to picture what it would be like out there in the field, and Fones was surprised to learn that I considered myself a conscientious objector. We had completely different ideas about religion, yet he was always interested in hearing me talk about it. "Every man must have the right to his own beliefs," Fones would say. "That's what we're fighting for, so that the Vietnamese can have the right to believe in what they want, too." Fones turned out to be one of the few guys who didn't argue against my being a conscientious objector.

At the end of the second day at LBJ, we were called out to hear our future assignments. None of us knew one company from another, yet we were all a little nervous just realizing that finally we'd be sent to our regular outfits, the ones with which we'd serve from then on in. And after the two days at LBJ, most of the guys were more than ready to make the move. As for me, I was perfectly satisfied to stay. As miserable as the place was, at least I wasn't out in the field killing Vietnamese.

Fones and I were to continue on together. We were both to report to Company A, 3rd Battalion, 21st Infantry. And now, like all the rest, we had both been promoted to Pfc.

As things turned out, we spent five whole days at LBJ. Each time we reported to the airport to catch our army plane for Chou Lai, the flight was canceled. Then we'd return to the camp for one more day of pulling details. The one I hated the most was called "burning shitters." We'd have to pour diesel oil into the latrine, light it, then stand by to see that it did a good job burning. The smell was really horrible and it always left my stomach plenty shaky.

One thing, though; we did manage a few hours now and then at the Jet Set Club. That helped a lot. The service club was right on base and had a great air-conditioning system. Volunteer nurses,

"Donut Dollies" we called them, were always friendly and nice to talk to.

In the club, we'd often run across GIs on their way to the States or R & R. Many of them had the number of days remaining in their tour printed on the front of their helmets, and they'd be quick to yell out at us, "Short, short," meaning they had only a short time to go. Or they'd point at one of us and shout with a grin, "There's my replacement, right there!"

When Fones and I told one GI just in from the field that we were going to report to Alpha Company, he shook his head with envy and said, "Man, you've got it made, all right. Those guys just check out ID cards all day long. They hardly ever get to see Charlie, the way I hear it."

On the fifth night, we finally made the flight to Chou Lai, about forty of us, all squatting side by side on the plane's floor. We arrived at Chou Lai Airfield about eight in the morning.

Before going to our regular company, however, we still had one more stop to make—one week of pre-combat training at the 196th Light Infantry Charger Academy.

It was totally different from A.I.T. Here you took special classes and were taught the real guts of jungle fighting. You learned about such things as booby traps and guerrilla ambushes. Also, you were taught to understand Charlie, the Vietnamese enemy. At least, you were taught to understand him as the U.S. military saw and understood him.

One thing that was constantly stressed, for example, was how all friendly Vietnamese farmers during the daytime could be "Charlies" at night. And how all Vietnamese looked the same. They even showed us pictures of the Cong, all dressed in black, to prove it.

"And always remember," the instructor said, "Charlie only attacks when the odds are overwhelmingly in his favor. That's why, when Charlie hits a company, it may damn well be wiped out completely—and usually is!" I kept thinking how that wasn't what we'd always heard on the news back in the States. Then, somehow, it was always the Vietnamese who got the worst of it.

Another thing they taught us at the Charger Academy was how Charlie was really "a smart little man who will make use of anything you throw away." Never discard a thing, we were told

—not even an empty can. Whatever it was, Charlie would pick it up and put it to use. He even made things out of B-52 scraps after a plane was shot down.

The more training I took at the Charger Academy, and the more I kept thinking how in a few days time I'd be out in the field where I'd be expected to put it to use killing Vietnamese, the more important it seemed to get out of the army any way possible. At one point, I felt so strongly about this I decided, right then and there, I'd be better off to be in prison. It was then I told the sergeant I was a conscientious objector and wanted to see the commanding general.

"You ever been out in the field?" the sergeant asked.

"No," I admitted. "Never."

"Well, let me tell you something, Daly—when you finally get out there and are being shot at, and you find you can't shoot back, that's when you can say you're a conscientious objector. Before that, it's just a crock of shit, hear!"

The general agreed to see me. He heard me out, then said, "Nothing we can do for you here, Daly. When you get to your company, you'll have to submit another c.o. application and wait until it's acted on. Until that time, you must carry out your duties as an infantryman."

"I can't do that," I said. "I can't go out there and wait months for the army to classify me as a conscientious objector—and all that time, I'd be fighting and killing. Sir, I've been doing a lot of thinking on it. I've decided that I'd just as soon go to prison before shooting at anyone."

"You mean you'd rather be in Leavenworth?"

"Yes, sir. I would."

He looked at me like he just couldn't believe that here was a man asking to go to prison. "You know, Daly, you just can't go to Leavenworth—or even one of our prisons over here, for that matter—simply by requesting it. A soldier is sent to prison because he's found guilty of doing something wrong."

"Well, sir," I said, "I don't believe in breaking the law. But I do know I'd rather be in prison than be forced to go out and kill somebody."

"Take my advice, Daly," the general said, "wait until you get to your company and see the chaplain. He'll try to help you. Meanwhile, keep in mind that some offenses out here will land you in Long Binh Jail for six months or more. Then, when you get out, you'll still have that time to make up as part of your tour. Think things over carefully."

"Yes, sir," I said.

"And, Daly," the general said, "believe me, if the Department of the Army approves your application, we'll get you out of here just as fast as we can."

So I stayed with it. I finished the week of learning about the enemy and how to fight him. Then, on the last day, everyone was assigned his regular weapon. I looked at the M–16 rifle without emotion. As far as I was concerned, I was never going to use it.

Just before we left, each man was given his Charger Academy Certificate. Mine read, "196th Light Infantry Brigade Charger Academy—Certificate of Completion. Pfc James A. Daly satisfactorily completed the Charger Academy course of instruction in pre-combat training given at Chou Lai this 16th day of October 1967. Signed—Commandant, Captain James G. Leckey; Commanding General, Brigadier General Frank H. Linnell."

So the trucks pulled in to take us to our companies. As far as the army was concerned, every graduate of the Charger Academy —and that included me—was now ready and prepared to face the enemy.

Four of us had been assigned to Alpha Company—Fones, myself, and two other guys. When our truck pulled up at the company area, the platoon leader was waiting. His name, I was soon to learn, was Lieutenant Fisher. No sooner had we climbed off the truck when he came over to the four of us, swept his eyes from one to the other, and asked, "Which one of you is Daly?"

"I am," I said.

He looked me up and down. "So, you're the conscientious objector. We heard all about you!"

I said nothing.

"Okay, Daly, the chaplain wants to see you. I'll catch up with you later on!"

I liked the chaplain immediately. His name, believe it or not, was Billy Graham.

"When did you first become a conscientious objector?" he asked.

Once again, I told all that had gone before. I explained how I'd never learned that my application had been turned down until after I had orders.

"What kind of conscientious-objector status did you apply for?" Chaplain Graham asked.

I told him I'd asked to be separated from the army.

He shook his head. "Well, that was all wrong, Daly. That was your big mistake."

"Well, the more training I took, the more I realized it was the only answer."

The chaplain nodded understandingly. "Yes, I can appreciate that. However, remember, you're in the Regular Army. That means *you* came to the army, not the other way around. A request for separation on religious grounds by a Regular Army man has about an eighty-five-percent chance of being turned down. There's only one thing for you to do at this point. You'll have to submit a new application—this time requesting noncombat status."

"But that could take a long time," I said. "Meanwhile, I'd be out in the field with the company."

"Well, I'm afraid there's no way around that," Chaplain Graham said. "At least, if you end up with a noncombat job, it may not be the perfect solution, but it will satisfy your more important beliefs."

It seemed pretty obvious to me that I really had no choice. Unless I refused to go out with the company and ended up in Long Ben Jail. Then, like the general at the Charger Academy had explained, I'd still have the same amount of time to serve in Vietnam when I got out.

"Okay, Captain, I'll take your advice," I said. "However, I must make it clear—I will not fire a weapon. I'd rather be killed than to have to kill anyone else."

"Well, I'm afraid that may be a very difficult decision to stick to, Daly. You see, in a combat situation there's the other men to think of, too. But let's not worry about that now—one thing at a time. We'll have to start from scratch on your application, so you'd better write home for a new batch of reference letters."

He walked with me to the door of his office. "You know, Daly," he said, "it's my personal feeling that we're doing the right thing fighting here in Vietnam. I believe that it is important to help the Vietnamese people to live freely. So you see, you and I think differently about the justification for fighting this war. Nevertheless, though we have different ideas, I want you to know I'll do all I can to help. Meantime, be patient—and do what is expected of you, as best you can."

"Yes, sir," I said. "And thank you."

Back at the company area, Lieutenant Fisher was waiting. As soon as I hopped off the jeep, he came over. "Okay, Daly—now tell me, do you refuse to go out in the field?"

"I'll go out, Lieutenant," I said. "But I want you to know, I'm not going to kill anybody."

He stared at me. "Look here, Daly—as long as you're in my platoon, you'll damn well do the same as every other man. You've got a weapon like all the rest of us. And you'll take care of it, clean it, baby it—and when the time comes, fire it. Otherwise, you'll have me to answer to."

I stared back at him and said nothing.

"And now I want you out with your squad, Daly. They're one man short—and waitin' for you."

About a half hour later, a jeep dropped me off in the nearby hamlet of Ngoc Nha. The squad—five men—were sitting in a small hootch taking a break for lunch. Sergeant Leshore, the squad leader, jumped up to welcome me. He was a short, friendly looking man with a warm smile. "Hi, Daly," he called out. "We're glad to have you with us." There was nothing at all sarcastic about how he said it.

He took me over and introduced me to the other four. Two of the guys looked up and barely nodded. The one called Nace got up and shook my hand. The fourth, Shriner, a heavy-set, red-faced Spec. 4, glared over and said, "So you're the c.o.!"

I had been given a supply of C-rations before leaving the company area, and I sat down with the others to eat. After a few minutes, a group of kids from the village crowded around and began to beg for candy or food. I really felt sorry for them—skinny, torn shirts and pants, bare feet, big, sad eyes just staring out at you.

"Number one, number one," the kids kept saying with a grin, which, I soon learned, meant they considered you to be okay. The bad guys, the ones they didn't like, were called "number ten."

I held up a small can of fruit to the others in the squad. "Anybody want this?" I asked.

They all shook their heads no. Then I motioned to one of the kids and gave it to him.

Immediately, Shriner jumped up. "Why did you give that to a gook?" he asked.

"Well, none of you guys seemed to want it."

"Man, you don't give anything to a gook. You throw it away first!"

"That's up to him," Sergeant Leshore said. "It's his right to give it away if he wants."

Shriner stepped right up close to me. "Wise up," he said. "You just got here, but before long you'll see things the way I do. You give gooks nothin'. Any one of 'em just as soon turn around right after you do and blow your fuckin' brains out!"

I didn't answer. Then, Sergeant Leshore told us it was time to move out. Our job, he explained to me, was to patrol the hamlet to check out ID cards. Just like I'd heard back at the Jet Set Club.

As we took off down the hot narrow street, more kids clustered around, begging, or calling out, "*Mỹ, mỹ*"—meaning Americans—"number one, number one!" But somehow, no matter how wide their grins, their eyes all held the same sad look.

CHAPTER 7

Chou Lai,
November 1967

Day after day, the squad patrolled the same few villages. If we stopped someone who didn't carry an ID card stamped "Chou Lai," that meant he was from another area and automatically a VC suspect. Then we'd take him in for questioning. The camp, set up on the outskirts of Chou Lai, was never very far away.

Much of the time we goofed off, killing time in some hootch —but always certain to be on the job when Lieutenant Fisher or Sergeant Capps, the platoon sergeant, was nearby.

The less time we spent walking around those Vietnamese hamlets, the better I liked it. Everything about them was really depressing, poverty everywhere, living conditions the worst. The people had to manage on very little food. Kids, always, were in rags, or less.

One thing I sensed immediately that disturbed me a lot was how most of the Vietnamese people resented our being there, acting like policemen. And they didn't bother covering up how they felt; you could even see it in their faces. Whenever they were friendly, it was because they had to be—and even then you could tell they didn't mean it. We were "number one" to only those groups of little sad kids begging for food or candy.

After a few days, I wrote home and said, "The people here are about a hundred years behind the Americans, and I feel so sorry for them sometimes. I give a lot of my food to the children. Please send hard candy so that I can pass it out to them."

A number of guys in the company let me know they weren't too happy at having a conscientious objector around. Most of the men, though, were okay about it, and I even struck up a few friendships. I liked Sergeant Leshore, and though Fones was in a different squad we'd often be out in the field together. And I ran across Meyers, one of the guys I'd taken A.I.T. with. He spotted me the very first day and called out, smiling, "Hey, man, don't you remember me? You shoulda come with the rest of us. You'd be gettin' short by now."

Every now and then, somebody would try to get me into a conversation about my being a c.o. The thing that bugged them most was just what the chaplain had told me it would be. They wondered how I'd react in a combat situation.

Often, I'd be forced into some questions and answers that went like this:

"Be honest, Daly, you mean you'd expect me to be out here and protect you in a battle, yet you wouldn't protect me if it meant firing your weapon?"

"It's a tough thing to answer," I'd say. "I'd much rather not get into it."

"C'mon, man, give it to me straight. If you see a VC about to shoot me, would you shoot him—to keep him from shooting me?"

"Look, I really don't think you'll understand. You'll probably just get angry."

"No, man, I won't get angry. Just answer the question."

"Well, I can only answer it like this. I don't believe in taking a person's life. I'd rather be shot myself than shoot someone else. According to how I believe, if I was to take a life, I'd give up all hope for redemption."

Most times, the guy would get really p.o.'d, like I figured he would. "In other words, you'd just stand there and let me be killed, Daly! That's what you're really saying, isn't it?"

Then I wouldn't know just how to answer.

I was in the company about five days when Lieutenant Fisher lined up the platoon one morning to brief us on the body-count system. I could hardly believe what I was hearing.

"For the benefit of the new men," he said, "let me remind all of you that it's possible for you to pick up a three-day pass out here if you're on the ball. Every dead Vietnamese body earns three days off for the soldier responsible for it. So, stay on the alert, and when the time comes to use your weapon, make it count!"

It was that simple. A three-day pass for every Vietnamese you kill. And it didn't seem to matter why or who—just as long as he was Vietnamese and he was dead.

Every so often, while patrolling a village or out in the field, we'd catch a few rounds of sniper fire. Whenever that happened, everyone was anxious to catch sight of the enemy and track him down. And I couldn't help but notice how all the guys around me always watched to see if I took the safety off my weapon. I never did.

Whenever information like that got back to Sergeant Capps, who passed it on to Lieutenant Fisher, I knew I was in for a chewing-out. Each time, Fisher seemed angrier than the time before. Once, I was even sure he was on the verge of hitting out at me.

What really got me was the day we picked up five Vietnamese women who were on their way to the market, carrying baskets loaded down with goods to sell. Both squads in the platoon were working in the village and Sergeant Capps was in charge. After herding the women together and looking over their ID cards, which were not in proper order, it was decided that we'd keep them with us the entire day instead of taking them back to headquarters for questioning.

So wherever we went, the five women—struggling with their full baskets—were forced to go along with us. Every time we stopped somewhere, one or more of the guys went over to feel them, squeezing, pinching, moving their hands however they wanted. The women protested as best they could and begged to be left alone. The squad never considered letting them go. It was a rare treat for them. Most Vietnamese in the hamlets were just old men and old women and children. If you came across a younger girl, she was almost always pregnant.

It went on like that hour after hour. Finally, the women began to cry. "What's botherin' you?" one of the guys asked. "You're all nothin' but a bunch of VC boom boom girls, anyway." Accused of being prostitutes for the Viet Cong, they cried all the harder.

A few times, when people in the village walked by, the girls tried to appeal for help. You could see how the passersby wanted to respond but were afraid. Instead, they just looked sad, turned their heads away, and kept on walking. When two old men did stop to listen, Sergeant Capps shouted out at them to keep moving.

The more I saw of Sergeant Capps, the more I disliked him. But the truth was, when it came to being in the field, he knew plenty more about it than Lieutenant Fisher. He'd always tell Fisher when he thought Fisher was doing things wrong. Unfortunately, most of the time the lieutenant wouldn't take his advice— not until it was proven right. Like insisting that the platoon trudge miles through an area of the jungle that Capps knew to be the wrong one, then finally taking everybody back again.

Our main purpose, always, was to find the VC, either in the hamlets or surrounding areas. Everyone was a suspect—farmers, workers, people in the villages. Scattered around as they were during the day, it was hard to realize that they operated as a highly organized military force, as much the enemy as the North Vietnamese Army.

Nobody doubted that the VC were there, all right. The only thing was, we rarely got to see them in action. Many nights we'd set up ambush sites in case any might come through. It never happened. The truth of it was, looking for and chasing the Viet Cong was almost always a lost cause.

Like the time when we heard some sniper fire and were sent on an all-day wild goose chase following a pack of dogs that were supposed to be hot on the snipers' trail. To me, those dogs were too old to do much of anything. But we were kept on their tails hour after hour in the hot sun with the guys bitching all the way. Of course, there was never even a trace of the VC.

Still, despite our lack of success at coming face to face with the Viet Cong, they never let us forget they were out there, ready to pick us off. During my first three weeks with the company, two men, both in another platoon, were killed by sniper fire. And one night in Ngoc Nha, while we were all bedded down under a canvas shelter, a guy in another squad took a round in his stomach. They had to bring in a helicopter to get him out, and all of us lit the area with flashlights to guide it in.

The first time I really and truly got scared, though, was one night in early November. We were out in a hilly, wooded area, ready to set up for ambush, when one of the guys spotted a fire in a village up ahead. We decided to change plans and find out what was going on.

As soon as we started down the trail, all at once firing broke out all around us. Everybody hit the ground.

It was impossible to see who was shooting at us or where it was coming from. I had no idea what to do. I just lay flat, head into the dirt, feeling very helpless and thinking how any second one of those bullets could burn its way into my back or head. It went on without letup for maybe five minutes. Then, finally, when it was quiet again, we slowly got to our feet. Just as quickly as they'd come, the enemy had disappeared.

The way Lieutenant Fisher was getting more and more p.o.'d with me, I knew it was only a matter of time before we'd end up having it out—and we did. It started the day I went into the field without any ammo.

Whenever we'd go through the camp gate at the start of the day, everyone was supposed to lock and load their weapons. On this one morning, I'd decided I wasn't going to take along any ammunition, and I left all of it underneath my bed before leaving the tent. As always, I carried two pouches with magazines in them —only this time, every one was empty.

When we reached the gate, Sergeant Capps called out, as usual, "Lock and load!" Shriner, who'd never stopped making wisecracks about my being a conscientious objector, had probably been waiting for just such a chance. Somehow, he must have seen me stashing away the ammo. He yelled over, "Aren't you gonna put a magazine in your weapon, Daly?"

I loaded the rifle and Shriner watched closely. Then he came over to me. "Hey, Daly, let me see that magazine, will you?"

"Why?" I asked.

"I just want to see it is all."

"I don't feel like taking it out," I said.

He shrugged, turned away, and went right up to Sergeant Leshore. Then the sergeant came over and asked to see the magazine. I took it out and showed it to him.

Leshore stared at the magazine for a minute, shook his head, then asked to look into the two pouches. When he saw that all the magazines were empty, he cursed under his breath, and I could see he was furious. It was the only time that Sergeant Leshore was really angry with me.

Within minutes, Sergeant Capps came over. He looked at the magazines, growled, "Well, this is it, Daly!" and demanded I follow him to see the lieutenant. When Fisher learned what had happened, he blew his stack.

"Goddamn it, Daly, what in hell is wrong with you, anyway? What if we were ambushed—what would you have done then?" I faced him and said nothing.

My silence infuriated him even more. He screamed at me. "Let me tell you something, Daly, if you ever do anything stupid like this again, you'll damn well regret it. And if anyone in this platoon gets hurt out there because of you—if somebody else doesn't take care of you, I'll get you myself!"

It was hard for me to believe that my life had just been threatened by my platoon leader. It upset me so much, I had a hard time to keep from crying. I took a deep breath, calmed myself, looked Fisher straight in the face, and told him, "Look, I made it clear how I felt before I got here, but no matter how often I said it, the Department of the Army wouldn't recognize me as a conscientious objector. Now I don't know how many people I gotta tell, but nobody is going to make me do what I don't believe in. And that means I will not kill anyone as long as I'm here in Vietnam!"

Lieutenant Fisher stared at me and his face was drained white with anger. "What you need," he said, finally, "is two weeks of KP to think things over!" He then turned and walked away.

In no time flat I was pulling KP. Out in the field, it's a lot different than in a mess hall. It never ends, from the minute you get up till you're ready for bed. Every night for the next week, I'd fall off to sleep completely fatigued, every part of me aching.

Then Lieutenant Fisher sent for me. "Well," he asked, "are you ready to do your job out here like you're supposed to?"

"If you're asking if I've changed how I think," I told him, "I still believe just as I did before. No KP is gonna change that. The army pays me for a full day, so if you want to keep me on KP twenty-four hours daily, that's okay with me. I'll just stay in it till I fall out. But you might as well understand, as far as my beliefs are concerned, I intend to stick to them. Like I told you before— I will not kill. I will not shoot a weapon as long as I am in Vietnam!"

One more time, Lieutenant Fisher screamed and raved at me. He went on for a full minute, and even repeated his threat to take care of me himself. This time, I didn't get upset like I had before. When he'd finished, I said very calmly, "You'd better know one thing, Lieutenant. If I ever do have to kill anybody in Vietnam, I hope that you'll be the first."

He didn't reply. He just looked as if he'd really like to squeeze my neck or something. And I realized, if he had the opportunity, he'd try his best to do it, one way or another. But at least now, finally, we understood each other.

The other guy in the company who continued to give me the most trouble was Shriner. I tried to avoid him whenever I could. But that was hardly possible the night we pulled guard duty together in Chou Lai. The squad was set up in two bunkers, one on each side of a small bridge that carried railroad tracks over a narrow body of water.

At first, we moved back and forth without talking, and I was perfectly happy to keep it that way. Then, after a while, Shriner said, "Daly, you don't mind if I ask you one question, do you? Tell me, why are you a conscientious objector?"

That was his way of getting into it. When I tried to put him off, he kept pressing me. "C'mon, Daly, tell me. I'd really like to hear."

"Okay," I said, finally, "but if you really want to know, then you'll have to understand about my religious beliefs, you'll have to know what the Jehovah's Witnesses teach."

"Sure, man, sure," Shriner said.

So we got into religion. I tried to explain how the Jehovah's Witnesses believe we're living in the time of the end, and that the worse things become in the world, the closer we are coming to it.

"Yeah, I see," Shriner said. "And what happens then, when the world comes to an end?"

"Then the Kingdom of Jehovah under Jesus Christ will rule over the earth and will replace all earthly governments."

"But meanwhile, man, we got an earthly government. And we got a goddamned job to do!"

So although I knew it was impossible, I tried to make Shriner understand, to see why a man who truly believed in the word of God could not live otherwise, could not fight wars, could not kill another human being. For such a man, I tried to make Shriner understand, the only hope was in the Kingdom of God.

Shriner didn't buy any of it. He was totally against everything I believed in. And the longer we talked, the redder he turned, and the angrier he became.

Suddenly I realized that for some minutes Shriner had been edging me nearer and nearer to the side of the bridge.

"Look, let's not argue, man," I said. "Let's knock off the whole thing, okay?"

He didn't answer then, just kept pushing closer. I glanced behind me and saw that it was impossible to move back. One more step and I'd be off the bridge and into the water.

"Hey, let's cool it," I said loudly.

And then Nace called from the end of the bridge. "Hey, Shriner, what're you doin'?"

Shriner backed away. "I'm not doin' nothin'! We're just arguing about religion, that's all."

"Well, just because you don't agree on religion, it's really crazy to let it go that far!"

"Hell, nothin' was going to happen, Nace. You didn't think I was gonna push him in, did you?"

I didn't say so—but that was exactly what I thought.

About four days before Thanksgiving, we learned we'd be moving north into the Que Son Valley. We didn't get the news from the army. We heard it first from the Coke Girls, a group of Vietnamese girls who came around selling Cokes when we were assigned to a lookout post.

Nace and I and one other guy were pulling observation duty just outside Chou Lai the night we found out. The girls came around like always, only this time they seemed very sad.

"Long time no will see," one said.

"Why? What do you mean?" Nace asked.

"Soon 196th go," she said. "Then—198th come."

The others agreed. "Yes, 196th go north," they said. "Too bad. When 196th here, no VC. When 196th go, *beaucoup* VC come."

The Coke Girls were right. A few days later, we were told to pack up—the whole brigade was moving into the Que Son Valley. And, as I found out weeks after, the VC did come into the area in very strong force as soon as the 198th arrived. That's the way it went, I learned. Things quieted down after one unit finally got an area well controlled. But as soon as it moved out and a new unit replaced it, that's when the Viet Cong moved in.

The word was that the 198th really made a mess of things before they settled down. Seems they shot some of their own men by mistake—and even managed to blow up their own mess hall.

The morning we left for Que Son Valley everyone was issued new weapons, and I was chewed out for not keeping my old one clean and free of rust.

The brigade moved by truck convoy to Tam Ky, where helicopters were waiting to fly us farther north. Hours later, we landed at our new camp—scattered bunkers on top of a mountain, or Fire Support Hill, as the army called it. We called it something else.

CHAPTER 8

Que Son Valley, Christmas 1967

Conditions on Fire Support Hill were really horrible. The rainy season was going strong, and I don't think I've ever seen so much mud at one place in my life. If you had to move any distance at all up or down the mountain, it was impossible without sliding every few steps.

For me, far from the most agile guy in the world, it was even rougher getting around. Sometimes I didn't even try. Like on Thanksgiving when I gave up a special meal. Rather than even attempt to climb down the hill to the mess hall, then back again in the dark, I stayed in the bunker and listened to the radio.

The bunkers were scattered all around the top of the mountain. Each one slept an entire squad. The floors were made of sandbags and the roofs were tin with more sandbags on top.

The big news that Thanksgiving night was how the Americans, supported by jets, won a great victory at Dak by taking Hill 875. What the account didn't tell, though—and I learned at a later time—was that it had been one of the bloodiest and most costly battles of the war.

After a few days, we started going out into the field to patrol villages, like we had at Chou Lai. Only here, it was very different. For one thing, in the Que Son Valley we were in a free fire zone. That meant no restrictions on firing, not even for helicopters flying over the area. According to the army, this was enemy territory. If a man was Vietnamese, there was a very good chance he was Viet

Cong. The possibility of this was so great, we were told, that it was perfectly okay to fire off everything you had every once in a while —just shoot away at nothing. If anybody caught one of those rounds, chances were it was the enemy. It brought back again what we'd been told over and over in training: kill everything in an enemy village. Women, children, animals, everything that's alive.

In the field, the rule to follow was a simple one. Shoot anything that runs. And the army couldn't be bothered worrying about why somebody might be running away. Like maybe because he was scared, or just a kid who didn't know better. In this area, to be Vietnamese was to be the enemy.

Actually, the Vietnamese in this part of the country did act differently toward us than those in the south. Their dislike for Americans seemed stronger—was more in the open. But I soon came to understand that almost all the Vietnamese people, wherever they lived, looked on Americans as their enemies; that the only ones who didn't resent our being there, aside from the heads of the government or the army, were the Vietnamese businessmen who had money or owned property, or who were making money on the war. No peasants among that crowd, that was for sure.

So, each morning, we'd divide up, several squads together, and head into the field. We'd stay out for many days, bedding down in one hamlet or another, then late that afternoon we'd move on to someplace else. Many of the villages were scattered far apart, and it often took hours to get from one to another.

Our job, as before, was to patrol the hamlet and check ID cards. We never worked at it too hard. Most days, we'd end up sitting around some hootch, eating, talking, smoking—just killing time. I guess it was hard for the guys to want to do a job that brought them into contact with the Vietnamese people all the time. Because, when we went into a hamlet, no one was ever friendly. Not even the little children. No begging for food or candy. No kids coming around to call out "number one." Just running away into their hootch, scared and silent, staring out at you. And if you offered the people anything, they'd refuse to take it—even a cigarette. Or if you asked a question, they'd just ignore you like they didn't understand.

The truth was, if you looked to see it, hatred for the Americans seemed to be just about everywhere. At first this really bugged me, made me angry in a way. Then, as I considered how miserably these Vietnamese peasants and farmers lived, how they'd suffered through so many years of war, how their small straw hootches had been destroyed so many times, or how they'd been forced to keep on moving from one place to another, I began to understand why they felt like they did.

As unbelievable as it seemed to me, the army's body-count system actually began to hook some of the guys, and they went all out to kill a Vietnamese whenever they could. Brigade Commander Gimlet was all for it, and it was his body-count pep talks that surely helped make possible the incident involving Lieutenant Fisher that—more than anything else up till then—made me hate what we were doing.

The brigade commander, who received a general report on the body count every night, was always pushing to see that it stayed up there. Whenever one company fell behind, he'd put the pressure on the company commander. It ended up a real competition between the companies, as if it were a basketball game or something.

After one of Gimlet's get-out-and-kill talks to the CO, the guys in the company would be pulled out for an instant replay. It was always something like, "What's wrong with Alpha Company, anyway? Charlie Company had fifteen counts today. Alpha hasn't even had one. How about those three-day passes? You guys love it around here so much you can't bear to leave the place—is that it? And the "Black Death" had another great day. Are we gonna let him make us look bad every damn day of the week?" This was a reference to the company commander of Delta Company, who was black. His company's consistently high body-count record had earned him the title of "Black Death."

So considering how Alpha Company was regularly bombarded about finding Vietnamese to kill, the incident in December wasn't all that surprising. The platoon, including Lieutenant Fisher, had just arrived in a hamlet and the squads were getting ready to go their separate ways, when a Vietnamese man was spotted running out of a hootch. Immediately, Fisher and a Spec. 4 from another squad took off after him.

The man was running slowly, stumbling along. It took only a

minute for Fisher and the GI to come up close behind him, and they both fired their weapons at the same time. The man staggered and fell onto the dirt street. All the guys ran up and crowded around him.

He was an elderly man. Fisher and the GI bent over him as he rolled in pain, blood covering his tattered shirt. Then a woman came running toward us, frantically waving her ID card. "He number one!" she shouted over and over. "No VC, no VC! Number one!"

Fisher and the Spec. 4 ignored her. They were busy arguing. "That's my man!" Fisher said.

"No sir," the enlisted man said. "He's mine! I shot him!"

The woman, who seemed to be the man's wife, was crying. She continued to plead, "No VC, no VC!" And the man, blood spreading in the dirt around him, moaned and begged for help.

As the entire platoon watched, Fisher and the Spec. 4 went on with their quarrel over who was to get the body-count credit for the Vietnamese man. Just as though he was already dead. And one by one the men began to turn away in disgust until, finally, the platoon medic interrupted the argument. "Are we going to call a medi-vac for him, Lieutenant?"

"Medi-vac won't fly in because of the weather," Fisher said.

"But what are we going to do with him?" the medic asked. "He's dying."

Fisher turned away. "Nothing we can do."

Then the radio man, who had been nearby, stepped up. "What would happen if one of *us* got shot, sir? Would they fly in a chopper then?"

"That's different," Fisher said.

"What do you mean, 'That's different'?" the soldier insisted. "If they'd come out for us, why can't they come out for a Vietnamese?"

"Because Charlie's different," Fisher snapped. "You're an American."

Meanwhile, the woman continued to cry and pointed to the sky—her way of pleading that we bring in a medi-vac to help her husband. Finally, Fisher shouted at her to go away—"*Di, di!*" When she didn't go, another guy in the squad held up his rifle and got across to her that if she didn't take off fast, we'd shoot her. At last, still sobbing, the woman ran down the street. She dashed into one hootch after the other, pleading for help. Always she came out alone. No one was willing to get involved.

Now three men were told to pick up the old man and carry him out of the main village area. A short distance away, still groaning in pain, he was dumped into a large clump of bushes. A group of guys stood off to one side and watched. Most of them were shocked and angry. But no one—including me—spoke up.

Later on, the Vietnamese woman returned and asked, over and over, where her husband was. We had been ordered not to tell.

That incident really got to me. I hated myself for not protesting. I thought how completely inhuman it had been—how we hadn't even left the old man with his wife so she could care for him. I'd rather have seen him dead than left lying in the bushes to bleed to death, to stay there until his decaying body smelled enough for him to be found.

And what made incidents like this one even worse in a way was that they went along with American military thinking. The life of a Vietnamese had no value—it was just something to argue over for body-count credit. Like Fisher had said, he was just a Charlie, and medi-vac would never have come in to help him.

It didn't take me long to find out that, to the army's way of thinking, Vietnamese lives, even hundreds of them, were not as important as the life of one American. As far as the military was concerned, forget the idea that we're all God's children.

Many of the guys didn't buy that. But the truth of it was, after what the GIs had drummed into them, most had little sympathy for the Vietnamese. Some even hated them And if they were ordered to do something, even if they believed it was very wrong, they'd do it anyway. Sometimes, when they were really bothered over an incident, they'd gripe about it for a time, and maybe that helped make some of them feel a little better. Like when, a few days after the killing of the old man, a sergeant shot someone running down the trail, only to find out it was just a small boy. The guys really blasted him for that, and the sergeant sincerely felt bad about it. Still . . . the little kid was dead.

As it came closer to Christmas, a tension began to build in the company. The reason was that everyone knew how, before long, Alpha Company was to be next in line to cross over a nearby river, and that the other side was thick in the middle of Charlie territory. A number of companies going in before had been completely wiped out.

It seemed the trouble was that the army tried to use the 196th Light Infantry Brigade for much more than it was capable of. During the past months, a few small companies at a time were moved into that area across the river—even though it contained a whole division of Viet Cong. When one company got ambushed or killed off, another would be sent in to replace it. It was really a crazy strategy, because the guy making the decisions had to know that even our whole brigade wasn't large enough to go up against that VC division.

Three days before Christmas, we returned to the camp on Fire Support Hill. We'd been back for short periods only twice since Thanksgiving. As I considered how, maybe the next time we left, it would be to cross the river, it seemed like a good time to write a letter home.

It was December 22, the day that President Johnson visited Thailand and Vietnam before his trip to see Pope Paul. I heard his words on the radio: "The enemy knows he has met his master in the field." As I put down some feelings about things in my letter, I thought how differently the President and I viewed the situation. The way one company after another had been getting it in Charlie territory, to me everything just didn't seem to be going all that fine.

I tried to reassure everyone at home that, no matter how it turned out for me in Vietnam, I was not afraid because I believed and trusted in Jehovah God. "I want you to promise," I wrote, "if anything should happen to me, not to let it get the best of you. Keep studying God's words, the Bible, so that, no matter what, our whole family can enjoy life together one day in God's new world." Then I wished all a Merry Christmas, and told them, God willing, I'd be writing again soon.

As terrible as the living conditions were at the Fire Support Hill camp, it was good to get away from the field for a few days, from the constant moving into and out of hamlets. And then, there were a few little things to be thankful for—like the fact that Shriner had been rotated and sent back to the States. Also, there was a new guy in the squad who was really kooky and always good for at least one laugh a day. His name was Kline, and he kept getting bounced from one company to the other.

Kline's beard was almost as long as my head, and he wore glasses. He used them more for getting out of details he didn't like than for seeing. Whenever Kline wanted out of something, he'd manage to lose his glasses for days.

One afternoon, the brigade commander came by. He walked up to Kline and asked, "How you doin'?"

"Fine, sir," Kline said, smiling.

"Kline, when was the last time you shaved?"

"This morning, sir."

I was standing nearby and had a hard time to keep from laughing out loud.

"Well, Kline, you'd better be clean-shaven the next time I see you."

Kline nodded, smiling again. "Oh, yes sir, yes sir. Clean-shaven, you bet, sir."

With Kline in the squad there weren't too many dull moments. He livened things up a lot those few days before Christmas. His buddy had been assigned to Alpha Company with him, and one night, as we sat around the bunker, they both thought they'd heard some shooting nearby.

"Maybe somethin' is goin' on out there," Kline said. He turned to his friend. "Why don't we make a little noise to let 'em know we're up and ready?"

"Sure, why not?" his buddy agreed.

"Well, go ahead, man," Kline said. "Shoot a couple of rounds."

"Right." His friend pointed his rifle up to the sky and fired. "Okay. Now you."

Whenever shooting like that started, it didn't take long before everyone got into it. Other guys, figuring something must be up, started firing, too. That night, before you knew it, GIs all around the mountain were shooting their weapons like mad. Shooting at nothing. All because Kline and his buddy had started it all going.

Christmas Day wasn't too great. That morning, an officer dressed as Santa Claus was brought in by chopper to distribute packages and gifts from the Red Cross. Then, a little later, my squad and one other were assigned the detail of setting up mines in an area near the camp. It was a scary job because all it took was one false step to set one of those things off. We were happy to get it over with.

As we started back, Tillman, a black guy from Brooklyn, suddenly realized he'd left his weapon out there in the mine field. He asked us to wait up while he went back for it.

Everyone watched as Tillman moved carefully across the area we'd just left, now spotted with live mines. He reached the rifle, picked it up, and started back. Then all at once the earth around him exploded! We looked on, horrified, as Tillman slowly sank down into the mud.

As it turned out, he was lucky it was Christmas. A few minutes later, the chopper that had flown in Santa settled down on the ground beside him. Tillman was lifted aboard, and in no time was taken to a nearby hospital. In a way, he could thank Santa he was alive to see 1968.

Others weren't that lucky. Out of the almost 42,000 American casualties in Vietnam during 1967, more than 9,000 of them had been killed and would never see the new year.

After we finished our special dinner that Christmas Day, we were told to pack up and prepare to go back to the field. As we sat around waiting for the order to move out, we killed the fifth of liquor that had been given each squad. I thought back to other Christmases, and to the last one, which in a way seemed so much longer than one year before. And I couldn't help wondering just where I'd be when the next Christmas rolled around.

I celebrated New Year's Eve by taking a bath. It was my first since Thanksgiving in Chou Lai. All that time, we'd just never been given the chance to wash up properly.

On New Year's Day, the cease-fire was still in effect. We were told to shoot back only if we received fire. And the word had come down that the very next day Alpha Company was set to cross the river into Charlie territory on search-and-destroy missions. The cease-fire would be over by then and we'd be back to normal—if it moves, runs, or looks Vietnamese, kill first!

The guys were really on edge New Year's night. We kept talking about the next day and the madness of it. The entire area we'd be moving into, we knew, was completely surrounded by an enemy division.

Green, one guy in the company who had only a short time left, was really nervous. Most of the time, he was a real worrier. But now, everything bothered Green, and the closer he came to finishing his tour the worse it got. On patrol, he'd always give me a hard time for walking knock-kneed, which I am. It concerned him that Charlie might be able to hear my knees bumping together.

That night, whenever anybody lit up a cigarette, Green went ape over it. "Put it out!" he'd demand. "Charlie can smell smoke a thousand miles away."

With only ten days to go, no one really blamed Green for the way he acted.

A couple of hours after dark, I was told to report to Lieutenant Fisher. During the past weeks, we'd hardly spoken a word to one another.

"Daly," he said, "I'd like you to pull OP down at the river tonight. I've assigned the two new men to take it with you."

The guys that Fisher had ordered to pull the lookout duty with me had both arrived in the platoon only the day before. It was impossible to be much greener.

Fisher waited for me to respond to his order. I just stood there and said nothing.

"I was sure you wouldn't mind the OP," Fisher told me finally. "Like you say, you'd rather be killed than kill anyone else. None of the other guys in the platoon feel that way about it."

So, like I'd figured, it had been just a matter of time before Fisher found some way to catch up with me.

A few minutes later, when Sergeant Leshore heard about the assignment, he told me not to go. Leshore realized I wouldn't be ready to fire my weapon on OP, and he believed it was wrong to endanger the two new men. So, at the sergeant's suggestion, we all stayed in his bunker that night. And though Fisher never said anything, I always had the feeling he knew we never pulled that OP.

The next morning, we crossed the river. It was so quiet, it was hard to believe hundreds of Viet Cong were right there in the immediate area. We walked up and down mountainous terrain for almost two days before we reached a village. Then the company broke up into platoons. Each squad set up in a hootch.

A number of days passed without major incident. It was a large territory to cover. The theory was that if any one company got ambushed, another company in the area could be brought in immediately to aid it. And that was just the way it happened to Charlie Company.

We were camped between two mountains that night. The company was put on alert, which meant we could be called to move out at any time.

Before daybreak, the order came through. Charlie Company, set up on a nearby mountain, was in real trouble. If at all possible, Alpha Company had to get through to them. And, it was made clear, every minute counted!

It didn't take us long to reach the area. Peering up the mountain, we could clearly make out where the battle was raging—streaks of bullets slashed through the blackness and our helicopters swung across the terrain, throwing flares of light over the enemy troops. The company grouped together. Then, the order. We started up.

Within minutes, it became impossible to advance. The entire area was blanketed in cross fire, and a continuing spray of mortars exploded all about us. We dug in—and waited. Finally, the order came through to move back down.

The battle continued throughout the night. Then, as morning came on, everything quieted down. Once again we started to make our way up the small mountain.

The silence now, compared to the intense noise of just a short time before, was weird and frightening in a way. As we approached the site of the battle, an open area on top of the hill, the smell of death was everywhere. We continued on a few more yards—and then I looked out on the most horrible sight I have ever seen.

It was just about impossible to even imagine what had taken place. On all sides of us, covering that entire area, were dead bodies and pieces of bodies—heads, arms, legs. The dead were all messed up together, Americans and Vietnamese.

We edged our way in. Somehow, it looked as if more Vietnamese had been killed than GIs. Still, we knew at once, with the exception of a few Americans who were still alive, all of Charlie Company had been wiped out.

The entire scene was unreal. At first, I could hardly move with the shock of it. And it wasn't like I'd never seen men battered up before. Growing up in Bed-Stuy, I'd known plenty of that. One time, I'd watched a man beaten to death right on my corner. But it had been nothing like any of this. It really shook me up. And, glancing around me, I saw it was so with many of the other guys, too—Fones, Green, Willie Watkins, Meyers. And just then I wondered how old Kline would have taken all of this. He wasn't with us. Just before the company crossed the river, Kline had reported his glasses lost again. He'd been sent to Saigon to have them replaced.

So I just stood there for a full minute, looking at all those ripped-up pieces of bodies that only the day before had been living men, with hopes and dreams and thoughts of loved ones. And it made me understand like I never had just how horrible war really is.

I remembered all the words I'd heard about war during my religious studies, but those words meant nothing compared to the scene in front of me. And I thought, if I ever live through all of this, no way will I ever in my life go to war again.

What made it all even worse was that what had happened to Charlie Company really never should have happened at all. The company had gotten resupplied the day before. Most always, after a helicopter brought in supplies to a company, it moved right out to another area; otherwise the enemy could zero in on it easily— they saw the choppers coming in and out during the day, and they knew exactly where the company was set up. But Charlie Company, for whatever reason, stayed right there in the same area. And that very night, the enemy hit them with everything.

A short while after we'd arrived on the battle site, choppers came in to take away the few live Americans—and the broken pieces of the dead. It was our job to pile up those bloody parts of bodies on the plane. It was like some horrible nightmare and I tried to turn my mind off, to stop thinking of what I was doing.

Later, after the bodies were evacuated, we moved out to another area on top of a nearby hill. Here we joined up with Delta Company and set up for the night.

The next morning, before we started out, Sergeant Capps informed me that I was being put in for a promotion to Spec. 4. "Everyone going out in the field should at least be a Spec. 4," he said, "and since there's still no word on your c.o. application, Daly, you'll be out here with the rest of us. Up till now, I think you've done your job as well as anybody else. How do you think you'll handle yourself in the future?"

I told him I still doubted I could kill an enemy soldier, even if I came face to face with him in a battle.

"Well, I'm putting you in for Spec. 4 just the same," Sergeant Capps said.

A little later, we moved out. The area was mostly quiet. Every now and then, we'd see one of our choppers overhead. That afternoon, one came down low a short distance ahead of us and fired off some rockets. When we reached the spot a few minutes after, we found what the chopper pilot had been shooting at. It was a Vietnamese boy. We figured his age about nine.

Before dark, we came across another helicopter, only this one wasn't flying anymore. It was wreckage, half-covered with water in a rice paddy. I didn't know it at the time, but the chopper had been piloted by Warrant Officer Francis Anton, one American soldier I was destined to get to know very well.

Finally, we set up for the night. We were all beat—not so much from moving around but more from having lived through the aftermath of the attack on Charlie Company. But this was not to be a time for rest, relaxation, catching our breath, or even calming down. And, somehow, everybody knew it.

CHAPTER 9

Captured!

We were put on one-hundred-percent alert, and that meant no sleeping for anyone. Every guy in the company was on edge, really nervous. No one talked. We just lay there, eyes wide open.

I knew one thing—they didn't have to worry about my falling asleep. I was much too jittery for that. And my mind was too busy thinking how I'd probably be getting my first real taste of action, wondering how I'd act. Would I be able to keep from shooting at anybody? Or would I get caught up like the others, ready to kill if I had to?

And then I couldn't stop remembering how the top of that hill looked, Charlie Company's hill, all of it fresh in my head, like I'd just seen it, pieces of all those bodies, and loading them up. . . .

About three in the morning, we started moving out. Everybody was bitching. Not because of the hour, or for lack of sleep, but because we hadn't been given time to eat. If any one thing could really get the guys pissed off, it was starting out on an empty stomach.

Our job was to look for bodies, a squad that was missing from Charlie Company, I think. So for hours we searched in the underbrush, behind bushes, anywhere the dead might be. It was a different kind of area than before—flat and bushy, no mountainous stretches like in the other part of the Valley. During the past week, I'd developed jungle rot on my feet, and at first I thought maybe not climbing up and down those hills would go easier on them. No such luck.

We went on for hours without any trace of the missing men. Tired and hungry, a lot of the guys began to slow up. But Sergeant Capps saw to it that our squad was right up there.

Finally, about noon, we stopped to eat. Fones and I settled down together for chow, not saying much.

Half an hour later, we started off again. Now, for the first time, they ordered both companies, Alpha and Delta, maybe a hundred and twenty men, to spread out side by side in line formation. Nobody could believe it. We moved out across these open rice paddies in one long line—and in full view!

Platoon Sergeant Capps was getting it from all sides, the guys yelling, cursing, shouting at him, "This is crazy! This is stupid, man! This is suicide!" "Knock it off and keep it moving!" he shouted back. So we just kept on, sloshing through the water, and before long the line wasn't straight anymore. As some guys moved slow, some faster, we were soon just a zigzagging string of GIs.

Then, up ahead, we could make out a narrow stream. And a short distance beyond it was a dike, the kind you'd see scattered throughout the rice paddies, one side of a small hill packed with mud. On top of the dike, the land stretched out flat again—but we had no view of it.

As we moved closer to the stream, you could almost feel the guys draw back. Everybody knew that if the enemy was up there on that flat area of ground we couldn't see, the company was really in for it. No way could we get away back through those rice paddies.

It was then I got a whiff of what I call the dead smell, strong and right nearby. I knew for sure we were coming into something.

As we approached the stream, I spotted the dead GIs, maybe nine or ten of them. It almost seemed they were drinking, all of them on their stomachs, heads in the water. And now, on the other side of the stream along the top of the dike, I could see barbed wire strung out all across.

We kept on. It was quiet and still, not even a breeze, the only sound a squishing of our boots in the water of the rice paddies. Little by little we moved up on those dead soldiers and the narrow stream sparkling in the sun.

The men up front jumped across. A minute later, it was my turn. I made the jump and was just starting up the hill when the two lead guys reached the barbed wire at the top. Then everything went crazy as a long burst of rifle fire exploded from the other side!

As soon as they opened up, Sergeant Capps shouted for us to get back. Everyone turned and ran, trying to get out of range, many firing, shooting rounds at they didn't know what. In seconds, we were scattered all over the place, some of us standing, others flat in the rice paddies. Then the firing from on top of the hill got heavier, and within seconds North Vietnamese in green uniforms came swarming over. I spotted Willie Watkins and another fellow named Ray trying to make it down. Suddenly, Ray caught it in the chest, but the two of them kept on running until they came on two large holes near the bottom of the hill. They both dove, one into each hole, like they were going head-first into a swimming pool.

Then I saw one guy—it was his first time out and I didn't know his name—standing flat-footed near the bottom of the hill, out in the open, firing his M–16 automatic at the oncoming Vietnamese. GIs kept passing him by, running back, but he just stood there like he could have been John Wayne in the movies, firing away and getting hit. The whole time he was standing there shooting, they were loading him up. He took maybe fifteen or twenty rounds in him. Then I could see him going down, real slow.

By this time, everybody seemed to panic, hollering and yelling, running back and forth, like nobody knew where to go or what to do. I was still on my feet, holding my rifle but not firing it, seeing guys getting hit all around—and scared as hell.

Then I jerked back with a sting in my arm, and a guy nearby yelled over to ask if I was shot. I told him no, it was only a rock that hit me. And then I heard Sergeant Capps, prone on the ground a few feet away, yelling at me to get down. I flopped on my stomach in the rice paddy.

All of a sudden, two GIs who were looking to the rear started shouting that some friendlies were coming to help. I twisted around to see a bunch of Vietnamese running toward us, waving so nobody would fire at them. A minute later, I realized they weren't really friendlies at all. They started setting up two machine guns.

Then my shoulder started hurting, and I looked inside my shirt to see blood spreading down my arm. I knew I was hit, but I hardly had time to think about it, for just then the two machine guns opened up on us. Now we were getting it from all sides. Even though it was during the day, it looked like night firing range, tracers shooting everywhere. We were boxed in. Enemy soldiers, firing and shouting, were coming at us from every direction.

Most all our guys were lying down by then, except for a few who were still standing and shooting, or throwing grenades. We weren't returning fire like we should have been. Our ammo was low and the company's one machine gun had run out. Even though we'd been resupplied the day before, it hadn't helped because somehow we'd been given the wrong ammunition for our weapons. Then, to make things worse, rifles were jamming all over the place. M–16s were still pretty new then, and it didn't take much for them to jam.

To one side, just a few feet away, I spotted Fones stretched out in a rice paddy like I was, the water almost covering him, too. I was facing the direction we had come from. Now, that entire area was also filled with Vietnamese, who were running past where the two machine guns were set up and jumping across the stream. Between that point and where I was lying, not very far from me, a long, deep trench provided protection for those GIs who had managed to jump into it, maybe six or seven. And every few minutes, a couple more came running back off the hill or out of a rice paddy to try and make it to that trench with the others.

I really didn't know what to do—whether to lie there in the shallow water and hope I didn't get hit, or to make a run for it. In training, we had been filled in on situations like this. Only thing was, I'd never paid much attention, just like with the other courses. That was when I still had no intention of ever going to Vietnam.

Now Sergeant Capps shouted over at Fones and me to stay put. "You guys provide cover for those tryin' to make it out!" he ordered.

I knew it was crazy to start firing our weapons then, or even to move, for that matter. Neither one of us had any cover, and it would take nothing for them to pick us off.

As it was, right then, the Vietnamese soldiers were more interested in getting the guys down in the trench. They weren't even shooting in our direction. Instead, they kept throwing grenades from up on the hill, trying to force the men out. Only thing was, the Vietnamese were too far off. The grenades continued to fall short, exploding near Fones and me, covering us with a spray of dirt and mud; luckily, no shrapnel.

Then I saw Fones lift his weapon, ready to shoot. Once he opened up, I knew they'd realize both of us were alive. They'd be able to zero in on us in no time flat. "Fones," I called over. "Don't shoot now, don't shoot!"

He only got off about two rounds. Then he was hit. But what really finished him off were the grenades. The Vietnamese on the hill had kept right on tossing them, and, like before, they'd land within a few feet of us. Until, one after the other, two grenades hit directly on top of Fones. Each time a grenade went off, I saw his body jump. And I knew he was dead.

I closed my eyes and lay without moving, arms outstretched. The water of the rice paddy covered most of me. My weapon was a little off to one side, and I left it there, figuring I'd look more like dead if I wasn't holding it. Heavy firing from the Vietnamese was still coming from every side. I just knew Alpha Company never had a chance. Aside from being caught in an ambush and almost completely surrounded, we were greatly outnumbered.

Movement around me seemed to slow down now, though every once in a while some GI ran by. Once, I looked up to see a sergeant, his head streaming blood, race to the trench and jump in. Then, I caught a glimpse of Meyers down in there.

It got very still after a while. Everything stopped. All around me just dead bodies, nothing moving. I thought how maybe I could make it down into the trench with the others.

I called out, almost in a whisper, "Meyers, can I come over there with you?"

After a minute, he answered, very low, "No, be quiet—stay where you are. If you move, you'll get shot."

I could feel the fear building up inside me then, and after a few minutes I called out to him again. "Meyers, can I come over there with you all?"

"Not now," he whispered back. "We're gonna stay here for a little while, and as soon as it gets dark we're gonna try and get out. We'll let you know then."

After a time, I called his name again. Nothing. I tried once more.

When Meyers still didn't answer, I got really scared. I whispered his name again, hoping. And then I realized that they were gone. Some way, they had all made it along the trench and escaped.

My first idea was to kill myself. I was frightened, not thinking clear, and I figured why not take one of my grenades off and pull it? It seemed like the only thing to do, when I thought back to what they'd told us in training—how if you're captured you're going to be tortured or killed, die a horrible death. They'd pounded that into us, like at A.I.T., repeating over and over again about Charlie and what he'd do to get information. Never forget, they'd told us—never surrender unless there's no other way out. Fight till the last before you let them take you. And I guess it wasn't too surprising that, with all of those words running through my head, I was actually considering taking my own life rather than be captured, thinking how if I had to die, better I die fast.

As I came to learn later on, all those tales of horrible tortures, like disembowelment, worked to make many American prisoners ready to tell everything they knew. When captured, they were so scared because of what our military had taught them, they'd reveal anything.

Meanwhile, I had my own battle going on right inside my head, like two people talking, one saying do this, the other saying do that. I knew I didn't want to die—to take my own life. Yet I really didn't think I could make it back at night by myself.

But the strongest voice in my head came right back to me from my religious training. To kill myself would be against everything I believed. And whoever takes his own life has no hope for resurrection. This idea, this belief, swept over all the other thoughts in my head. And then I knew I wasn't going to pull the grenade, no matter what happened.

The question was—what *was* I going to do? I considered how maybe I should stay right there and wait until dark. But what then? I'd have no idea which way to go, even if I was lucky enough to make it out without getting shot.

Then I heard their voices—North Vietnamese soldiers moving among the dead bodies. I lay motionless, arms outstretched, one eye closed, the other halfway open, my head down in the water.

I could make them out as they went from body to body, taking packs, weapons, watches, rings. Suddenly, I realized one was heading directly for me. I tried to hardly breathe and hoped I looked dead.

When he came over to me, he lifted my arm up, like he was trying to feel my pulse. I kept it limp, and when he let go, it flopped down into the water. Then he shoved one foot under my stomach to turn me over. I didn't want him to bend down, so I made it easy for him. As he lifted his foot, I rolled over.

Once I was on my back, he quickly took my pistol belt with the grenades and ammo pouch on it, pulled off my watch and ring, picked up my weapon, and walked off.

At first, I felt great relief. Then, I became really upset at the thought of trying to find my way through the jungle after dark, or getting shot down by the North Vietnamese Army, which was sure to remain in the area. Right then, it seemed like it made much more sense to let them know I was alive.

I started moving in the shallow water, just a little. Two soldiers spotted me right away and shouted out to the one walking away. Then all three came running over.

They motioned for me to get up and put my hands over my head. One pulled off my helmet and threw it down into the mud. Then they pointed in the direction they wanted me to walk.

I looked around. Bodies were everywhere. Later, I learned that only six men out of our company had survived.

We started off in the very direction the company had come from, back over that same stream. I was really scared, and I guess it showed. Maybe they wanted to make sure I wouldn't try and run, because they kept repeating over and over, "No kill, no kill."

Before long, not far from where the attack had taken place, we came to a hootch. When I stepped inside, I felt a little bit relieved. In the far corner, sitting on the floor against the straw wall, was Willie Watkins. I remembered how when I last saw Willie, he and Ray had jumped head-first into the two big holes on the side of the hill. I was happy to know that Willie had made it. And right then, it was really good to see that familiar black face looking across at me.

I was always like that even when I was small—feeling much better if someone was with me if I ever got in trouble. Like if I was caught doing something I shouldn't, I was always scared if I was by myself, but it was a lot easier if someone else was there, too. So when I saw Willie, it was like—whew, golly, somebody else is with me at least.

I sat down beside him and we started talking. Willie wanted to know if anybody else was alive, and I told him I didn't think so.

Meanwhile, there were about ten Vietnamese soldiers inside

the hootch, going through packs, smoking and laughing. After a while, one came over to us—the only one, it seemed, who spoke any English at all. "No sweat, we no kill," he said several times, as though he was trying to reassure us. Then he offered us a smoke.

After that, a number of NVA came over to give us cigarettes. Soldiers kept coming in and out. Every once in a while, one would look over in our direction, then step over and offer each of us a smoke. Then they began to open up the food they had gotten from GI packs. We had the idea they planned to wait around until dark.

They really loved the food—even the cans of C-ration. Each time they opened a can—cheese, peanut butter, jam—they gave us some. They opened the bread last, and we wondered why they didn't think to give it to us before with the cheese or peanut butter and jam. As we sat there, eating and smoking, every now and then one of them would come over and ask, "Okay, huh? Okay?"

We'd nod back. "Sure, okay."

About an hour later, one soldier who spoke English came into the hootch. He gave each of us a booklet—"NLF's Lenient and Humanitarian Policy Toward American Prisoners of War."

"You read this," he said, then bent down to us. "Understand —we will not kill you. Do not worry." He studied our faces, and I guess we didn't look too convinced. He repeated, "No kill, no torture. We take you to camp. You will be reeducated. Maybe we keep you four or five months to teach truth. Then we let you go."

We nodded back, still not believing.

After dark, they took us outside and ordered us to take our boots off. Then, surrounded by about ten guards, we started walking.

Something I came to understand later was that when the Vietnamese took you someplace, it was never straight to where you were going. They didn't want you to have a sense of direction.

We walked barefooted for over four hours, round and round, through open rice paddies, up and down a number of dikes—mud hills, much like the one where we'd been attacked. Sometimes it seemed we were back at the same dike we'd just climbed over a little while before. And all the time, I was feeling really miserable —the jungle rot was killing me, and though my shoulder had stopped bleeding it never quit paining.

At last we came to a small village, more like a camp where soldiers stayed. Most of the houses were big blocklike buildings, side by side, all lined up in a row. Hootches were scattered out behind them.

They led us into one of the buildings, an empty room with a few wooden benches, and a closed door on the far wall. Sitting on a bench, barefooted, his boots on the floor beside him, was Ray.

He looked to be in bad shape. A blood-stained bandage was wrapped around his chest where he'd been hit before jumping into the hole. We looked over at him and smiled. He just stared back.

We sat on one of the other benches and waited. After a while, they called each of us into the other room, one at a time. Willie went first, then Ray.

Finally, it was my turn. Inside, a Vietnamese officer sat behind a large desk covered with folders and papers. The only light in the room was a candle on the desk. A guard, holding a rifle, stood at the door.

I waited as the man at the desk read through some papers and puffed on a cigarette. Then he looked up and asked in a French accent, "Are the other two in your company?"

I found out later that all the GIs who were captured had been questioned by this same officer. He was called Frenchie.

He waited for me to answer the question, tapping his fingers on the desk. I wondered whether Willie and Ray had told him what company we were in. Finally, I said, "Yes, we are in the same company."

He nodded. "What is your company commander's name?"

"I don't know," I said. It was the truth. A new company commander had just come in, and though I'd heard his name, I couldn't think of it.

He suddenly banged his fist down on the desk and shouted at me, "You will tell me your company commander's name!"

"Sir, I really don't know." I explained why.

He then told me the name of my company commander.

"How many men in your company?" he asked.

"I don't know," I said. "I was never with the whole company at one time."

"I will tell you," he said angrily. "You had about sixty men in your company. With the exception of only a few who were cap-tured, all have been killed. Now then, how many M–16s and how many machine guns were there in your company?"

"I have no idea," I answered.

He stared at me, ready to explode.

"Let me explain one thing," I said. "I'm a conscientious objector and really never paid any attention to what they had and what they didn't have. I just don't know."

He studied me for a moment, then asked, "What is a conscientious objector?"

"Because of my religious belief," I said, "I think it is wrong to kill. I believe that all wars are wrong."

"But you were captured on the battlefield with a weapon, so how can you say you are a conscientious objector?"

"I had a weapon but I never fired it."

He thought for a minute. "If you believe what you say, then why did you come to our country?"

"I came to your country to keep from going to jail," I said.

He seemed to cool down a little. "That's right," he said, "that's why all GIs come—because they are forced to. But if you are a conscientious objector, why did you not cross over to our side?"

"What do you mean—cross over to your side?"

"We have a special program for GIs who cross over. If you knew the war was wrong, you should have done that. We would have sent you anywhere you wanted to go."

"Oh, I didn't know about anything like that," I said. "Besides, I wouldn't have known who to go to, anyway."

Suddenly he seemed angry again. "I don't believe you. You were still carrying ammunition that other men could use."

I looked straight at him and said, "You can believe it or not. It's the truth!"

He leaned back and lit another cigarette. Then, softly, he asked, "Do you know why you're here in Vietnam?"

"For the same reason as any other war," I said.

"What's that?"

"Riches. All wars are fought for riches."

"Who told you that?"

"I learned that from the Bible."

"It is often true," he said. "But that is not why our country is fighting. We are fighting for our freedom and our independence. Your country is the aggressor and is trying to take control of our country. That's why we have no choice but to fight."

I said nothing and he continued. "But you will be educated," he said. "You will learn all about the war, and then, after you understand, we will let you go home. Only a short time ago we released some prisoners, and that was after only two months. When you shall be released—all depends on you."

It was the first time I heard that expression, "It all depends on you." I was to hear it again often. Many times was I to be told it depended on me how fast I was to go home. If I progress fast, I go home fast. Maybe two months, three months, four months. It would all depend on me.

My interrogator then placed a sheet of paper and a pencil in front of me. "Can you draw a map?" he asked. "Draw a map of your Fire Support Hill for me."

"I can't draw at all," I said.

"Well, then, describe it."

I shook my head. "I really can't describe things very good."

"Try your best."

"You see, I haven't even been on the whole hill," I said. "I've only been on one side."

Then he glared up at me, thinking, almost as if he were trying to decide whether to be angry or not. After a minute, he reached into a folder and took out a map. He opened it on the desk. "Come look at this," he said.

I stepped around to the side of the desk.

"This is your Fire Support Hill here," he said. "And this is Gimlet right here." He pointed to the headquarters of the brigade commander. He then told me how many companies were out there at a time, how many companies were in the field, how many men were in each company. It was very clear that Frenchie knew everything. He replaced the map, obviously pleased with himself.

"So, you will now be taken to a camp with other Americans. You will learn. Then we will send you home. How long will depend on you."

What I told him then was something I truly believed. "I don't think I will be going home soon," I said. "In fact, I think I may never get to go home again."

He looked up, surprised at my words. "Why do you say that?"

"Because my religion teaches that in a few more years this entire way of life is going to come to an end. This war, I believe, is only the beginning of the big war that is coming, and it will go on for many years. I have been taught that life will become bad and horrible things will happen—like in this war. And then, it will get even worse. Until the War of Armageddon."

"What is that?"

"That is the day God takes His revenge on all of mankind. When He separates the good from the wicked. It will be God's battle. And He will be the victor."

"What religion believes what you say?" he asked.

"Jehovah's Witnesses."

"I do not know this religion," he said. "But I tell you this—it will never happen as you say. And this war will not last long. The United States imperialists will be defeated."

He then motioned for the guard to lead me out.

A short time later, I was taken outside the building with Willie and Ray. I kept thinking of what Frenchie had said—how we would be released in only a few months. I didn't believe it. I kept remembering what we had been taught in training, of what Charlie always did to American prisoners of war. And I thought how they would now take us someplace else and try to get information. And then, if they didn't get results, how we'd be tortured.

Now five guards formed a circle around us. Still in our bare feet, we started walking.

We walked for seventeen days. I walked about fifteen. The last two days, they carried me.

CHAPTER 10

South Vietnam, Tet, January 1968

That first night, we kept moving without a stop, barefooted, carrying our boots. I was tired, yet in a way I didn't feel it. I was too charged up, shaky inside. And, despite all the reassurances, I still kept thinking how they'd probably kill us before very long.

That morning, when we finally stopped to rest, Ray tried to ask Willie and me about getting a message to his wife in California. He was in very bad shape and must have known he might not make it. We never got the information. No sooner had he started talking to us than the guards came over and led him off.

A short time later, when we started again, Ray was not with us. We were told he was unable to continue. Then, that night, one of the guards informed us that Ray had died.

The days of walking followed a pattern. Every morning at eleven o'clock, we'd rest and eat. At one, we'd be back on the trail. About an hour before dark, we'd always stop for the night in a small village. Then the guards cooked dinner and we'd squeeze into a hootch to sleep.

Each evening, while the guards cooked, our interpreter visited us. During the day he always traveled up ahead, and when we stopped for the night he'd be waiting.

The interpreter was a young, friendly man who never failed to ask us if we needed anything, but there wasn't much point in requesting what didn't exist, like medicine for the jungle rot on my feet, or something for my shoulder wound, which was no better at all even though it had been dressed and covered with some kind of black ointment. So we'd just sit around waiting for the rice dinner—and talk. Always about the United States. He never tired of asking questions about places in the United States, or how we lived there. He wanted to know about our families and what the schools were like. "America is a very beautiful place," he'd say. "Someday, I wish to see it. I'd like very much to visit Niagara Falls."

Day after day, no matter how many times it happened, we were always amazed at our reception when we first entered a village. People came running out from all over just to look at us; you'd have thought somebody had caught a reindeer or something. Some of the villagers shouted out, "Number ten, number ten!" and called us names in Vietnamese. Still, a few always tossed out a cigarette or candy, and by the way some of the older people nodded or smiled, you could tell they were really sorry for us. So we caught some of each—friendliness and anger. Even with the kids. Some followed us from one place to another and called out, "Okay, G.I., okay!" while others jeered and laughed.

I soon came to realize that now, for the first time, I was seeing the Vietnamese people as they were, acting toward us as they really felt, not as we'd known them on patrol. We passed through one hamlet I'd been in a number of times before. The people had been friendly. Now, these very same men and women shouted at us in hatred. It bugged me to think how we'd been taken in. But then, as the days went on and I came in contact with more and more people in the hamlets and on the trail, I understood it better. I sensed that none of these Vietnamese really liked us *as Americans.* The only difference was, while some took out their hatred of the United States on us, others somehow just viewed us as two men, two human beings.

So we kept going, one day much like the other, and most always with plenty of air traffic overhead, American helicopters suddenly swooping down, forcing us to stop and take cover.

What really disturbed Willie and me, though, was seeing the kids, the ones that had been wounded during American bombing raids. One little boy of about eight came up to us one day and pulled down his pants to show the scars that covered his legs and thighs. *"May bay,"* he repeated over and over, to let us know it

was American planes that had done it. We just nodded sympathetically. "Johnson number ten," he said. Then he patted me on the
shoulder, smiled and said, "But you okay. You number one!"

Several times, women in a village carried their children over
to us and held them up to let us see the scars or unhealed wounds.
"Look, look!" they'd shout, then call us all kinds of names in Vietnamese.

Wow, how it upset me to see those kids!

On the trail between villages, we passed at least a thousand
people each day, women and little children, mostly, all of them
carrying supplies. We just couldn't get over how happy they all
seemed, laughing and singing songs. It really surprised us. In the
army, or even back in the States, I'd always been told how the
Communists had to use force to get people to work.

Many of the men and women on the trail—and even a scattering of North Vietnamese soldiers—seemed genuinely concerned
about us. Some stopped to offer us candy, cigarettes, and sometimes a potato-like vegetable that grew in the area. I didn't realize
it at the time, but this vegetable, called *co'm mi* by the Montagnard tribes that grew it, was to be a major part of my diet in the
times ahead.

When passersby gave us food or cigarettes, the guards never
interfered. Actually, they were very friendly, constantly reassuring us that we'd be treated well and given time to recuperate. And
always, it seemed, they were ready to talk, especially about America. Often, they'd tell us something about themselves, or try to
explain some point about their country. Then they'd ask, "*Ông
hièu Khong?*"—Do you understand?

Two days before we reached the camp, I found it impossible
to continue. The jungle rot on my feet had turned really bad with
the days of barefoot walking. When the interpreter examined me,
he said immediately, "You will not walk anymore. We will carry
you." And before we started out again, the guards put together a
makeshift stretcher.

The camp was huge—big enough to hold a couple of thousand
men. It was divided into three sections, each a half mile apart.

When we arrived, the camp commander greeted us. "You will
stay here until your health is better," he explained through his

interpreter. "Then, when you are strong, you will continue on to another camp."

We were given a hootch—just for the two of us. Within an hour, a doctor came to look us over and prescribe medication. I was to receive penicillin shots every three hours. Willie was given pills for the malaria he had contracted. To promote the healing of my wound, it was important for me to exercise my arm regularly, the doctor explained. For the next two weeks, he came by to visit us every day.

Later that first afternoon, an interpreter came to see us, a very little man who Willie and I got to calling Shorty. He seemed concerned that we'd have a problem communicating with the guards, since very few spoke any English at all. To help us, he wrote out a list of words in both Vietnamese and English. "I will come again tomorrow," Shorty told us. "If you do not receive enough food, you will tell me then."

If there was any one thing Shorty needn't have been bothered about, it was how much food we got. The portions were enormous. The soldiers at the camp ate community style, eight or nine out of one large bowl. Our servings, just for Willie and me, were the same as for eight Vietnamese—fish, rice, red sauce, and some kind of green vegetable. And we always ate by ourselves in the mess hall, after the six hundred soldiers in that section of the camp had finished. Our guards would stand off to the side and wait for us.

For the first few days, we managed to get most of the food down. After that, it was impossible. I wanted to tell them it was just too much for us, but Willie was worried they'd get angry.

"Why should they get angry? They oughta be glad if we tell them," I argued. So finally Willie agreed, and I told Shorty how the food was great and all, but our appetites just weren't that big. The next day, the portion was cut down one half.

Willie and I lived a really lazy life at the camp. Though we did nothing more than sit around in the sun, the days passed quickly. Normally, I think I would have been bored out of my head. But between my burning feet and aching shoulder, I was far from myself, and it was good to just take it easy, moving from one spot to the other to keep up with the sun.

What also helped a lot to make the days better was the way the area we sat in turned into a kind of social scene, with guards, camp workers and a few soldiers gathering to talk. There were always many soldiers around the camp. Only half were out in the field at one time, because that was all they had weapons for.

Most of them, we figured, were part of the organized VC rather than the North Vietnamese Army. Every now and then, one might call out or make some sign to let us know what he thought of us, but most just went about their business and ignored us. The few who were friendly came over regularly, and one stopped by every morning for an hour's visit, always prepared with cigarettes.

Five women, officers' wives, worked in the camp kitchen, and two of them had little boys about two years old. I always liked kids a lot, and whenever I spotted the boys I'd wave and call out. They'd always laugh and wave back.

We'd been at the camp about a week when our guard decided to bring over one of the boys to play. Willie and I had a great time with him, and he just loved climbing all over us. While all this was going on, the kid's mother came out. Immediately, she ran over, very upset.

The guard talked to her until she calmed down. Finally, she seemed reassured and returned to work, leaving the boy behind to play.

After that, both mothers began to bring their kids over. Before you knew it, we had ourselves regular jobs as babysitters.

Still, despite good things like this, being treated okay, receiving medical help, and getting plenty of food, we couldn't give up the idea that, sooner or later, we'd be interrogated again, tortured, or even killed. Willie never seemed to get it out of his mind. He was always afraid to talk about things, or worried he'd be overheard by the Vietnamese. As a result, he just didn't do much talking at all. And this sure didn't make for the greatest social relationship.

One afternoon near the end of January, Shorty came up to us, all smiles. "Tonight you eat big meal," he said. "Then you go to the big house."

Later, when we went to the mess hall for dinner, we couldn't believe the spread of food—pork, chicken, fish, noodles and large bowls of rice.

"Wow, look at it all!" Willie whispered. "I bet our time has really come and this is the last meal."

What we didn't know then was that it was the first day of Tet, the Vietnamese lunar new year. The special dinner was part of the celebration. Following the meal, all three sections of the camp, almost two thousand men, were to come together in the building that Shorty called the "big house."

It was wild. All these soldiers sitting on wooden benches in this huge hall that had been set up for entertainment and a movie. When the guards led Willie and me inside, you'd almost have thought we were the stars of the show. Everyone turned around to look, and, as soon as we were seated, one of the guards came over and asked if we'd like something to drink. To me, "something to drink" meant alcohol, and I told him, "Great, I sure would." It turned out to be hot tea.

Soon the entire room was filled, men squeezed onto every bench, many sitting on the floor. Then the camp commander made a speech. Everybody applauded. Next, several of the officers took turns in leading songs. Everybody sang. And after that a song-and-dance group, four men and two women, came out to entertain.

The girls, dressed in colorful costumes, were great-looking. They sang without any accompaniment—and they really didn't need any. Their voices, clear and bell-like, carried throughout the hall. And when they finished a song, every man in the audience clapped and cheered. Those to either side of us turned and asked, *"Dep,* huh?" meaning "Beautiful," and Willie and I both answered enthusiastically, "Oh, yes, *dep, dep!"*

During the intermission, a number of men walked over, patted us on the back and said, "Okay, okay," some handing us cigarettes and cookies. Then, we could hardly believe what we were seeing as an officer led over the two girls!

Close up, they looked even prettier. When the officer introduced them, they both blushed and giggled a little. Then, one offered us some Ruby Queen cigarettes, a real treat. During the few minutes we stood together, it was impossible for us to communicate with them, of course, but that didn't really matter. They just kept staring at us, and, every now and then, one reached out to touch our skin or hair. *"Dep, dep,"* they whispered, giggling and blushing again.

When the song-and-dance group finished their performance the movie was shown. It ended about midnight, and the guards took us back to our section of the camp.

After settling into bed, Willie said, "Well, I guess maybe they wasn't gonna do us in, after all."

And then we went to sleep—talking about those two blushing girls, and how it was really okay the way these Vietnamese soldiers had taken time out from the war to celebrate Tet.

Many others didn't, though. It was on that very January 31 that the Tet offensive had been kicked off. Swarms of Viet Cong hit United States marines at Khe Sanh. Battles raged at Saigon, and VC forces held the city of Hue for twenty-five days. And General Westmoreland, head of the United States Army in Saigon, asked for 206,000 more American troops. All this I learned at a later time.

After one month at the camp, we were told it was now time for us to move on, that we had regained our health and were up to traveling again. It was true—Willie and I were both in good shape. He was rid of his malaria. My wound had healed and the jungle rot had cleared up. I could put on boots again. During the four weeks at the camp, I had worn only cut-off slippers.

The night before we left, another American prisoner was put into our hootch. His body was covered with bandages, and he smelled so bad it was impossible for us to sleep. All night long he kept moaning and pleading for water, but we had been instructed by the doctor not to give him any. The prisoner's name was William Port. Many months later, I was to meet him again.

Early the next morning, Shorty came by to give us instructions. We were to be walking through the jungles for a number of days, he explained, and it was most important that we stay close to our guards at all times, to follow them step by step. The area was filled with wild animals and snakes. Separation from the guards, who knew the trails well, could be extremely dangerous. As for any thoughts we might give to escape, Shorty pointed out, we'd best not even consider it.

At last we were ready. Shorty, several guards we'd come to know, and the two mothers with their boys watched us go. As we started off, I waved good-by and smiled. They all waved back.

In a way I was sorry to be moving on. The camp had become familiar. We had always been treated well—plenty to eat, a clean hootch, a bath in the stream every day. There was no telling what awaited us at the next stop—a real detention camp for prisoners, we learned.

So the seven guards spread out around us and the two up front set the pace. And as we moved down the dirt road and out of the camp, I sensed that same old uneasiness, a kind of fear. I kept remembering again how Charlie was supposed to take care of American prisoners of war.

CHAPTER 11

On the Move

At the new camp, for the first time, I began to question the war in a different way. Up until then, I had always considered it morally wrong, like any war or killing. Now, with the help of classes every day for two weeks, I looked at the war from another point of view. Political.

We had traveled four days to reach the camp, and it was during that time that the full impact of being a POW struck me. When you're walking through the jungle hour after hour, there's plenty of time to mull things over. I think it was then that I first really realized how fighting the war was no longer a problem for me. Maybe now, plenty of other things were. But at least as a POW, chances were I'd never again be forced to consider the need for killing another man.

The new camp was strictly a detention camp, tiny compared to the first one. It held sixteen Vietnamese prisoners and thirty Vietnamese guards and officers. Willie and I were put into a long hootch, separated from the Vietnamese prisoners by a partition.

When the classes started on the day after we arrived, I was determined not to be taken in by any of it. Anyone with any sense at all, I figured, just had to know that whatever an American POW was taught here had to be nothing more than plain Communist propaganda. None of it, I told myself, was going to reach me. It didn't turn out like that.

What I soon came to understand was that our Vietnamese

instructor, a pleasant, soft-spoken man we secretly called Cross-Eyes, had no idea of filling us with propaganda the way we might have expected. Instead, he was very careful to tell us mostly what we knew to be true. And that made it really tough not to accept it.

Cross-Eyes started out teaching us some Vietnamese history. "It is important for both of you to understand how our country has suffered through wars for four thousand years," he said. "And how today we are still fighting for our independence and freedom."

Then he traced the history of Vietnam—back from the Bronze Age, when the Mongols moved down from China and mingled with the Indonesians, who were already in the Red River delta region, to produce the Vietnamese. Cross-Eyes described how the Vietnamese resisted invasion from China on the north for almost two thousand years, and how the country came to find its name in 207 B.C., when a Chinese general brought in his troops and set up a new kingdom which he called "Vietnam," meaning "land-of-the-south." We learned how for two hundred and fifty years Vietnam fell from one Chinese ruler to another, and we then followed the life of the tiny nation through centuries of wars and invasions.

Continuing on, Cross-Eyes showed how the French first established influence in Vietnam in 1802, then invaded the country in the late nineteenth century. We were told how Vietnam fell to the Japanese during World War II, and how the French returned again to fight the Vietnamese in a disastrous war that saw them defeated in 1954 at Dienbienphu.

And finally, Cross-Eyes brought us to the present—how, with Vietnam divided along the 17th parallel, and the North and South fighting an internal war, the United States forces—"aggressors" was what Cross-Eyes called them—came into the country.

As Cross-Eyes told it, you couldn't help being moved by this history lesson, and I experienced a sense of where I was—of what Vietnam was—like I never had before. Neither Willie nor I could really evaluate all of the politics involved in Vietnam's bloody history. Still, one thing came across—that here was one place war and suffering had never stopped.

After a few days of classes, Cross-Eyes asked us to write down some questions. "Tomorrow, we will try to answer these," he said. "I wish for you both to talk and think about them tonight first."

Many times during the months ahead, I was to be asked questions very similar to those put to us by Cross-Eyes: What was the war really for? Why was the United States in Vietnam? How much aid had the United States given the French? Why had the French been defeated? How could we claim to be in Vietnam to stop communism, when it existed politically in our own country?

It was in answering these questions that Cross-Eyes was able to get across all the points he wanted to make about the war—and about the U.S. government as well. He would not go deeply into things, he explained, for we were to be moving on to another camp soon. But he wanted us to be prepared for the classes to come, for it was to be at the next camp that our education would really begin.

So for one week, in a very easygoing way, Cross-Eyes tried to disprove everything we had always been told about the war—and about the United States' purpose in coming to Vietnam. He'd provoke us with questions like "How can Americans be here to fight for freedom when so many of you are not free in your own country? Isn't that so?" "Sure, man, it's so," Willie would respond to a question like that, and go on to tell about his life in the South and how bad it had always been for his family.

When Cross-Eyes described conditions in the United States, it was mostly how we knew them to be. He talked about the struggle to get a good job, how education was out of reach for so many of the poor, how slums were common everywhere.

"That is the way it must be under capitalism," he stressed. "And it is not only the problem of the black man—but of every poor man. The ruling class in your country—the rich—do not care about color when it comes to making money from your labor. As long as black is against white, white is against black—there can be no unity. This is why racism is important to the ruling class, for it allows them to rule easily."

As I listened to Cross-Eyes speak, putting down capitalism and describing conditions that I knew to exist, I thought of school and things I had learned in economics—and how, when I was small, most people always referred to politicians as no-good men, just out to make money or serve special interests at the expense of the people.

I tried to protest when he insisted that the United States, like all capitalist countries, can only survive by exploiting other countries, that we send our troops into foreign nations, not to protect freedom of the people, but to protect American business interests. He listened, allowing me to speak my piece. Then he said softly, "Well, you will learn. You will understand. You will come to question why the United States has troops in 108 different countries throughout the world—and how it came to power from the poor country it once was."

Each night, Willie and I would talk about that day's lesson. We really wanted to debunk much of what Cross-Eyes had told us. Sometimes, we managed. Yet both of us were now confused about many things. Many questions were left in doubt.

During the fourth week at the camp, Cross-Eyes asked us, "Well, how would you like to visit some of your friends in another camp?"

Always wary of the unknown, we both insisted we were perfectly satisfied with our treatment and liked it fine right there.

"Will you go with us?" Willie asked.

Cross-Eyes smiled, pleased by the question. "No, I cannot go," he said.

And so, a few days later, we were off once again. The camp we were heading for had no name, as did none of the POW camps in the south of Vietnam. And I wasn't quite certain where it was located, except that it was in the mountains, somewhere between Chu Lai and Tam Ky.

CHAPTER 12

POW Camp, South Vietnam, March 1968

We could have reached the camp that night but decided to stop. With darkness coming on and fifteen hours of traveling behind us (we'd taken off at three o'clock that morning), setting up for the night was just fine with me.

The next morning, after we'd been back out on the trail a while, we were startled to suddenly see a group of Americans move out of a wooded area and head right for us. They were dressed in loose-fitting pajama-like outfits, much like ours, and, hearing them tease and poke fun at one another, we could not mistake them for anything but Americans. Each man toted a basket on his back. A Vietnamese, carrying a rifle, followed close behind.

"Hey, are you the new guys comin' to our camp?" one man called out to us. For a second, I didn't know how to figure them. My first reaction was that they were Americans helping the Vietnamese. Then, it clicked. They were POWs too.

"Right—I guess so," I said.

The four crowded around and put down their baskets, filled with *co'm mi*, the potato-like vegetable we'd eaten many times since first being handed one on the trail.

"We've been out on a *co'm mi* run," the one with the long beard explained. "I'm Russ—Russ Grisson."

Then the others introduced themselves: Pheister, Strictland, Weatherman.

"Hi, I'm Daly," I said. "And this is Willie Watkins."

I thought how at ease they seemed, carefree almost. If it wasn't for the Vietnamese with the rifle, you might have thought they were out on a leisurely stroll to gather vegetables. Then, our guards acted a little fidgety, like we should be moving on.

We all grinned at one another. "Well, guess we'll be seein' you all again soon," Willie said.

"Right," Russ said. "We're taking a shortcut, so we'll be back ahead of you." Then they picked up their baskets, left the main trail, and moved off into the woods again.

About an hour later, when we stopped for a break, we were surprised to meet up with another group of Americans. Three were prisoners. The fourth, though he was American too, carried a Chinese-made AK–47 automatic rifle and wore a plain dark uniform. He stopped and exchanged words in Vietnamese with our guards. Then he turned to us.

"So, you must be the new POWs. We've been expecting you," he said. "Meet three more. I'm bringin' them into the camp now."

At first I was confused. I wondered how come this American was guarding three POWs. Then I remembered what Cross-Eyes had told me just before we'd left. "You will meet the American who carries an AK on the trail," he'd said. "His name is Garwood. He too was a prisoner, and he was released. But he refused to go home to the United States to see little children playing and being happy when he knew Vietnamese children were dying."

"You must be Garwood," I said.

He nodded, like he took it for granted I should know him. The three prisoners told us their names: Hammond, Ski, Burns.

"Okay, then, let's move it," Garwood ordered. The three POWs smiled over at us and started down the trail. "Be seein' you soon," Burns said.

We continued on, up one small hill, down the next, climbing all the time. Here and there the ground was still soggy from the last rainy days of the monsoon season, even though it had ended weeks before, in February. Finally, high on a hill ahead of us, we spotted the entrance to the camp. By now we were so far up that when you looked off to the sides you could see scattered clouds down below.

The camp commander was at the gate to meet us. He was

old-looking with a sad, tired face. Beside him, stern-faced, was his interpreter, a slightly built man, erect in a clean, neatly buttoned uniform. Four guards stood behind him.

One of our guards stepped up to the camp commander, spoke to him for a minute, and handed over some papers. Then the camp commander faced us. The interpreter translated. "You will now be taken to the prisoners' compound," he said. "There you will meet your squad leader, who will tell you everything you must know and read to you the camp rules. Then you may wash and rest."

The four camp guards led us inside the gate. Now we saw a scattering of hootches, some tiny, some bigger, spotted about the flat, barren area. I thought how dingy and depressing everything looked.

At the far side of the flat area, we followed the guards down a small hill to another section of the camp that was set off with a long, uneven bamboo fence. As we came closer, Russ came out through a small gate to greet us.

"Hey you guys, welcome to the prisoners' compound! We've all been waitin' for you."

Now that I got a good close look at him, at the scraggly beard and deep lines in his face, I'd have bet Russ was in his fifties. Actually, I found out, he was no older than most of the guys. "I didn't tell you on the trail," he said, grinning; "I'm your squad leader. You see, I'm the veteran POW around here. The VC captured me in 1966."

Just inside the gate, all the prisoners were waiting, including the other new ones that Garwood had brought in. The first guy to catch my eye looked even older than Russ—Williams, the first sergeant. His hair and beard were completely gray, and the way he moved you could tell he was badly wounded.

Everyone crowded around. I recognized Pheister and Strictland and called hello. Then all the guys started shouting out questions at us. It seemed like there wasn't anything they didn't want to know. No sooner had we answered one question than someone would yell out another.

"When were you guys captured?"

"January ninth."

"Hell, two days after me," Strictland said. "Same as Harker, here."

"When do you think the war will be over?"

"Oh, I'd guess about four or five months," I said, not knowing where I got my information from.

"What's happening back in the world, anyway?" "The world" meant the United States.

We started moving across the compound area. The questions kept coming. How and where did we get captured? How many days did we walk? What was each area like that we went through? And as we supplied the answers, they tried to piece them together with other bits of information they had in an effort to figure out where the camp was located. Most everyone had been captured in different places, and the more distances and descriptions they could compare, the better chance they had of pinpointing where they were.

They asked about the inquisition after we had been captured and what the interrogator had looked like. Every guy there had been questioned by Frenchie, too.

At the far end of the area, we came to a long hootch. Another hootch nearby, we were told, served as the kitchen—and one other, smaller, was a classroom. Russ explained that all the guys slept in the one hootch—and with the new arrivals that day, the total was now fourteen.

We went inside. The hootch was unbelievably filthy. Most of the room, from one end to the other, was taken up by a huge bed that stood about one foot off the floor and had been constructed by criss-crossing split bamboo poles. The poles were bound together with vines, forming a kind of mat.

"You mean we all sleep on that there?" Willie asked.

"Sure as hell do," Russ said. "And with all you new guys, it's gonna be a mighty tight squeeze."

"Hey, you all got any tobacco?" Pheister asked, grinning. "I sure could use a smoke just about now."

I opened my sack and pulled out the tobacco I'd been given at the last camp. As I offered it around, Russ said, "I wouldn't do that if I was you. We only get a regular supply of tobacco once a month here. When it runs out, you got to request some from Mr. Holmes, the interpreter. You probably saw him when you arrived, a little guy who does the talking when Slime spouts off in Vietnamese." Russ grinned. "Slime—that's our name for the camp commander."

"And when it comes to moochin' tobacco, you'd better be on

guard against Junior Flip, the smoke fiend," a man named Kushner said.

"He's talkin' about ol' Pheister there," Williams said.

Pheister, who I figured was called Junior Flip because he was short, took a deep drag on his butt and grinned. "Pay no mind to all that bullshit," he said.

The guys laughed.

"When do we eat chow around here?" I asked. "I'm starving."

"We only eat two meals a day," Russ explained. "We cook for ourselves, so we have breakfast and one big meal late in the afternoon."

Willie and I had been given food supplies before we'd started out the morning before. Most of it had not been eaten. I opened my sack again. "Maybe you guys'd like some of this," I said. Willie opened his sack also.

Everyone dove in and grabbed at the rice, *co'm mi*, and *nuoc mam* fish sauce like they hadn't eaten in months. The only two who didn't want any rice were the two officers, Captain Floyd Kushner, a doctor, and Francis Anton, a warrant officer. Neither of them ever ate it, they said—even at meals. It was Anton's chopper, I learned later, that we'd seen wrecked on the hill before we were captured.

Then Russ explained the camp rules. No fighting. No disturbances. Keep the area clean. Respect all guards. Salute the camp commander and officers by nodding your head to them.

So we grouped around on the bed, eating, smoking, shooting the bull. At one point I asked, "What do you guys do here all day long, anyway?"

"Hell, we jus' sit aroun' an' talk 'bout food, is all," said a tall, lanky guy named Cannon.

At the time, I never realized just how true Cannon's words were, how we'd spend many, many hours doing exactly that— talking about food. Especially Cannon. In his hillbilly way, he could talk on and on about food forever. And nothing ever stopped him from eating an enormous meal, as long as it was there to eat. Not even the wound in his back—a festering hole the size of a baseball.

It didn't take very long to get into the routine of things. Except for maybe the bed—that took a lot of getting used to. It was so jammed with the fourteen guys that you had to sleep in a perfectly straight position. You could never bend, curl up, roll over, or stretch an arm or leg.

At least there was plenty of space in the prisoners' compound, a large area for walking around in. And we were free to move anywhere inside it, as long as we didn't go through the gate without getting permission.

We took turns as cooks, two guys each day. Breakfast and dinner were much the same, *co'm mi* and rice. The only thing that varied, really, was how you prepared it, and I planned to try out some good ideas I had about that.

Twice a week, a group of us would take turns going out on *co'm mi* and wood runs. We scheduled these ourselves by telling Mr. Holmes the night before we wanted to do a run the following morning. Then, a guard would be assigned to accompany us. It took about six hours to go into the field, get a supply of *co'm mi* or wood, and return.

Some of the guys, like Kushner and Anton and a few others, never wanted to go out. Nobody pushed them. But I could sense that it wasn't going to go on like that forever, not as long as they wanted to keep warm at night around the burning wood, or eat *co'm mi*, our main food.

As far as the camp officers were concerned, they couldn't care less whether or not we went out for *co'm mi* and wood. Mr. Holmes, translating for Slime, told us, "The wood is for you, and it is up to you whether you get it or not. If you don't want to go out and carry *co'm mi*, you don't have to. But do not complain about being hungry."

Of course, we needed both. And we had to get it.

During the day, if you weren't out on a wood or *co'm mi* run, you either slept or sat around talking, playing cards, or playing chess or dominoes with sets the guys had made themselves. About three every afternoon, Mr. Holmes brought down the radio so we could listen to the "Voice of Vietnam." Then, at five, we'd all collect at the compound gate and stand at attention for head count, which Russ gave to the guards in Vietnamese. At night, the guards did a bed check every three hours.

For the most part, the guards didn't give us a hard time about anything. A few did, though, like the one we called Frankenstein because the way he walked reminded us of Frankenstein in the movies. Of the other guards, the worst of them were Montagnards, recruited from the primitive dark-skinned tribes of people whose villages were spotted throughout the highland areas. One of them, the one we disliked the most, we called Savage.

Even though the guards took orders from the camp commander, they had their own guard commander and operated independently in many ways. Later on, this division of authority resulted in plenty of trouble.

As for the officers, they didn't go out of their way to make life easier for any of us, but actually they could have been worse. Slime, the camp commander, was older than the others. He took his job very seriously, and was plenty strict when a POW did anything wrong or broke the camp rules. Still, he was just as strict on the guards as he was on any of us, and you couldn't help respecting him for that.

Slime's assistant was a pleasant, chubby man who seemed always ready to smile. He treated everybody okay, and we gave him the name of Jolly.

As for Mr. Holmes, nobody liked him. He was conscientious about doing his job—he'd always report any of the prisoners' needs, like if someone was sick, or asked for tobacco—but you couldn't help but know that Mr. Holmes did only what he had to. He really hated Americans, and it showed in many ways, like how he wouldn't answer questions sometimes, or would give one of the guys a hard time about something, or would keep us waiting out in the cold before he'd start one of his weekly criticism meetings.

Observing Mr. Holmes, you knew he was really intent on getting ahead, that he looked to advance to a higher rank in the Viet Cong. Whenever you got a glimpse of him, he was studying something, and he'd stay up late into the night, reading by candlelight. But even though we admired him for wanting to learn, we sensed how he felt about us, and we hated him for that. And many of the guards really disliked him, too. More than once, after he'd punish one of the guys for breaking some camp rule, a guard would come over to us and say, "Mr. Holmes—he number ten!"

Of the guards, the one we liked the most was Quang, a young guy in his twenties who always hung around us asking questions and trying to learn English. We'd kid him all the time and call him names in American slang. Finally, he caught on. After that, he learned all the slang words. Before long, we could talk or joke around with Quang the same as we did with each other, and he'd understand.

Mr. Holmes's weekly criticism meetings were really a drag, but there was no getting out of them. As squad leader, Russ would start off the meeting with a report on everything that had happened during the week—the health of the men, which of us had gone out on details, what arguments had taken place. He then had to do a thorough job of criticizing each of the men, including himself. Each of us had to do the same. At that time, we were even encouraged to criticize the guards.

All of us, of course, would give a good report, even though there seemed to be more and more petty arguments among the guys, and every so often one that wasn't so petty. But standing up there in front of Mr. Holmes, we'd say things like, "This week I didn't break any of the camp rules, had only one little argument which was really nothin' at all, and went out on a wood run."

It wasn't the kind of criticism that Mr. Holmes wanted to hear. Often, he'd remind us, "These meetings are to help you understand what you do that is wrong—and to correct it. Often, one does not realize his own mistakes. Someone else can always see them better."

I'd been in the camp about one month when two happenings livened things up. One was the arrival of two new prisoners, Thomas Davis and Isaiah McMillon, who we called Ike. The other event was our first political course.

New POWs coming in created excitement, just like when Willie and I had arrived, because it meant changes—new guys to talk to, new stories to hear, all the questions, seeking out new information, getting in touch with the world outside the camp. And just the fact that it changed the overall situation in some way, that was important, too. Any change from the routine of things was important.

So with the arrival of Davis and Ike, everything picked up for a while. We played cards more often and sat around trading stories all the time, even into the night. When we got to talking about home, both of them always had plenty to tell, since they were black and from the South. And as far as the problem of sleeping space was concerned, we solved that by putting up two hammocks. No way could they have squeezed into our community-style bed.

As for the political course, which lasted a full week, I learned one important nonpolitical lesson: sometimes, it's better to keep your mouth shut. Mr. Ho, who ran the course, came to the camp with three other teachers and several observers. During the day, the guys were divided up among the teachers for classes. Then Mr. Ho would take over for a general session with all of us.

Mr. Ho had been a professor in civilian life. Now he was a regional commander for the entire district, and one of the top officers in the VC. Days before he was to arrive, the guards were after us to clean up the prisoner compound area and the hootch.

It was the first time that Mr. Ho had been at the camp since the increase in POWs. When he saw how we were sleeping—fourteen on the bed and two in the hammocks—he issued an immediate order to build an additional hootch.

I had Mr. Ho for the first class, and it started out much like the one Cross-Eyes had given, a lecture on the four-thousand-year history of Vietnam, right up to the war. Mr. Ho had a British accent and spoke English very well, except that every now and then he'd use some old-fashioned word you never heard anymore. He covered the country's history, period by period, and when he came to the present time, he discussed the war in great detail, even the various United States Army policies under President Johnson such as "search and destroy."

After his lecture at the general session, Mr. Ho would always open up the class to a debate period, during which everyone was free to argue or disagree with any of his opinions. "You do not have to agree with me," he explained solemnly. "If you feel differently about something, you must speak out." He repeated this every afternoon; however, after three days of classes, no one had questioned or debated with him—except for one brief outburst by Earl Weatherman, one of the guys I'd met on the trail the day we arrived. One day, Weatherman suddenly jumped up and yelled out, "It's all lies and propaganda, that's what it is!" Then, a minute later, he admitted he was wrong. I learned later that Weatherman had always been like that, and nobody took his opinions on things too seriously.

Mr. Ho had just finished one of his long harangues about the

United States—how United States armed forces had intervened in countries throughout the world, even before World War II, and even as recently as 1965 had sent 23,000 troops to invade the Dominican Republic against a force of only 4,000. He insisted that it was by the use of such methods that the United States had become the power it was—and that the United States would support any government, no matter what it was, even the worst dictatorship, if such support would be to its advantage.

Before I realized it, I was on my feet arguing with him. The guys looked at me like I was out of my mind.

When I finished speaking, Mr. Ho nodded, then said, "Well, I see I did not make my point, Daly. Let us go over it all once again. Perhaps this time I will do better."

Then, for the next hour, Mr. Ho reviewed everything he had said before. Then he asked me, "Well, Daly, do you understand now? Do you agree with what I say?"

I was tempted to argue, but the stares of all the guys stopped me.

"Yes, I do," I said.

"You are not just saying that because you know I want you to, are you? Remember, there is freedom of speech and freedom of debate."

"No, I'm not just saying it," I said.

"Then you agree?"

"Yes, Mr. Ho. I agree."

Later, the guys really chewed me out. "Daly, don't you do that no more, hear!" "Mr. Ho woulda kept us there forever if he thought any of us didn't agree that all he said was true!"

So the one thing I did learn from that first political course was that you never disagreed with Professor Ho if you wanted to get the day's class over with fast.

After Mr. Ho's visit, we were back to the routine again. After weeks at the camp, what bothered me most, I think, was that there was just nothing at all to do. It had been that way at the recuperation camps, too. But then, at least, there'd always been plenty of food, and conditions had been good. Not like here—sixteen of us sleeping in one hootch, and the place so thick with filth that it was crawling day and night. And nobody looked to clean it. Not even when Williams, sick during the night, filled his pants and his portion of the bed, so that the stink of it woke us up in the morning.

Another thing I couldn't stand was how the guys who were cooks for the day never cleaned out the pot. We just kept on using it, day in and day out, and it was always swarming with bugs.

But at least during the day you could get outside and wander anywhere you wanted, as long as it was within the fenced-off area. Not that there was anything there to do or see—but the air was fresh, and now the days kept getting warmer and sunnier.

Davis, who had been a hard worker from the day he arrived, turned out to be one of the guys most everyone looked up to for making decisions and organizing things. He became sort of an unofficial leader. Also, to my surprise, Willie Watkins was different than before. He was still very careful about what he said when any Vietnamese were around, much like he had been in the recuperation camp, but now he was always telling the guys what he thought should be done, taking things over. So, little by little, Davis and Willie became the heads of the group. Each one was strong as an ox, and nobody wanted to go up against either of them. And they were smart enough never to get angry at each other—only at the other guys.

Though nobody said so straight out, their rise to power didn't sit too well with everybody. After all, both Davis and Willie were from the South. And they were both black.

Each day the bickering got worse. All of us became caught up in it, including me.

Like the one time I told off Captain Floyd Kushner. He was always bitching, refusing to sweep the floor or go out on *co'm mi* runs. It was as if he saw himself as better than the rest of us— especially the black guys, I suspected.

This one afternoon, we were trying to clean up the hootch, which was even cruddier than usual. We asked Kushner to give us a hand.

"Hell, I didn't go to school for eighteen years to learn to sweep a floor," he snapped.

"Wait a minute, Kush," I said, "I may not have been to college or anything—but I went to school for twelve years, too, you know. And I graduated high school. I didn't go to no school for twelve damn years to sweep no floor, either!"

He turned away and I followed him.

"Look here, man," I said, "you're a prisoner like the rest of us

—and you're gonna sweep the floor like the rest of us, too!"

Kushner bitched some more. But he helped sweep up the hootch.

On March 31, everyone was really surprised at the news on the "Voice of Vietnam." At first we didn't even believe it. President Johnson not only declared a limitation on the bombing of North Vietnam, but he announced his withdrawal from the presidential race.

Mr. Holmes stopped by that afternoon. "So you see," he said, "Johnson has finally come to understand that this is a war the United States will never win. Finally, he realizes that the American people do not support him—or the war!"

Later that night, we sat around for hours drinking hot tea and talking about it. It was difficult for us to evaluate what it really meant, whether it might make a real difference in bringing the war to an end.

I don't suppose I was all that optimistic, though. At least it didn't seem to matter none the following morning, April 1, when five of us, including me, tried to escape.

CHAPTER 13

The Escape Attempt,
April Fool's Day, 1968

It was a good clear morning, and I was looking forward to the *co'm mi* run so I could get out of the camp for a while. When we started out about seven-thirty, it seemed no different than the other times I'd gone out. Except—our bad luck—this time our guard was Frankenstein.

As usual, we followed the trail up into the hills. There were five of us: me, Bob Sherman, and three of the guys I'd met that very first day on the trail—Earl Weatherman, Dennis Hammond, and Ski, whose real name was Joe something-or-other, a long Polish last name that ended in "ski," which was the only part of it anybody could remember. Frankenstein set a fast pace, his dog from the camp chasing up and back beside us as we walked.

We had just gotten up into the hilly area when Bob Sherman said suddenly, "You know, it looks like a beautiful day to try and make a bird. What do you think?"

Nobody answered, and Bob pointed off into the distance. "See that mountain over there? If we can make it to that mountain, I'd know my way back to the base camp."

When Sherman had used the word "bird," all of us had understood it meant "escape." Actually, he could have said it right out. Frankenstein didn't understand a word of English.

Still, none of us answered. Maybe it was because Sherman was the kind of guy no one took seriously. Everyone was always poking fun at him, and he was the butt of jokes all the time. Not only because of the way he looked, like an old-time Western barber with a full scraggly beard, but also because most of the time he just didn't act like he was right. Kind of way out. Saying silly things, like the way he'd always insist he could eat a five-gallon pot of goulash nonstop if given the chance.

It was only later I learned from Kushner that Sherman had originally come to Vietnam a long time back, and had been assigned by the marine corps to duty in a morgue in some city in South Vietnam. After a while, working with dead bodies all the time really began to bother him. Finally, he had had a mental breakdown and was sent back to the States.

After many months in a mental hospital, Sherman was released. The very first thing he did was to reenlist in the marines.

Sherman's immediate assignment was not only right back to Vietnam, but into the very same job he had had before, doing the exact same work that had brought on the mental breakdown in the first place.

"Well, how about it, you guys?" Sherman repeated, looking from one of us to the other.

Weatherman was the first to answer. "Sure, it's okay with me. You guys know how I feel about getting out of here."

Actually, nobody knew how Weatherman felt about anything. The guys realized he was always changing his mind—like when he had jumped up to argue in Mr. Ho's class. There had been times when Weatherman hated the VC, then other periods when he was so anti-U.S. that he had actually lived with the guards. So what it really amounted to was, the more you knew Weatherman, the more you saw him as two different people, with two different minds. The trouble was, you could never know for sure which of the two was going.

When we reached the edge of the *co'm mi* field, Sherman turned to me. "Well, how about it, Daly?"

I suddenly thought back to the miserable conditions at the camp. I considered how impossible it was becoming for the guys to get along with one another, how the arguing and squabbling were more and more frequent. Getting away from all that—and maybe, with luck, having the chance to return home before too long—seemed like the greatest thing in the world just then.

"Sure," I said. "You can count me in."

Next, Sherman faced Joe. "You with us, Ski?"

Joe hesitated. "Look—it's a good idea, all right, but I think the time is wrong. We'd be better off trying it from the camp, with some of the others going along."

Then Dennis Hammond spun around. "That's a crock, Joe, an' you know it! We'd never stand a chance from the camp. I say we blast that fuckin' Frankenstein with his own piece, then take off!"

The way we were all talking back and forth, Frankenstein sensed that something was going on. He slowed up and looked over at us. Then, after a minute, he decided it was nothing worth bothering about.

Now Sherman went to work on Ski. "Look, man, you're the only one holding out. You're not gonna fuck this up for all of us, are you?"

Joe said nothing.

"Goddamn it, what do you say?" Hammond asked him.

"Okay, okay," Joe agreed.

Then Weatherman turned to me. "You know, anything might happen, Daly. For one thing, we've gotta take care of Frankenstein. Bein' a conscientious objector an' all, do you think you can help kill him if you have to?"

All the guys looked over at me, waiting for my answer.

I didn't let myself really consider it. Instead, I told them off the top of my head, believing it, "Look, right now, I want to go home. If you want to get to the other side of a wall, you gotta go over it. If what's between me and going home is that guard, I can do anything."

We continued on, talking it over. It was decided we'd wait until after we started pulling the *co'm mi,* then we'd jump Frankenstein and kill him. Once we'd made up our minds about this, though, the question was, which one of us was going to do it?

When I thought about shooting the guard, I went completely cold inside. I figured the guys might be really pissed off, but I told them, "I don't know about the rest of you, but the truth is, I could never kill a man just like that."

"Neither could I," Joe said. "Not that way—in cold blood!"

Then, one by one, everybody admitted to the same thing.

"Well, someone's gotta do it," Sherman said. "You know, Weatherman, it really oughta be you. You got more reason than any of us—you've been here the longest and suffered the most."

Weatherman nodded. "I really do hate that Frankenstein, all

right. But I don't know if I could kill him."

We were well into the field now. Frankenstein was sitting a short distance away, not even watching us.

"Well, if nobody can do it," Hammond said, "let's just forget about it." And we all agreed. Except Weatherman. As soon as he heard we were ready to give up the idea, he spun around and headed for Frankenstein.

We could tell by the way he approached the guard that he was scared. He asked Frankenstein for some water, then bent down to pet the dog a few times. Frankenstein had left his weapon propped up against a tree a few feet away, and we saw how he looked over to it once or twice. He must have realized then that something was up, and he seemed very edgy. Then, after a few minutes, Weatherman came back.

"Man, I just can't kill him," he said, shaking his head.

"C'mon, let's forget it," I said.

He thought for a minute. Then, without a word, he turned around and headed straight back to Frankenstein.

The weapon was still sitting up against the tree, and this time when Weatherman asked for some more water, the canteen was actually shaking in Frankenstein's hand. Then, he must have known for sure that something was going on, yet he was just too scared to move or do anything. Weatherman handed back the canteen, then played with the dog again. He kept this up for a while, and you could almost see his mind working, trying to decide. Then, once again, he turned around and returned.

"I tell you, I just can't do it, man," he said. "I just can't kill nobody in cold blood. Did you see how that guy was shaking?"

None of us said anything. Then, very suddenly, Weatherman turned away and started back to the guard for the third time. He came up on him fast, and, without any hesitation, this time he jumped him. Immediately, Dennis Hammond leaped up to help.

Frankenstein was down in the dirt, and Weatherman and Hammond pounded him without stopping. He just lay there, squirming and moaning, blood covering his face. He kept calling Weatherman's Vietnamese name. "Ton, Ton," he cried, "please!"

Then Dennis yelled out. "Hey, Bob, get the rifle, get the rifle!"

Bob charged to the tree, grabbed the weapon and ran the short distance to where Hammond and Weatherman bent over the guard, kicking and beating him. Once there, Sherman just stood without moving, the rifle at his side.

"Shoot him, Bob, shoot him!" Hammond and Weatherman shouted.

Bob lifted the rifle. "I can't, I can't, I can't!" he screamed back. Then he turned away and ran to me. "Here, Daly," he cried, "you take it!"

My arms were frozen. "No, Bob," I said. "I can't kill him either."

Suddenly Hammond yelled out, "Bob, if you can't shoot him, then pull the bayonet out and stab him!"

Sherman didn't budge. "I can't, I can't!" he called back, and threw the weapon to the ground.

Then the guard broke free, screaming and hollering. Hammond and Weatherman ran after him, caught up, threw him to the dirt, and started pounding his face all over again. All at once, battered and covered in blood, the guard tore loose once more. This time they let him go.

None of us moved—just stood and watched Frankenstein run off wildly through the fields, arms waving, screaming for all he was worth, his dog chasing after him. Then Sherman, still shaking, asked, "What are we gonna do? What are we gonna do now?"

Hammond and Weatherman raced back, shouting as they ran, "Come on, you guys, let's get out of here!"

"We can't, we can't!" Joe shouted back. "Now that the guard got away, there's no way we can make it!"

Hammond turned away angrily and faced Bob. "What about you? You comin' with us?"

"I ain't goin' either," Sherman said weakly.

Then they swung around and looked at me.

"Joe is right," I said. "We'd never make it now."

Weatherman's face twisted in anger. He grabbed the rifle. "Let's go, Dennis—the hell with them!"

"Cowards, nothin' but fuckin' cowards!" Hammond screamed at us. And then the two of them turned and took off running.

Then Joe said, "We might as well sit down and wait a while to give them a chance to get away."

"Hell, no," I said, "no use to stay here now. If we don't beat that damn guard back to the Montagnard village, they're gonna be out here like ants on sugar and there ain't gonna be no questions—they're gonna shoot first."

"He's right," Bob agreed. "It's only a couple of miles, and he'll be there in no time."

So the three of us took off, running as fast as we could. I had been to the village once before. Maybe a couple of hundred Montagnards lived there, judging by the straw huts and hootches scattered all around. Each tribe owned the land surrounding its village, and that's why the camp had to trade with them in return for permission to pull the *co'm mi.*

We kept running without letup. But before we reached the main part of the village, we knew Frankenstein had made it there ahead of us. From a slope, looking down, we spotted him way off, a large crowd of Montagnards swarming all around him. Even from where we were, we could hear his shrieks and cries, telling them all what had happened. Yet there was nothing for us to do but keep on going and hope we could make them understand in some way that we didn't take part in beating up the guard.

When the first villagers spotted us, a loud cry went up. Within a minute all the people started yelling out, running everywhere, as if King Kong was coming through. Women grabbed their little children to get them out of the way. Even some of the men ran off in fear. And then, very cautiously, a group of men in loincloths, holding spears, came slowly toward us. We just stood there and waited.

Suddenly, they rushed in, grabbed us, and dragged us off toward Frankenstein. When he saw us, he started screaming louder than ever. Then he picked up a piece of wood and came running over to beat us with it. Several men held him back.

They tied up our hands and legs—Bob and I were tied back to back—and pushed us down in the dirt in front of one of the hootches. All the while, men came charging into the village from all sides. The word had spread to the neighboring villages, which were within only running distance for the mountain people. While it might have taken us forever to get from one of their villages to the other, somehow they made it in minutes.

The village chief kept waving them in, and before long they were out there like I didn't know what, maybe five hundred or more. As I learned later on, one of the reasons they even allowed the VC to set up POW camps in the area was because of a promise that prisoners would make no trouble. Now, with that promise broken, the tribes were in a fury.

Finally, the village chief gave a signal. Then the entire mob —howling, yelling, jabbing their spears into the air—took off for the mountains in search of Hammond and Weatherman. It was hard to believe—right out of a Tarzan movie.

With most of the men gone, the women in the village now turned their attention to us. They crowded around, stepping up one at a time, poking a spear or stick in our faces.

Bob Sherman had it worse. Frankenstein had explained who we were, and the story was that Sherman had been captured while having sex with one of the mountain women. Now, the women of the village cursed at him, each stepping up to him, one at a time. Most of them were chewing on some powdery stuff called betel-nut. It turned their teeth black and gave off a horrible dark red juice. They kept spitting like a ballplayer with chewing tobacco, and now they took turns spitting at Bob. This red blob kept hitting him in the face, and before long he was covered with it, his hair, his eyes, everywhere.

Sherman kept pleading, "Can I have some water, please?" over and over, until I just couldn't stand hearing it anymore. Finally, I twisted toward him and said, "You might as well quit it. There's no sense begging for what you're not gonna get anyway."

As the women poked at him or spit in his face, Bob jerked from side to side, and every time he moved, the ropes cut deeper into my arms. Soon, I had a numbing ache from my shoulder down to my hand. I knew it was a waste of time, but I asked them to loosen the ropes. I don't know if they understood or not, but not one of them paid attention.

Then, one woman stood right in front of me, and I could see the hate in her eyes. She kept poking her spear at my face, trying to make me flinch or pull my head out of the way. I made up my mind not to move, and I didn't. Infuriated, she jabbed the point of the spear closer, grazing my cheek. This went on and on until finally I lost all control. I started yelling and cursing at her, and spit at the ground in front of where she stood. When I did that, she exploded in anger.

Just then, we heard a gun go off from a nearby hill. Everything stopped.

A short while later, they brought Dennis in. Four mountain people dragged him along, and a circle of men surrounded them. Two of the VC guards from the camp were there, walking off to the side. When they came to the center of the village area, the Montagnards pulled Dennis to his feet and, one after another, started beating him. Dennis staggered back and forth, his face split and bleeding, yet he never made a sound. When he fell to the ground, they picked him up again.

Finally, Slime arrived. I never thought I'd actually be happy to see the camp commander's scowling face anywhere, but this time I was. Mr. Holmes and five guards were with him.

When they came up to us, I told them about my arms, and they immediately loosened the ropes. Dennis was brought over, and for about ten minutes Slime and the village chief argued over him. Every time Slime directed the guards to take Dennis away from the men who were holding him, the village chief blocked their way. It was clear he had no intention of letting Dennis go. At last, we started for the camp without him.

On the way back, Joe asked me, "What do you think, Daly, maybe we should admit the whole thing?"

"Don't admit that we did anything," I said. "If Frankenstein tells the truth—that neither of us were in on the beating—maybe we'll get a break. When they get Dennis back, he's gonna be in for it one way or the other. As for Weatherman, we'll soon find out what happened to him."

Dennis returned to the camp one week later. The Montagnards had kept him in the village for seven days. He had broken their trust and therefore had to be punished—their way. Every day, he'd stood outside in the village area, bound hand and foot. And every day, all the women of the village had lined up to take turns beating him with bamboo sticks.

He told us about Weatherman, too. They had both been hiding in the bushes when the mountain people spotted them. The men crowded around, holding them to the ground with their spears. Then one man with a gun came up to Weatherman and put the weapon to his head.

The first time he pulled the trigger, the gun didn't go off. Then he fired it again. This time it blew Weatherman's head completely open.

Just as the man turned the gun on Dennis, the two guards from the camp, on their way to the village, came upon the scene. One guard knocked the gun from the Montagnard's hand.

After Dennis told us that story, we learned that fifteen NVA officers had arrived at the camp. They were there to carry on an investigation of the incident and, when they had the facts, to help conduct our trial.

Garwood questioned each of us individually every day, asking for a detailed description of all that had happened, the same thing, over and over. The one point he kept coming back to was whether we had planned the escape. I told him no, we hadn't planned it. Somehow, it had just happened.

Mr. Holmes made a big thing about that, too. "Did any of you talk about trying to escape before that morning?" he asked.

Then, after I insisted we hadn't, he pressed me: "What about later? Which one of you suggested it?"

"I really can't remember," I said. "It seems as if we all started talking about it at the same time."

The day before the trial, Slime called us in. Again, each of us had to go over all of it. As I stood before him, with Mr. Holmes interpreting, I told the story for what seemed like the hundredth time. I could see that the camp commander was really worried. The emotion showed in his face—tired and drawn with the strain of the past days. I realized that he would be held responsible for all that had happened, and his report on how Weatherman had been killed was certain to go to the NVA top brass. In a way, I couldn't help but feel sorry for the old guy.

Then, the trial. They used the classroom—the four of us standing up front, the chairs occupied by Slime, Jolly, and the fifteen NVA officers. Garwood and four guards lined the walls. Mr. Holmes did the questioning.

Once again, each of us had to testify as to what had happened, only this time we were asked to plead guilty or not guilty. Trials at the camp, I'd been told, were held whenever anyone broke the rules. Usually, though, the POWs themselves were asked to decide on guilt or innocence—and what the punishment must be. Our case was considered too serious for a trial like that.

Frankenstein told his side of it. He explained it all in Vietnamese, without any translation, and we couldn't be sure just what he said. But judging from the expression on his face—and the anger in his voice—we had little doubt he painted as bad a scene as he possibly could.

Then Joe. He was nervous and his voice was shaky. He pleaded not guilty, and his main defense was that he hadn't taken part in the escape in any way, didn't even talk to the rest of us while it was going on. They seemed to go along with this, and I figured that Frankenstein had told it that way, too.

I was called next. I stressed that I had not beaten up Franken-stein.

"But you understood what was going on, isn't that so?" Mr. Holmes asked.

"Yes," I admitted.

"And you made no attempt to stop the escape—or the beating?"

I shook my head. "No, I didn't."

When Bob Sherman testified, he explained how he had refused to kill Frankenstein, how even though he had held the weapon, he had thrown it on the ground rather than use it. So far, the fact that the idea of escape had been Sherman's in the first place had not been revealed.

Dennis Hammond had no choice but to plead guilty. He admitted beating up Frankenstein, then running off with Weatherman.

"Was the escape your idea?" Mr. Holmes asked him.

"No," Dennis said.

"Then whose idea was it?"

Hammond hesitated, deciding what to say. He must have figured it wasn't going to make any difference to him anyway. He answered finally, "I just don't know whose idea it was—everybody's, I guess." Then he added, "It was a bad mistake. I'm sorry about it."

The deliberations didn't take very long.

Dennis was given ninety days in stocks, a really tough sentence. It meant that for all that time he'd have to stay in his bed, locked into a wooden board with holes in it that secured the ankles. In stocks, it was possible to sit up, but there was no way of turning over or getting out. Even meals had to be eaten right there.

Sherman was sentenced to sixty days in stocks.

Joe was given no punishment at all.

I received thirty days probation. The reason for the sentence, it was explained, was because I did not try to stop the escape or attempt to take the weapon away. "Remember, Daly," Mr. Holmes announced, "if you do anything wrong during these thirty days, you will be severely punished!" He stressed the word "severely" to make certain I understood that he didn't mean just the usual punishment for breaking some small rule, like standing at attention for two or three hours.

Then, Slime and Mr. Holmes faced the four of us in front of the classroom, with all the NVA officers watching. Slime paced back and forth, stopping to look squarely into each face. With Mr. Holmes translating, he said, "Each of you must understand—when the time comes for prisoners of war to return home, you will be the very last Americans to leave Vietnam!"

So the trial was over. The NVA officers left the camp. And Hammond and Sherman began to serve their sentences.

Dennis managed okay. But it was really rough on Sherman. As the days went on, he began to say way-out things. After a while, he refused his meals, and finally would eat only when one of the guys sat beside him with a spoon and put the food into his mouth.

About forty days later, Mr. Ho returned to the camp to conduct another political course. After inspecting the area and observing Hammond and Sherman in stocks, he decided, as he put it, to "liberate" them. Both were released.

But it was already too late for Bob Sherman. By then, he was weak and sick most of the time. And as much as we hated to admit it, it was pretty clear to all of us that he had just about lost his mind.

CHAPTER 14

The Letter, South Vietnam

It was just like a bunch of cats and dogs living together. Not a day passed without an argument over something. Maybe, after the new hootch was built, some of the problems would be eliminated. Meanwhile, though, we were still all together in the same dirt and filth, sleeping like sardines on that wall-to-wall bed.

One of the few bright spots, an event that we all looked forward to, was when Mama Son came into the compound to cook for us. About sixty or so, Mama Son worked in the camp kitchen, and in a way she was like a mother to all the prisoners. She'd always be ready to give us extra food—not at all like the camp cook, Hannah, who'd never give up an extra crumb. Whenever Mama Son cooked, it was really great because she'd bring along many spices and things we'd never have gotten otherwise, like onions, green peppers and garlic. Her specialty was *co'm mi* soup, which she made with one and a half pounds of ham and half a bottle of oil, more than our normal two-day supply. So whenever Mama Son asked us what we'd like to have her cook, all the guys would yell out for the soup, knowing we'd get the ham that way. And the more you praised Mama Son, the more she liked it. We'd always be sure to tell her, over and over, "Oh, Mama Son, soup number one, number one!"

Sitting around the hootch at night before sleep, talking about home and family was one of the few ways the guys related to one another. We were allowed to keep a fire going during the colder nights, so often we'd settle around it with a big pot of tea and trade stories.

Sometimes the storytelling was real entertainment—like listening to Davis, who had lived in a world none of us knew, not even the guys who came from the deep South as he did. Davis was always ready with some tale about his home life, and it was exciting to listen to him, like seeing a movie. He could be really funny the way he'd mimic all the characters, and after a while it seemed like we knew all his wild friends. It got so we could just about see those backwoods places where Davis lived, like Billie May's, a club where moonshine was sold, fighting and cursing never stopped, and people got themselves shot up regularly. Before long, I felt I knew Billie May—this burly gal, huge and husky like a man, bossing everyone around and beating up her husband every weekend.

It must have been tough living in those cotton fields and backwoods of Alabama, and, as rugged as Davis looked, the hard life showed on his face. Sometimes he'd talk about that side of things, too, like how his father died right when he was born, and what a large black family without a man was up against down there.

Willie Watkins was beginning to open up some now, too, and he was another one who could keep all the guys interested by telling what he remembered about growing up in a small South Carolina town. One story that shocked all of us was how his grandfather was lynched after some white woman accused him of molesting her.

Willie had a lot of hatred in him, and I knew he didn't trust whites much by many of the things he'd said to me when we'd been together all those weeks in the recuperation camp. Now he was always very sensitive to anything one of the white guys might say, like if they made a crack about him and Davis running things, or how the five of us blacks had too much control over what went on. In a way, we did influence many things, since, most of the time, when Davis and Willie decided on something together, Ike, Lewis and I went along with it.

Actually, I don't think I sided with the guys because they were black; it just often worked out that way. If I thought of anyone as a friend, it was Cannon. Ike was okay, but it kind of bugged me to hear him talk about his life in Miami, trying to give the impression that he came from a middle-income family, when I suspected his people just about managed to get along. Maybe it bothered me because it had been the kind of thing I'd always felt the need to do, like letting people think we owned that old house in Bed-Stuy, when all the time we'd be lucky to scrape together the rent for it each month. And it had always been that kind of struggle, ever since my grandmother had leased the place in 1929.

Robert Lewis was much like that, too—embarrassed about being poor and about the conditions his family was forced to live under in Houston. Lewis was a nice enough guy, but just plain lazy. Ever since he slipped on the mountainside and hurt his back, he used it as an excuse to lie down all the time. Lewis just wouldn't do one single thing he didn't really have to.

As for Cannon, it's hard to know why I took a liking to him the way I did—except, I suppose, because he was just a tall, lanky dude who always did the best he could and never griped about anything, even that horrible wound in his back that never seemed to get any better.

I couldn't figure how Cannon had gotten into the army, though. He'd never gone past the fifth grade and could barely write his name. At first, he even refused to take a bath, until it got so bad we had to force him. I told him straight out he wasn't sleeping in the hootch unless he did.

And all the time, just like on that first day, Cannon always talked about food. Even though he'd smoke up his entire allotment of tobacco the very day he got it, Cannon was the only guy never to be without some. He managed this by walking around all day on his hands and knees looking to police up any butts the prisoners or guards had thrown away. So, even Pheister, the smoke fiend, didn't have tobacco as regularly as Cannon. When Pheister ran out, he'd make it down to the gate and act like a clown for the guards for fifteen minutes or so, then ask them for a little tobacco. He'd put on a whole show, then keep repeating "*It, it,*" a little bit. Most times, they gave him some.

But you really had to hand it to Cannon. No matter how much trouble that wound in his back would give him, he'd never complain about it. Not even when Jane, the camp medical worker, came in each day to clean it. She couldn't care less about making it easier for him—and it was horrible to watch. To clean the wound, she'd take a piece of gauze and stick it all the way down into it. Cannon would just sit there and grit his teeth in pain, the sweat pouring off him. Sometimes, I'd go outside so I wouldn't have to see it.

What made it all the worse was that even though Cannon had to go through this same ordeal every day, it did no good at all. There just weren't the proper supplies and medicine available to treat him. So the wound never healed. After a while, it started getting maggots in it.

I managed to get along with most of the guys all right, with not too many arguments. I suppose, though, my refusing to sign a letter protesting the war, which most everyone else agreed to sign, couldn't have helped my popularity any too much.

They started buttering us up days before. Mr. Holmes and Jolly came around with candy and passed out regular cigarettes instead of the usual tobacco. Garwood must have been in on it too, acting nice and joking like he did.

Finally, Mr. Holmes came into the compound and said he was going to appoint a group to write a letter about the war, and, when it was finished, he'd like all of us to sign it. Then it would be given out to the press.

Six men were chosen as writers, each from a different unit— Kushner, Anton, Strictland, Joe, Willie, and David Harker. I was surprised at Harker being picked, since he was the one guy who was always answering Mr. Holmes back and giving him a hard time. Somehow, Harker always got away with standing up to Mr. Holmes, maybe because he was such a hard worker. The Vietnamese respected that. So Harker was never punished, even though sometimes he'd make Mr. Holmes so mad during a criticism meeting that Holmes would go storming out of the room.

For three days, the writers went off by themselves. Mr. Holmes made it very clear to them what the letter should say. Its purpose, he told them, was to try to bring pressure on President Johnson to end the war. Without coming on so strong that it wouldn't be believed, they were to tell in their own words how wrong they thought the war was and how unhappy they were at being away from home.

Just before it came time for everyone to sign the letter, an NVA officer visited the camp to meet with us. Speaking in English, he gave it to us straight.

"You must all understand that no one will be forced to sign

the letter," he said. "What each man does is entirely for him to decide. However, you should all keep in mind the fact that you are prisoners. Your government does not know you are here." Then he paused and emphasized his next point.

"You must also remember that your life is now in our hands. What happens—all depends on you!"

Everybody got the message. Back at the hootch, the guys were really pissed off about it.

"Like hell they don't use force!" Ike said. "What else is it when you get threatened that way?"

Everyone agreed. But then, as we kicked it around, a few of the guys came up with another point of view. It was true that they were trying to intimidate us by making it very plain that we'd never get out of these mountains alive if they didn't want us to. Still, in one important way, it could be to our advantage to sign the letter. If it were to be broadcast, that would get out the news that we were POWs, and our families would learn we were alive.

Then, as we discussed what the consequences of signing the letter could be after our release, the arguments were very much like others I would hear many times in the future. Everyone realized we could always say we had had no choice—that we had done it to protect our lives. That was the one explanation, the guys knew, that would be accepted by the military, which was always ready to believe the Communists used methods of force and torture.

After going around with all the pros and cons, most everyone decided to sign. The only three who refused were Fred Burns, First Sergeant Williams—and me. I wasn't all that certain why I was unwilling to go along, yet I felt that I owed them an explanation, and I tried to explain the reasons I considered it a mistake for me.

Even if nothing happened to the others, I told them, I was almost certain to be in for a ton of trouble. I had everything going against me. The fact that I was a conscientious objector and had tried to get out of the service, that my army records must be loaded with reports of my protests right from the start, that in the eyes of the army I was a problem and a troublemaker all along the line—all this would mean that the military would be mighty quick to single me out for discipline.

But I considered even then how all this was a way of thinking I'd seriously have to question sooner or later. Here I was, truly against the war and everything it represented, probably with stronger convictions than any other POW at the camp—yet I was refusing to sign a letter protesting it. And what really bothered me was the knowledge that, somewhere along the way, I had allowed the system to intimidate me. Somehow, I had been made to act contrary to what I believed in—just like when I joined the army and came to Vietnam in the first place.

Anyway, even with all the questions and doubts, I still stuck with it. I refused to sign.

"Man, when you decide to do somethin'—or not to—you sure *will* stay with doin' just what you want to," Ike told me. "You're a real *will* Daddy, that's what you are." And from then on, that was a nickname I never got rid of—Will Daddy.

Mr. Holmes arranged a ceremony for the event. Movie cameras were set up. The prisoners were lined up and told to step before the table one at a time to sign the letter. I waited with the others. When my name was called, I walked up as those ahead of me had done—but I just paused at the table, did not sign the letter, and continued on.

I couldn't miss the flash of anger on Mr. Holmes's face. The guards around the room stiffened, staring after me. From then on, one of those guards was to get back at me many times, pushing me along the trail, or slicing at me with his stick during a supply run, saying, *"Di, di."*—Go, go fast!

So the letter went out missing three signatures. And Williams, because he hadn't signed and was a first sergeant, was given the blame for having influenced the other two of us.

If the guys were really down on me for not signing the letter, they had their chance to get even after the orange-stealing incident.

I was out on a wood run that morning with Ike, Harker, Strictland and Dennis Hammond, who ever since the day of the escape had made it plenty clear he didn't like me any too much. We were just getting ready to return to the camp when Strict and Harker spotted some orange trees a short way from where they were collecting wood. Our guard, Dang—always ready to give us a hard time if he could—was sitting off near the trail. The guys ran the few yards to the trees, gathered up some oranges, and dashed back. Dang never even noticed.

As they got ready to go, I called out, "Hey, wait a minute, let me get at least one before we take off!"

Just as I reached the orange trees, someone called my name. It was Kushner, standing on another hill nearby. He waved and hollered over to me, "Hey, Daly, get me some o-r-a-n-g-e-s, too!" as if nobody would hear or understand him because he spelled it out.

Immediately, Dang came charging over. I quickly made it back to where the other guys were grouped. I noticed that the oranges they had taken had been dropped to the ground, like hot potatoes.

"Who took oranges?" Dang demanded to know.

No one answered.

He asked each of us the question again. One by one, everyone denied it.

Now Dang stared at me. "I saw you there, Daly—did you take oranges?"

I told him no.

He turned to the others. "Did Daly take oranges?"

Dennis Hammond answered, "Maybe he did, maybe he didn't!"

With that, Dang decided I did. He picked up a big bamboo stick and handed it to Hammond. "Hit Daly for taking oranges," he ordered.

Dennis hesitated, then moved toward me.

I faced him. "Hold on, Dennis—you're not going to hit me with that stick!"

"I ain't gonna hit you hard," Dennis said.

"That's not the point. The point is, Dang wants you to beat me 'cause he thinks I'm guilty of taking these oranges, and you know damn well I didn't take 'em!"

"Oh, I'll do it easy—"

"Like hell you will!"

Suddenly Dang pulled the stick out of Hammond's hand and came down with it on my head as hard as he could. I saw stars.

I spun around. Screaming at Dang, calling him every name I could think of, I started after him. "I'm gonna kill you!" I shouted.

Dang backed off. "Stop, Daly, stop!"

I kept moving toward him. Dang lifted his rifle.

"Cool it before he shoots you!" Joe called out.

Dang loaded his weapon. I had all I could do to stop from

hitting out at him—but I held back, realizing how if I took one more step he'd pull the trigger. Then, hardly knowing what I was doing, I turned and took off down the hill at ninety miles an hour, screaming louder than a siren.

I was still yelling when I ran into the camp. Garwood grabbed me and asked, "What happened?"

"That son of a bitch hit me in the head!"

"Why? What did you do?"

"Nothin'—that's what I did!"

"Get back to the compound, Daly!" Garwood ordered.

That afternoon, I was put on trial for stealing oranges. Everyone was there—officers, guards, all the prisoners, and Slime—a total of nineteen. After Dang told his side of it, the camp commander took over.

"This is not your first offense," Mr. Holmes translated for him. "You must be punished if you are guilty. It will be for the prisoners to decide. Tell me, Daly, did you take the oranges?"

"No, Mr. Holmes, I did not take the oranges."

He faced the prisoners. "Those of you who believe that Daly took the oranges raise your hand."

Every hand went up.

Later, the guys told me how they figured I'd be punished anyway, so it seemed best to find me guilty fast and get it over with. I just couldn't buy that.

After the vote, Mr. Holmes asked, "What should be the punishment?"

It was necessary for everyone to agree on how I was to be punished.

Dennis answered immediately. "He should go ten days without any food."

Slime replied, "To go ten days without food in the mountains, a man can die. You must think of punishment where we do not take away food that may cause Daly to lose his health."

Someone called out, "How about missing three meals and being tied up overnight?"

Mr. Holmes asked if everyone thought this was a fair punishment. All agreed.

Then Slime turned to me. Mr. Holmes interpreted. "Daly, do you think this is fair punishment?"

With all the guys voting for it, I knew it would be senseless not to go along. "Yes," I said.

"Then you will be tied up for twenty-four hours and receive no food. However, you will be given water."

With that, the trial was over. Off in the corner, listening to everything with a hard, expressionless face, was a new officer we hadn't met yet. No one realized it at the time, but he was soon to be our new camp commander. And he was to be given the perfect name for how he looked and acted—Rat Face.

That night, I was tied up outside the hootch. Not one of the guys even thought to give me water. The next morning, I questioned them about it.

"We just forgot you were out there," everyone explained.

And I suppose it was true. The way things were, nobody really cared much about anyone else. Each guy was out for himself. Like the way each pair of prisoners, when they took their turns as cooks, always cheated on the others. It became an accepted rule. If it was your turn to cook, everyone understood it was also your day to screw everybody else—your "fuck-everybody day," as it came to be called.

So when you got right down to it, we were just a bunch of guys living from day to day in our own ungiving world.

May 15, 1972

ar Mom & Family,

am fine & in good health & hope that all of you are
same. I received your letter & was very glad to know
t you received the tape of my voice & my letter. Tell
ryone in the family & my friends that I send my best
ettings. In your next letter I would like to know if Chy,
n., or Ren. is married & how many children. I would like
you to send me some pictures of everyone & the house.
r letter means very much to me. So continue to write & tell
ryone else too. I love you all so very much & I hope & pray that
war ends so that I can see you all again soon.

> Take Care & God Bless You All.
> Your son Bubby.

NOTE: Whenever you or anyone else writes to me
please make sure the letter is the same as mine,
with ten lines for the body of the letter. Your
letter must have this address inorder for me to
receive it —

James A. Daly RA 11815566
Camp of Detention for U.S Servicemen
Captured in South Vietnam
c/o Special Mission of the
Republic of South Vietnam
In the Democratic Republic of
Vietnam, Hanoi. (via - Moscow)

The letter Jim wrote to his mother in May 1972. Prisoners were restricted to ten lines in each letter, and few letters were permitted out of the camp.

Above: *Conditions in the camp were not ideal, but prisoners made the best of it. Here are all the eating utensils in the camp.*

Below: *Plantation Gardens, Hanoi. These men are soon to be released, and they know it! Jim will go with them.*

Left: *First leg of the journey to freedom. The bus to Hanoi airport.*

Below: *The formal repatriation ceremony, Hanoi airport. Mr. Bad sits at center, watching, flanked by camp guards. He will not see Jim again.*

Left: *Hanoi airport, just before boarding the plane. Gaunt and tired, the men still wear their camp pajamas and sandals. They are now in American custody.*

Below: *On the plane to the Philippines. We made it!* (U.S. Air Force Photo)

GOD LOVES U WE

Above: *Group portrait at Clark Air Base in the Philippines. All the members of the Peace Committee are here. Jim is third from right, standing in the rear. Riati is standing at center, wearing glasses.* (Joint Information Bureau, Operation Homecoming)

Below: *The next leg of the journey. The group arrives stateside. All's well that ends well. But for some, it was not quite the end. . . .*

Left: *Jim, back in uniform, arrives at McGuire Air Force Base. Here he is, flanked by Major General Foster, Base Commander, and Colonel Price, director of Operation Homecoming. Quite a hero's welcome. Soon, Jim would even shake the president's hand. But what lay ahead after that?*

Right: *A reunion of the Peace Committee, hosted by the Veterans of Foreign Wars, in Kentucky, January 1974. (Photo by Nancy Moran)*

Below: *All the way home! Jim back in Bedford-Stuyvesant.*

Jim, back to the window, discusses his problems with Peace Committee members John Young, Michael Branch, and Fred Elbert, at their 1974 reunion. (Photo by Nancy Moran)

CHAPTER 15

Rat Face and Mr. Thieu

Rat Face's real name was Dang, too, just like the guard, but nobody called him that. He was the worst. Old Slime had been an angel compared to him.

At least Slime had been straightforward, and he didn't try to scare anyone into doing things. Sometimes, he'd even joked around. Of course, when Slime told a joke, we all listened and laughed when he laughed, funny or not. It reminded me of the Al Capone movies where, when the bad guy laughed at something, everyone standing around laughed with him. And when he stopped laughing, so did everyone else.

So in a way we were sorry to see Slime go, because all of us knew that things had to get rougher with Rat Face. Just by the way he acted and spoke to us, you could tell how much he hated Americans. I thought of him as the kind of person who was so evil, he found it just about impossible to smile, even when he tried to.

Rat Face looked to make sure that none of us got anything more than we were entitled to—not one extra can of food or ounce of tobacco. He did what his job obligated him to do—nothing more.

And nobody messed with Rat Face or talked back to him, like they sometimes did with Mr. Holmes. We were just too scared. Whenever Rat Face got angry, you could imagine just by his look that he was perfectly capable of torturing a man without flinching. Nobody was about to test out that theory.

One thing that made up for the arrival of Rat Face, though, was the new second interpreter, Mr. Thieu. Everyone liked him right off, and he seemed to really enjoy spending time with the prisoners.

Many times, Mr. Thieu came down to the compound to eat with us. Like one day when I was cook and he just wandered into the kitchen and asked, "What you cook, Daly?"

"Oh, some baked *co'm mi* today. Want some?"

And when we sat down to eat, Mr. Thieu was right there with us.

When he first arrived, Mr. Thieu knew only a little slang English. The guys called him names for fun, like they used to with the guard, Quang. They'd say things like "Hey, stupid. Buffalo head!" It took Mr. Thieu a while to catch wise.

From the very start, Mr. Thieu did all he could to help the POWs. When we requested something, like tobacco, he'd never make us wait for it, as Mr. Holmes always did.

One time, a couple of us spotted Mr. Thieu coming from the supply room with soap for the prisoners. Before he reached the compound, he slipped a piece of it into a back pocket. Knowing how little soap the guards and officers were allotted, and liking Mr. Thieu the way we did, nobody said anything.

Mr. Thieu would even tell us in advance when we were to receive some special food—just to be sure that Hannah didn't cheat us out of it. Once, when we were supposed to get two cans of sardines, but didn't, Mr. Thieu went down to the supply room himself and came back with them. "Hannah forgot the fish," he said. Then, smiling, he told us, "But you must be careful. Hannah forgets many times." After that, if he was around when we were to pick up food supplies, he'd go along to make sure it was all there.

As the general condition of the hootch turned worse, more of the prisoners came down with dysentery. Finally, Mr. Holmes and Mr. Thieu got after us about it.

"Americans are supposed to help one another," Mr. Thieu said. "It is most important that you keep the hootch clean!"

So we tried—and the place was a little better than before. But without medicine or drugs, the sickness raged unchecked.

Up until then, I had been lucky. The only thing really wrong with me was an itching rash that had spread over my body and formed little pus-filled bumps. My hands had become scabby, and

I had to keep them under water often to make them soft. At night, the itching nearly drove me crazy sometimes, but Kushner said it was a heat rash and there was nothing they could give me for it. It was rough, but nothing compared to some of the others.

One guy who was really in bad shape was new in the camp, but Willie and I knew him from before. He was William Port, the man who had been brought into the recuperation camp all bandaged up just before we'd left. There just wasn't much that anyone could do to help Port.

He had been hit in a mortar attack and seemed no better than when we had seen him last. Chances were he'd been kept at the recuperation camp all this time, since there were no better equipped hospitals in the area. Now, he could hardly see. In order for him to hear us, we talked to him through a rolled-up paper put up to his ear.

Port was always depressed. And with his hearing and sight as bad as they were, he kept imagining that the guys were stealing his food. As a result of lying in bed all the time, patches of skin on his rear had turned to tissue paper. And bedsores, many infected, were crawling with maggots.

It was obvious to all of us that the only possible way to save Port was to get him north to a hospital in Hanoi, or release him. And nobody had hopes for either.

We didn't hold out much hope for Cannon, either. Even though he continued to eat like always, dysentery had turned him into a skeleton.

One morning, I cooked a huge pot of rice for that day's dinner and left it in the kitchen. When I returned later, the pot was empty. Cannon swore he hadn't eaten it, but we knew better. He had been the only one around.

Finally, Kushner told Mr. Thieu about some medicine that could control the dysentery and stressed to him that it was urgently needed. Mr. Thieu went to Rat Face about it, then came back to explain that the medicine was very difficult to get. But Rat Face had agreed to try.

Before everyone started getting sick, it had been common for the guys to goof off, claiming illness. At one point, refusing to go out on supply runs happened so often that Hammond, Willie and Joe came up with the rule that from then on, anyone who didn't work didn't eat. But now the claims of illness were all too real.

Guys were flat on their backs and really couldn't do a thing.

In addition to the dysentery, we were getting hit with a sickness that Kushner called "hunger edema," something like beriberi, caused by lack of vitamins. The disease was really terrible —painful, body all puffy and swollen. At its worst, Kushner explained, a man just wasted away—and even a temporary supply of vitamins wouldn't help. The body didn't store them up, and a few weeks after taking them, he'd be right back where he started.

So the hootch was practically a hospital ward. Cannon and Port continued to deteriorate. Williams, Russ, and Bob Sherman came down with hunger edema.

At last, the medicine for the dysentery arrived. That same morning, Cannon had been as hungry as ever—the more we'd given him, the more he'd eaten. But he never got to take any of the medicine. He was already dead when it got there.

I'd expected it, of course. Still, when it actually happened, it was a heck of a shock. I'd really liked Cannon.

Then, about a week later, First Sergeant Williams died, too.

Digging graves and burying men was a new thing for most of us. We learned fast.

When I volunteered for the job of regular cook, the guys took me up on it. I started out working with Ike. It meant getting up at three each morning, but that was perfectly okay with me. It took me off the field trips, in addition to getting me away from the constant quarreling.

Aside from the string of stories at night, the closest any of us ever got to anything sexual was knowing about how our friend Quang, the guard, was making it with Ti Son, an attractive woman of about thirty who worked with Hannah in the kitchen and supply room. Ti Son was the wife of an elderly former camp commander who had been transferred to another camp long before. Ti Son had stayed on.

Several times we found Quang and Ti Son together. Now that he understood English, everyone teased him about it all the time. Like when we'd ask him for tobacco and he'd say, grinning, "No tobacco now. My sweetheart take all."

"Who is your sweetheart?" we'd ask.

Then he'd laugh and say, "Oh, Ti Son, she keep me warm."

It was a happy romance. Until Rat Face caught them. Three days later, our friend Quang was gone—sent far off to another area.

Finally, the second hootch was up. The men were divided, half in one hootch, half in the other. I was in with Ike, Kushner, Anton, Harker, Strictland and Russ. The other group consisted of Willie, Lewis, Davis, Hammond, Burns, Pheister and Joe. So the new hootch managed to separate us all right, and provide more room, but it didn't help much to put an end to the arguments. Everyone, it seemed, had some angle going.

Joe and Kushner became very tight buddies, but that didn't last for too long. Joe, who played up to Garwood all the time, traded him a ring for eight bundles of tobacco, which none of us knew about at the time. When Kush asked Joe if he had a cigarette, Joe insisted he was all out of tobacco.

Then, a couple of days later, Willie spotted Joe getting tobacco down from the rack where he'd concealed it. Later, when Joe was out, Willie pulled out the bundles. "See here, Kush," he called out, "just look at this, will you? And Joe's your man!"

So from then on, everyone was down on Joe for a while—and Kushner raged and called him a no-good Polish son of a bitch.

Funny thing about Kushner, he didn't consider himself to be prejudiced at all, but it didn't take me very long to figure out that he really was. Like the time I noticed how he avoided using the same spoon and cup that I did.

Soon after, I got into a long talk with him on his feelings about blacks. Throughout the discussion, Kushner kept repeating how he had nothing against Negroes. But then he'd admit to things like how he wouldn't want to live next door to one. One time, with a group of us sitting around, he even tried to illustrate how unprejudiced his family had always been by telling us how a black handyman had worked for his father, had never had to buy food or pay rent, had had a girl friend he saw regularly, and had lived a happy life. He had been paid all of ten dollars a week.

"Hell, that's worse than slave labor!" I charged. "What can a grown man do for ten dollars a week—he couldn't even take his girl out to eat and a good movie for that!"

Then, when a couple of the guys started to side with Kushner, I really got stirred up. I said, "Well, you can sure come to work for me when we get back—I'll be glad to give you a job for ten bucks a week!"

For the most part, though, Kushner was like most of the guys in the sense that you could like him for some things and be bugged with him over others. And I realized how frustrated he was as a doctor, knowing he couldn't help the guys who were sick.

One thing about him, he mostly tried to play it cool and be on the "right side"—and only once in a while would he spout off his real feelings of the minute. Like the time he was debating politics with Mr. Holmes and was told how Nguyen Van Thieu, the president of South Vietnam, was a puppet of the United States. Without thinking, Kushner snapped back, "Well, Ho Chi Minh is a puppet of Mao Tse-tung!" Mr. Holmes was so furious he just about exploded.

As for his letter-writing for the Vietnamese, I always questioned whether Kushner was really as strongly against the war as he made out. Just like I did with Anton. As the only two officers, the VC obviously considered it very important to have both of them write and sign the letters. Mr. Holmes often praised them. But personally, I couldn't help but think that they really were trying to deceive him. That maybe they did have some misgivings about the war, but nothing like they wrote it.

As for Anton, I think what bothered me most was how he always cursed at God whenever anything went wrong. Like when he fell down once on a supply run, looked up at the sky, and yelled out, "Son of a bitch! Yes, I'm talkin' to you, I'm talkin' to you!" All my life I'd known people who didn't believe—but still they never cursed at God like that.

And when any of the guys would talk about what had happened to the Vietnamese kids during the war, or when I would describe some of the children who'd been maimed by American bombings, Anton would say things like, "Bombing is good for these people, they deserve it. It's the best way to solve the problem— bomb the hell out of 'em!"

We actually saw, right from the camp, American planes dropping bombs a number of times. The bombing was seldom close enough for us to have to get into the shelter that had been dug right outside the hootch, so we'd just stand there and watch it, off in the distance, the bombs looking like ants in the air. And it was always Anton who'd be shouting them on, "Drop it, drop it, kill 'em all!"

Part of me, the part that had been indoctrinated with American patriotism all the years in school and as a kid, wanted to cheer those planes on, too. But when I thought of the people dying, when I remembered those little Vietnamese kids, rooting for those bombers didn't come too easy.

Then, when all had settled down, Anton might describe how much he had liked to fly around, spotting people on the ground and shooting at them. And I'd get a flash of the wreckage of his chopper, as we'd seen it the day before being captured, smashed up on the side of a hill. Somehow, I wasn't very sorry that that chopper had been knocked out of the sky.

Our two hootches were still covered with plenty of mess and dirt, and Rat Face cracked down with stricter regulations for cleanliness. And now we were required to get out for PT every morning.

"You know, we judge all Americans by what you do!" Mr. Holmes told us. And Mr. Thieu kept after us in the same way—"Is this how Americans live? Are all Americans like this?"

And when the guys would become lazy, sleeping and lying around all day, Mr. Thieu would explain, "Maybe in your country it is different because you eat proper food. Here, you must stay active. When you do little in the mountains—when resistance is low—you will become weak and sick."

Some guys, like Fred Elbert, couldn't seem to help lying asleep much of the day. He'd work in spells, then suddenly be out of it, go off by himself, sometimes just sit daydreaming.

As more of us began to come down with malaria, and with the constant reminders of how Americans should know better, we finally began to work at keeping the hootches clean. I think we were embarrassed into it.

But the bickering went on. It was just impossible for us to get along without some kind of squabble or argument. In fact, for the first time, Mr. Holmes seemed pleased with the criticism meetings. Little problem now in getting one guy to criticize another. Who knows, maybe it was out of his satisfaction with the way the meetings were going that he decided to teach us the popular patriotic song, *Giâi Phòng Mien Nam!* meaning "Liberate South Vietnam!"

All of us were familiar with it already from the afternoon "Voice of Vietnam" radio broadcasts. In addition to putting on

American rock and roll, Vietnamese music was often played. This particular song came on at least once every three or four days.

We had to stand at attention while we sang it, even though it wasn't any kind of national anthem. The teaching of the song went on for days, and Mr. Holmes told us that every man would have to continue with the class until he could repeat every word. Only then could he go.

Actually, I liked the song. It had a very pretty melody, and it spoke of the beauty of Vietnam, its mountains and rivers, and how all of it was part of one country and belonged to all the people. And, of course, Mr. Holmes made certain we all understood what else the song expressed—how victory would be theirs when they defeated the United States imperialists. And we were taught some of the words in English—"All together, forward march/to liberate the South!"

It took a while, but we all learned to sing *Giâi Phòng Mien Nam!"*

The day before Thanksgiving, Bob Sherman suddenly turned worse. By night, he was really bad. Before morning, he was dead.

In mind and body, it had been downhill for Bob ever since all those days in stocks. Aside from that, he never should have been in Vietnam for a second tour. Not after that first time around, when he'd flipped out and ended up in a mental hospital.

Another guy who had nothing at all to be thankful for was William Port. Unless it was for dying, for suffering no more. Following Bob, he never made it through the day.

It wasn't a very happy Thanksgiving.

When all five black prisoners were called in to see Rat Face, we didn't know what to make of it, especially with Mr. Ho there to lecture us about the racial conditions in the States. He talked for almost an hour, going on about the Black Panther Party, Black Power and its meaning, the murder of Dr. Martin Luther King, Jr., which had taken place just days after our escape try that past April.

Mr. Ho was on top of everything that affected Negroes in the States, and he ticked off racial crimes like a calendar of events. Listening to him, we all began to think that maybe it was some kind of indoctrination in preparation for releasing us. No such luck.

Mr. Ho went on to tell us how the Vietnamese people in many ways had to face the same kind of problems that blacks did in the United States. That is why, he said, the Vietnamese were sympathetic to us.

As he spoke, I considered how often the guards *did* seem more responsive to us than to the others, always a little more willing to give us help.

What it all came down to was that the camp was building a third hootch, just for the five of us. In doing this, maybe they meant well, or maybe they saw other advantages in having us separated from the others. There was no way of knowing.

Personally, though, I didn't much care for the idea. The truth was, I'd just as soon have been living with some of the other guys. And no matter what they called it, it was still segregation.

Having our own hootch made little difference in anything, except that now the others began to resent how several guards, well supplied with cigarettes, came around at night to visit. Actually, aside from the nights, the five of us were hardly ever together —each went back to the group he'd been with before. The sense of familiarity that came in being with the guys you were most used to was important. Even if there was an argument now and then.

So, for the most part, the routine of the weeks hardly varied. One of the few differences was getting shoes and washcloths for the first time. Up until then, we'd always been barefooted, except during a supply run when we were allowed to wear our boots.

Also, I had now become the only cook. Ike and I had argued so often when we were cooks together, it seemed we'd spent as much time yelling at one another as we had working. Finally it was agreed that two cooks were too many.

As regular cook, I followed the same daily schedule. Up at three, my first duty was to get a light from the guard to start the fire. This had to be done very early, since spotter planes circled around the camp every morning and would have seen the smoke. These were the planes that picked the areas that were to be targets for the U.S. artillery—directed each night from nearby fire support hills. So far, mortars had exploded all around the camp, but had never hit it directly. It made me wonder if the army knew it was a camp for POWs.

Since becoming the single cook, I had come up with many varieties of *co'm mi* and rice, enough so that it almost seemed we were eating something different each day. Breakfasts were almost always the same: rice, *co'm mi* and *mam*. We used the *nuoc mam* sauce for flavor all the time, as the food itself was often unseasoned.

Each morning, the guys were up at six for breakfast. Then, everyone washed his own plate. I was supposed to have a pot of boiling water for cleaning the dishes, but most of the time the plates were washed under the spout from the bamboo water line that ran from the mountains down into the camp. It was a large, round bamboo, split down the center from end to end, and it served as well as any pipe could have. The water was for all purposes, such as drinking, cooking, and—squatting under the spout —bathing.

It was really amazing how many ways I learned to cook the same *co'm mi* and rice—roasted, steamed, baked, boiled. Sometimes, I made them both together, with the vegetable cut up like hash brown potatoes. If I had enough oil, I made rice soup. Every now and then I'd save the cooking oil and grate the *co'm mi* into a batter, ending up with something like potato pancakes. If I wanted to go overboard, I'd cook fried rice—that was special because it meant we'd be without oil for several meals.

One of my specialties, when bananas were available, was a *co'm mi* patty that was like an apple turnover. I'd grate the *co'm mi* and make a dough, then take the bananas and cut them up, season them, and cook them mixed with meat, if we had any. All of this went inside the *co'm mi* patty, which was then wrapped with a banana leaf. The patty was then put into a pot with bamboo at the bottom and just enough water to make steam. It was a great recipe that I learned from Mama Son. And when you could stuff the patties with peppers, onions or cooked cucumbers, it was even greater.

One dish that wasn't so special was my soup made with grated *co'm mi*. In fact, it was really awful, and the guys refused to eat it. Except for Kushner. It was crazy, but he seemed to like it. I really realized how terrible that soup was when we tried to feed it to the pigs and they turned away.

Certain times during the year, we could get cucumbers, corn, pumpkin, and a juicy tropical fruit that tasted like mangoes. It could all be cooked with oil, salt and *mam* to make a food we called "bread fruit."

I was always on the lookout for some new food or a new way to prepare it. The guards didn't help much. They had just about the same food as we did, only they almost always cooked it exactly the same way—just plain *co'm mi* and rice.

A real treat, which we weren't supposed to have, unless it was a holiday or some special occasion, was chicken. When we got one, it was only because one of the guys had stolen it. Every now and then we'd see a chicken walking around the camp and try to coax it into the hootch. While it was being cleaned, someone would stand guard.

One day, Lewis spotted a chicken outside the hootch. He dove right through the air after it, looking like Superman. Just that minute, Rat Face walked by. He stopped in his tracks and stared at Lewis like he could hardly believe what he'd seen. Then he just shook his head and walked away.

The monsoon season started again—no sunshine, days of rain. It was a sad December. Russ developed bronchitis on top of hunger edema. The combination was just too much for him, and he died.

Christmas meant nothing to the Vietnamese at the camp, most of whom were Buddhists. Still, they tried to help us celebrate with a special dinner cooked by Mama Son. We had white rice (instead of the usual red), pork, chicken, vegetables, *co'm mi* wine, candy, Ruby Queen cigarettes, and real tea instead of the tea leaves that grew on trees in the area.

The friendlier guards came by to wish us a Merry Christmas. Rat Face sent his greetings with Mr. Holmes. Mr. Thieu visited with us for a long while, and we sat around telling him of Christmases at home.

"One day I will come to see America," Mr. Thieu said.

"Tell me, Mr. Thieu," I asked, "if a helicopter landed here right now to rescue us, would you go, too?"

"Of course I would go," he said, smiling broadly to let us know he was kidding.

"Be serious, Mr. Thieu—would you really?"

He shook his head. "No, I could not go with you. You see, I could never leave my family—"

And so, Christmas passed. And a few days later, Burns became sicker, pounds of flesh seeming to disappear by the hour. I remembered how he had been when I'd first met him that day on the trail with Garwood, and it hurt me to look at him now.

After Kushner came in to examine him, he asked, "What do you think, Kush? How bad am I?"

"You need medical treatment," Kushner said.

"It doesn't look too good, does it?"

"No," Kushner said.

"But what if I don't get any help?" Burns asked.

There was nothing for Kushner to do but tell him the truth. He said he believed that, without proper medical treatment, he would die.

For days, Burns pleaded with Mr. Holmes and Mr. Thieu to get him released and sent home to be hospitalized. Had it been up to Mr. Thieu, I think he would have tried to do it. But the military mentality—whether it's Vietnamese or American—doesn't allow for an individual's concerns, or a sense of compassion. There was nothing Mr. Thieu could do.

On New Year's Day, 1969, Fred Burns died.

Listening to the "Voice of Vietnam" that afternoon, as we always did, the announcer appealed to all GIs to wear some peace symbol, and asked, "Why die for Old Glory?"

And then, without really wanting to, I suddenly thought of Cannon, Williams, Sherman, Port, Russ and Burns. I considered the endless war. And I couldn't help but ask myself that very same question.

CHAPTER 16

1970: Camp to Camp

We almost never got peanuts, and cucumbers only once in a while. But after the American planes sprayed the crops, we had plenty of peanuts and all the cucumbers we could eat.

The morning it happened, we were sitting around the table after breakfast, when Willie asked, "Do you guys smell something funny?"

He was right. A sweet odor had drifted in over the area, so strong after a few minutes you could almost taste it.

A short time later, Mr. Holmes came into the compound. "Americans are spraying crops with chemicals to destroy food," he said.

"Impossible!" Kushner said. "I know for a fact that the United States doesn't use chemicals like that—it's against the law!"

"You will see," Mr. Holmes said. "Soon the planes will come closer."

About twenty minutes later, we heard them. They came in low, three small planes, and we could actually see the chemical substance being sprayed to all sides. They continued to circle nearer and nearer the camp, yet no attempt was made to shoot at them. To do so would have revealed exactly where the camp was located. It was so well camouflaged that it could not be seen from the air unless a plane was to fly directly over it at treetop level.

That afternoon, Mr. Holmes returned with two guards. "You will all come with me," he said. "I want everyone to see what American planes have done to the crops."

We followed him a short distance outside the camp to an area spotted with rice paddies. All the rice was dead.

Then we moved on to a field of *co'm mi*. Usually the vegetable was white inside. Now, when you peeled it, the inside was black.

"So you see," Mr. Holmes said, "this is all part of the American strategy. It is based on an old theory—if you take water from ocean, you can catch fish. Americans believe that if they destroy food in the countryside, people here will be forced to move to the cities they build. Then, they believe, they will be able to control the people—and catch the enemies."

I recalled having seen a number of small areas, called "new life hamlets," being built by the U.S. Army in and around the bigger cities, and realized that this was what Mr. Holmes was referring to. Vietnamese from outlying areas were continually being brought into those hamlets—and even entire villages were relocated. The idea was to keep the people where they could be observed, and in that way prevent them from supporting the VC.

Seeing those American planes killing the crops that day came as a shock to all of us. Of course, we didn't know then what the entire world was to learn years later. It all came out when newspapers printed the results of a study by the National Academy of Sciences. I wasn't really surprised when I read how the United States dropped more than a hundred million pounds of chemicals on South Vietnam, destroying areas that would never be the same for a hundred years. What really upset me, though, was finding out that the chemical poisons caused deaths among the children of the Montagnard tribes—some only babies, carried on their mothers' backs while the mothers tended to the crops.

But even then, after this short time in Vietnam, I started to realize how the United States was ready to take just about any step at all to get to the Viet Cong, that the VC guerrilla operation was making it plenty rough. That much I knew from my own experiences—and from those search-and-destroy patrols into enemy territory.

The Vietnamese fully understood the importance of the Viet Cong in the war, and they were ready to talk about it with us. In fact, Mr. Ho spent several classes during one week of political sessions lecturing on it. Of course, he never called them VC—but the National Liberation Front.

To make his point, Mr. Ho explained how the population of

all Vietnam together—North and South—was only forty million people, as compared to the over two hundred million in the United States. And not only was North Vietnam, a small underdeveloped country with no modern weapons, fighting against the United States—but against fifteen other countries as well. Under such circumstances, Mr. Ho stressed, it would be impossible for North Vietnam to try to fight such a war army to army.

"In this war, the only way for us to win is for all of the people to fight," Mr. Ho said. "For us, this is a 'People's War.' All of the Vietnamese understand that they must fight for their freedom— that it is not only a job for the army. And that is why men and women, young and old, in villages all over our country, are ready to help, however they can."

"The United States knows this," Mr. Ho continued. "It realizes that Vietnamese people everywhere support the National Liberation Front. That they will hide any weapon to fight with, even picks and shovels. That they save rice for those who defend the country. And this is why the United States is so determined to find members of the Front—to force the people into the hamlets they build, even by destroying their crops."

Then Mr. Ho paused and looked at us for a long, silent minute. He ended that class by saying, "But it will be of no use. Even though the United States is a much more powerful country than Vietnam, it can never defeat us! You must understand, no matter how small a country is, it can stand up against the most powerful army—if all the people have unity and work together."

In a way, we still saw those political classes as brainwash. But more and more, we found ourselves discussing them back in the compound. It was obvious to most of the guys that a good part of what we were told in class was true. Still, we were reluctant to let the Vietnamese know we thought this way.

We also continued to resist the criticism meetings, though now the guys were much quicker to chew one another out than they had been. With the prisoners split into three groups, we now had three squad leaders—Willie for my group, Joe, and Harker. And Harker, squad leader or not, continued to speak his mind and drive Mr. Holmes crazy.

Like after we'd been lectured to about keeping the hootches clean, Harker might say, "But Mr. Holmes, you're always tellin' us about sanitation an' keepin' things clean—then how come whenever I see the camp kitchen it's really dirty? If you don't practice what you preach, Mr. Holmes, it's all a lot of baloney. You're supposed to set the example, you know!"

And Mr. Holmes would blow up. "Harker, you are not to criticize the camp!" We kept telling Hark how he was pushing his luck too far. In fact, it was really because of him that it became an official order—no criticism of the camp or any of the guards.

Most of my gripes in the meetings were about Hannah. Things like how I was missing cans of food, or soap. Mr. Holmes probably realized that Hannah was swiping supplies for herself, but he defended her. "It is up to you, Daly, to count everything at the supply room!"

Hannah was really a terrible person. Just about everyone hated her—the guards, Mama Son, and Ti Son, who fought with her all the time. Once, just after Ti Son had had her daily bath, Hannah dumped a bucket of rice all over her. So Hannah was a problem for everyone, and it was mostly because of her that the entire camp had to be moved to a new area.

Hannah kept cheating Marty, the chief Montagnard, until he refused to trade with the camp anymore. The major items the camp traded to the tribes, in return for the *co'm mi*, were salt and cans of food. The canned goods, which were also available to the prisoners and camp personnel, had originally been shipped as aid to South Vietnam by the United States. It never reached the people for whom it had been intended. Instead, the food had been sold to black marketeers, then bought by the VC. That's how, as cook, I'd come across cans of hot dogs, hamburgers, spiced beef— all food I recognized from U.S. Army mess halls. Or sacks of wheat marked "Donated by people of U.S.A."

All of this food was bought in the market by Quang Lee, the camp supply director and Hannah's boss. Of the money spent, there was an allotment of eight piastres per day for each POW. At that time, one American dollar was worth 125 piastres, so each of us was being fed for one dime daily. Actually, enough *co'm mi* could be bought from the Montagnards, in exchange for only one can of salt or three cans of food, to feed all the prisoners for a week.

The problem was, Hannah never gave the Montagnards the number of cans of food they were entitled to, especially when the chief sent his wife or children to the camp to collect. If Marty came around to complain, Hannah always claimed the food must have been lost on the way back to the tribe.

So it was only a matter of time before the Montagnards refused to trade at all. And that left Rat Face no choice but to make plans for moving the entire camp to a new area.

Right about then, Cory arrived, just about the biggest guy I'd ever seen. When they brought him in, we could hardly believe how huge he was.

Cory had been wounded in the shoulder and spent the first few weeks recuperating. Everybody took to him right away—not only the prisoners, but some of the guards, too, and especially Mama Son.

Every day, Mama Son would come down to cook a meal for Cory, and at first, when he was really weak, she'd sit by the bed and feed him, asking all the time, "*Dau, dau?*"—Does it hurt?

Of course, whenever anybody new came in, that meant a whole new crop of stories, and Cory always had one to tell, rambling on in his hillbilly way about all the things he was supposed to have done and how he'd lived back in his hometown of Backroad, Tennessee. It didn't seem to matter to any of us that Cory always seemed to contradict himself and that his stories couldn't possibly all be true—like how he'd been a truck driver, or taken airborne training, or was raised in an orphanage, or then came from a family of seventeen. But no one cared. They liked Cory, and so did I. He reminded me of Cannon, in a way.

It was about two weeks before we were to close down the camp that I started feeling weak and tired, and finally had to spend a part of each day in bed. None of the officers at the camp seemed particularly concerned, though, and I think I got a clue why, when one of the Vietnamese prisoners I'd been friendly with came by. He told me how the Vietnamese believed that Negroes were so strong they could overcome illness without even needing any medicine. Great! I hoped he was wrong about the Vietnamese thinking that way.

Days before we were to leave the camp, all prisoners were kept busy cleaning up the area. Now the compound finally began to shape up—but we weren't going to be living there anymore.

Then, about three o'clock one warm morning in May, the entire camp packed up all belongings and took off down the hill. Avoiding the regular trail, we went out the back way through the woods instead. In the dark, it was slow, rough going—guys stumbling, falling, dropping pots and pans. We reached the first Montagnard house in about two hours, a spot that usually took us about twenty minutes when out on a wood run.

It was just about then that the sickness hit me again, and I realized I had malaria. Even under the best of circumstances, it didn't take much to get me tired—one reason the Vietnamese gave me salt tablets all the time. Now, moving along that rocky trail was impossible. I fell farther and farther behind.

Finally, Rat Face assigned the Savage, the Montagnard guard, to stay back with me. He was as mean as always and kept snapping at me to move faster. I knew I couldn't continue, and I tried to get this across to him. No way.

Then I decided the best way to make my point was to fall out on the trail, which I did. Stretched in the dirt, shaking with the fever that now came over me, I actually felt like I'd rather die than take another step.

The Savage was furious. "Daly, *di!* Daly, *di!*" he screamed. And when I didn't move, he tried to pull me by the arm. I was dead weight.

At last, in a rage, the Savage lifted his weapon. My eyes were closed but I squinted just enough to watch him. As he pointed the barrel down at me, my stomach flipped around in fear. But I didn't move.

The Savage shot a round. It struck the dirt—inches from my head. Still I remained motionless, one eye open only a sliver, enough to make out the form of his Ho Chi Minh sandal. He stood there for a minute, doing nothing. Then, I guess he finally realized I was not faking. He turned, and I heard him start off down the trail.

Suddenly I thought how I didn't want to be left alone out on the trail, that I'd never make it to the camp on my own. I called out, "Wait, don't go!"

But the Savage kept on walking, cursing me now with every step. *"Do mami!"* he shouted, motherfucker in English. Then he called me "Johnson!"—and that was considered even worse.

About forty minutes later, Mr. Holmes returned for me. "Daly, you must try and walk," he said. "At the camp you will be given medicine."

I struggled to my feet. He told me it was only half an hour.

Actually, it was over two. Every time I stopped to ask how much longer, Mr. Holmes insisted it was now only a short way.

So, stumbling along, spurred on and conned by Mr. Holmes, I finally made it to the new camp.

The camp was on a plateau, and the prisoners' compound was set up in a large, level area. All the POWs, thirteen of us, were back together again in one hootch, but it was spacious and sturdier than the others. Our kitchen was nearby. And just to the other side of a fence that set off the compound were hootches for the Vietnamese POWs.

Down the hill, a number of smaller hootches housed the twenty or so guards, and still farther down were the quarters for the camp personnel, all those responsible for food and supplies.

Four new prisoners were brought into the camp—two men, and two women nurses, all German. They had worked on a hospital ship near Saigon. One day, they went into the country to take pictures and were captured by the VC.

I wondered why the Vietnamese would want to hold these Germans as prisoners. Kushner had a theory about that.

"The VC refuse to draw the line when it comes to foreigners coming over here," he explained. "To them, the fact that these people are hospital workers doesn't matter at all, just like they'd never consider letting me go only because I'm a doctor. As far as the Vietnamese are concerned, anyone who comes to Vietnam to offer aid to the enemy, no matter where they're from or what they do, is contributing to the war."

All four of the Germans were very sick. Even though the women were in really bad shape—and looked it—their just being around turned all the guys on. Everyone tried to catch looks at them through the fence that separated the two areas, especially when they went to the latrine.

It was our job to wash their clothes, since they weren't up to doing it themselves. Whenever one of the guys would get his hands on a pair of panties, anyone would have thought it was the most exciting, valuable piece of cloth in the world. He'd hold it up, wave it in the air—even pass it around to be smelled.

For the first month at the new camp, I was completely out of it, bedded down with malaria. Joe was very sick, too. Kushner looked us both over. Then, he immediately told Garwood that Joe required special food. As for me, he said nothing.

If it hadn't been for Mama Son, I'd have been in much worse condition. When she missed my daily visits for food supplies, she came to the compound to see what was wrong. From then on I received the special food that Kushner hadn't asked for. Mama Son went straight to Mr. Holmes about it, and that very day I started getting things like white rice and mackerel.

As for Kush not getting me the food, the guys didn't let him live that down for a long time. Harker kept after him about that for months; he seemed to enjoy baiting Kushner, like bugging him about his friendship with Garwood, accusing him of "kissing ass" all the time. Finally, one day, after Hark had been putting him down about the food thing again, asking him for the hundredth time why he'd gotten it for Joe and not for me, Kushner blew up and shouted, "Harker, please leave me alone! How long you gonna hold that against me anyway?"

Kush was a funny guy, all right. Of course, he always kept on insisting how unprejudiced he was, when many of his ideas showed exactly the opposite. Like when we got onto the subject of intermarriage and he admitted he was totally against it. Then he tried to soften it a little by saying how he was really against *any* kind of intermarriage because the children would be sure to suffer.

Another thing that bothered me about Kush was his always acting friendly with Garwood when the guard was around, then putting him down like the rest of us when he wasn't there. One time I noticed a guard stealing a raincoat and soap, and made the mistake of telling Kushner about it. Next thing we knew, Kushner had reported it to Garwood, even though he knew that now we were not allowed to criticize the guards, and anyone accusing a guard of stealing was sure to get punished.

In no time it got back to Rat Face, and he immediately asked us who stole the soap. All of us said we didn't know. Finally, Rat Face tried to make a joke of it and said, "Well, maybe it was a rat with two feet!" We all laughed and agreed. "Sure that must have been who—a rat with two feet!"

For the most part, though, everyone got along better and the living conditions were much cleaner, all of us—camp personnel and prisoners—having learned a lesson at last. When any of us really got pissed off at something one of the guys did, we had a routine for bugging the guilty person if he wouldn't own up. We'd all sit around, and without actually naming the offender, we'd curse out "whoever" it might be. The guilty one, of course, had no doubts as to who we were name-calling.

We did it with Anton one time, when he shit into the water. Each night, I placed a large pot outside at the water spout, to fill up by morning from the bamboo water line. Then one night I saw Anton get up to go to the latrine, but instead he just went out to the area where the water line ran, and squatted. From where he was, I knew for certain that the water would carry it right down into the pot. And, sure enough, next morning, there it was!

Later, I let some of the guys know what had happened—and who had done it. Then when we were all sitting around together, I asked who was responsible for shitting at the water line. Anton never said a word.

Then we all started to denounce "whoever" it had been. The name-calling went on and on, each of us taking a turn, saying things like, "Whoever shit in the water is a no-good son of a bitch!" "Whoever did it is a mother's whore!"

When it came to Anton, he joined in, too, adding his curse to the rest. Right then, no one came out and directly accused him. But when the time was right, when he angered one of the guys enough, he was sure to hear about it.

With the preliminary peace talks now going on in Paris, we were often rapping about how maybe the war would be over soon. That this was now a real possibility was probably of some help in putting the guys in a better frame of mind, making it easier to get along with one another. Not so for the guards and camp personnel, though. The tension and bitterness that had been building a little at a time between the two groups now exploded into a full split.

One faction consisted of Rat Face, Jolly, Mr. Holmes, Mr. Thieu and the women workers. The other group was made up of the guards and the guard commander.

Before the split, food and supplies were brought into the camp for everyone together, and the guards and personnel joined in cooking. But now food was more expensive at the new camp, not as accessible as before. The Montagnards were not as friendly as the other tribes used to be before the cheating—and it took more cans of salt or food to trade for the baskets of *co'm mi*.

What really brought on the break, though, was how Quang Lee, the supply director, and Hannah continued in their thieving ways. When they made food deals during the trips to the markets in Tam Ky and other cities, they always managed to keep food for themselves, at the expense of the guards. Finally the guards had enough and decided that from then on they'd carry their own supplies, grow their own crops (the camp had always tried to grow some vegetables on its own), and cook separately.

All of this made it really rough on the camp personnel, a much smaller group. Like when it came to carrying supplies for themselves and the POWs, who were their responsibility. The split made it rough on the prisoners, too. Now there were constant arguments between Rat Face and the guard commander, and many times when we'd be ordered to do something by one, the other would give us a counter order.

Mr. Holmes tried to make light of it all. "We are civilians—they are military," he said. "However, we get along."

Nobody argued with him. But we could see how things were.

Two of the German prisoners—one man and one woman—died within a few weeks of one another. It was a surprise to no one. The only surprising thing, really, was how the other two managed to stay alive.

One hot summer day, Cory, Willie and Strictland were told by Mr. Holmes that they were to attend a series of classes. Cory had never taken an indoctrination course, and we figured maybe they'd finally gotten around to it for him. As for Strict and Willie, we had no idea why they were asked. After the classes started, none of them offered us any explanation.

A few weeks later, it all became clear.

It was just after breakfast, and we were sitting around the hootch when Rat Face and Mr. Holmes came over. Both were smiling.

"Somethin' must be up," Harker mumbled. "Look, Rat Face is smiling!"

"Everyone must go to a criticism meeting this morning," Mr. Holmes announced. "It shall begin immediately."

The meeting started out like always. We went around the room, each man taking his turn at criticizing himself, then the others. Now that everyone was getting along better, there was little criticism—just unimportant incidents that meant nothing and would result in no trouble or reprimands. Then, as always, we had the health report. Following this, instead of receiving the old news bulletins that Mr. Holmes usually passed around for us to study and which were supposed to help us to understand the war, Rat Face stood up to address us. Mr. Holmes translated as he spoke.

"Today," he said, "we have some good news. Good news for some, bad news for some. Does anyone have an idea?"

We all shook our heads. Then Rat Face announced: "The Front has decided to release some prisoners—and this area has been chosen!"

We all sat there, stunned, surprised as hell.

"I have been asked to recommend who will be released," Rat Face said. "Now, what do you think of that?"

The significance of the news finally hit. All the guys shouted out approval and applauded wildly. Rat Face watched, smiling broadly.

"Three men will be released," he said. "Who do you think?"

We all had a good idea. It had to be, we figured, the three squad leaders—Strictland, Harker and Willie.

"I will now tell," Rat Face exclaimed in Vietnamese, as Mr. Holmes translated his words. The camp commander was obviously enjoying himself.

"Number one—William Watkins!"

Everyone cheered. For all Willie's ways, and his open distrust of whites, the guys liked him. When someone was sick, there was nothing Willie wouldn't do to help him—give up his food, bathe him, take him to the latrine.

"Number two—James Strictland!"

Again, everyone applauded. Strict had always been a really hard worker and got along pretty well with everyone.

"Number three—Cory Kinsley!"

Once more the guys responded, but you could sense the surprise. Especially Harker.

Then Mr. Holmes explained that the release of the men was to show appreciation for the efforts of peace groups in the United States that were working to end the war. "Soon, we will have a party to celebrate," he said.

As it turned out, we ended up having two parties. Mr. Ho was supposed to have arrived at the camp for the event, but he never made it. When he came two weeks later, Rat Face decided to give the party again. They killed a pig for the occasion, and all the guys had as much rice as they wanted.

On the day that Willie, Strict and Cory left, it was raining heavily. All of us acted happy, laughing a lot, wishing them good luck.

Still, underneath, we were all a little sad. It was good to know that now our families would learn we were alive and safe. Yet, seeing the three of them take off for home, and not knowing how long before we'd be going, too, we could not help feeling a bit low. And I kept remembering what Slime had told us after the escape attempt—how I was to be one of the last Americans to leave Vietnam.

We stood at the gate and waved them off. As happy as I was for them, it was a hurting kind of thing to see the guy you came in with take off, while you stay behind.

On September 3, 1969, Ho Chi Minh died. All of the guards, and even the South Vietnamese prisoners, wore black armbands. I asked one of the South Vietnamese, a short, friendly man we called "Mighty Mouse," the reason he'd put on the band. Without the slightest hesitation, he answered, "Everyone knows that Ho Chi Minh was president of all Vietnam."

Since the release of Cory, Strict and Willie, Harker began to change. Now he didn't work as hard as before and was often surly. As a religious guy, he had never cursed like all the others. Now he swore as much as anyone, and started to bait Mr. Holmes more than ever.

Joe got sicker. Kush told us he didn't expect he could hold out too much longer.

And all the while, food became harder and harder to get in the area. Often we picked wild vegetables, and sometimes ate a grass that looked like spinach but tasted terrible.

Before long, everyone realized that it would be only a matter of time before we'd have to move on again.

We left in late December, on the anniversary of the National Liberation Front. The entire camp was closed down, just like it had been before. Joe couldn't walk. We carried him.

It took less than a full day of walking to reach the new camp. The site was better than the last one, on a hill and out in the open. However, it didn't take very long for us to realize that the food accessibility was no better than before. We could not pick the *co'm mi* in the fields but had to get it directly from the Montagnards. It was really bad. Often, they took it from the pig pens to fill our baskets.

I could hardly believe that Christmas had come around again. And with the holiday season, I found myself thinking of home even more than usual, wondering how everyone was. I tried to imagine what it would be like back in New York, Christmas shopping, getting caught up in the excitement and spirit of the holiday. So far, I had not received a reply to any of my letters.

Recalling the holidays at home made me realize how much I'd changed since leaving the States. My ideas about things—and my values—were much like they had been. Still, some basic feelings just weren't the same.

For one thing, I really saw the war in a different way. How much the political courses we still had every three months influenced my thinking was hard to figure. And the constant reminder, "It all depends on you," didn't spur any new understanding. It was just that something about the war, and about the Vietnamese people, was beginning to get to me.

I'd still refused to sign any letters; only now my reasons didn't seem as convincing to me as before. With each month I found it more difficult to answer the question that Mr. Ho and the other teachers continued to put to us: "What did you come here for?" Somehow, the reason—that we were there to help the South Vietnamese people and to stop communism—didn't hold up too good any more.

Many times, I'd think back to that time before being captured. The competition for body counts. The shooting of that old Vietnamese man, and the dumping of him in the bushes.

And although I often talked religion with the guys, it didn't seem to occupy my thoughts as much as it used to. At least, not in the same way.

Christmas Eve was a sad time. Joe died.

Ski's death didn't seem any less significant when the next day, on Christmas, Mr. Holmes told us about the casualty figures released by the United States. Forty thousand American deaths in almost nine years of war. And I wondered how many more "missing" Americans had died whom they still didn't know about—like Joe.

For Tet, the camp put on a small celebration. A few of the guys stood up to speak, saying how they hoped for the war's end soon, how they wished everyone would be at peace. Then, Anton, trying to be smart, got up and offered his remarks. He said, "Mr. Holmes, I want to tell you one thing, I hope the Vietnamese people get everything they deserve!" Some of the guys snickered. The Vietnamese couldn't understand why.

Very often we could hear small-arms fire and knew it was only a few miles away. Every now and then, an American copter circled nearby. It was wild to think that the U.S. Army was all that close. We learned more about it from Jose, who'd been captured right in the area.

Jose had been on an operation that had taken place so near the camp he couldn't understand how the army had missed us. The Vietnamese must have been wondering the same thing about then, for now they started digging fighting holes all over the area surrounding the camp. Also, an emergency camp was set up nearby in case it became necessary for us to get out fast.

Jose was another good storyteller. His tales made Cory's lies seem like nothing at all.

Often, Jose talked about his Mexican family in Texas, who were supposed to live on a ranch. Sometimes it was a big ranch, run by his father, with cows and chickens. Other times, he said his father had a plumbing business. Then, at the same time, his father was supposed to be a disabled vet receiving one-hundred-percent disability. The one true story was that he had studied to be an interpreter in California, and could now speak and understand Vietnamese.

Jose and I didn't hit it off at first, mostly, I guess, because of his attitude on religion. We argued about it all the time. Jose was always ready to sum up all religion as just a money-making business. As far as he was concerned, he insisted, he didn't buy one bit of it.

Then we had an argument over his supply of quinine pills. Jose refused to allow Kushner to hold his pills like the rest of us did. I tried to explain that Kush kept the pills until one of us needed them. Jose said to hell with that, he was taking all of his right then.

"Okay," I told him. "Go ahead and take them. But I'll tell you one thing, if you get sick later, you won't be gettin' any of mine!"

"Before I'd take anything from you, Daly, I'd die first!" Jose said.

About one month later, he got malaria. All the guys had used up their supplies of pills, and the only ones Kushner now held belonged to me. I told him that Jose was not to be given one single pill of mine.

Then, after a few days, as Jose's malaria turned worse, I relented.

For a time, things went along smooth and quiet, except for the constant shelling that sometimes zeroed in close by. Otherwise, the routine went on: the same supply runs, same classes, same storytelling bull sessions at night, same hopes that maybe something great would happen in Paris. One thing that was different was the food—now worse than ever.

But we really couldn't bitch too much about the food, because the truth was, that's all there was available. It wasn't as if the guards or anyone else ate better than we did; sometimes they ate worse.

As for the guards and Rat Face, as long as we didn't give them a hard time, they weren't too tough on us. There'd be some punishment sometimes, but nothing we couldn't handle. Just disciplining, really.

Whenever the guards acted against the rules, there wasn't much that could be done about it. Garwood had been sent north, but there'd never been any point in reporting things to him, anyway, since Rat Face just refused to hear any criticism. Same thing went for Mr. Holmes or Mr. Thieu. The best that could happen if they took our accusation back to the camp commander was that we'd get punished for telling it.

That's why I never bothered to say anything about what I saw the assistant guard commander do to Ti Son's little boy. How he pulled out his penis and stuck it in the boy's mouth!

Ti Son's kid was really cute and likable, and I felt terrible watching how the guards treated him. Like when they taught him to lie down and move like he was having sex, then told him to climb up on top of his mother, who he slept with, and do the same thing to her. He did—and Ti Son gave him a real beating.

The other kid at the camp was Hannah's little boy. He was old enough for the guards to play with, but they were really rough with him, banging him around all the time. He could have been a happy little boy, I thought, and it killed me to see how he was treated.

Then, on St. Patrick's Day, Dennis Hammond died.

Ever since the escape attempt, Dennis and I had never been the best buddies. Still, when you live with a guy for almost two years, it's hard not to think of him as a friend.

Now the weather started getting warmer again. One morning, when a group of us left the camp to go on a wood run, we came to a sudden stop just a short distance from the gate, hardly believing what we saw.

All the trees in one section had been cut down to make an LZ landing area for helicopters.

"It's a perfect LZ," Anton exclaimed. "Believe me, I know, I've landed on many of them."

Looking further, we discovered boot tracks. It was obvious that a group of men had come in to do the job. Since it was so close to the camp, we just couldn't figure out why no one had heard anything.

From then on, there was more and more talk about using the emergency camp. And the mysterious LZ was all we talked about for days after.

Then the shelling increased. Most nights, we jumped in and out of the bomb shelter three or four times. Even though no shells hit directly, shrapnel traveled a long way, and plenty of it landed in or near the camp. Staying in the straw hootch made no sense.

The shelter was a large hole covered with rows of logs, big enough for all of us to squeeze inside. Sometimes, when the bottom filled with water, we'd end up soaked, pressed one against the other, listening to the whistling noise of the shells as they sailed by. It was the noise that let us know just how much danger we were in. When you heard it clearly, you knew how, seconds later, a shell was going to hit plenty close.

And it was during times like that when Jose, who'd claimed he had no religion, could be heard mumbling over and over, "Oh, my God! My God!"

With every day much like the one before—card playing, sleeping, killing time—you'd think the weeks would have just dragged by. Sometimes it seemed that way. Yet, with our hardly realizing it, months just disappeared. A few new prisoners came in. None were released. And, thankfully, none went out any other way.

Then, one day in November, Mr. Holmes announced that he was being transferred to the north, and we realized something must be up. One of the last things he did before going away was to stop by and tell us how he'd just gotten the news of U.S. forces failing to free POWs at Son Tay prison camp near Hanoi. Seems the raid had been a complete failure, and that all the POWs had been moved out before the American attack took place.

There was no farewell party for Mr. Holmes. No one was especially sorry to see him go, except maybe Rat Face. And though he didn't say so, I knew that Mr. Thieu was happy to be rid of him, too.

It was a raw, cold day, and I had just started the cooking fire when a guard came running up. He told me to put out the fire immediately. Minutes later, I realized why. Six U.S. helicopters came sweeping in right over the area!

Everyone—guards and prisoners—went charging for the bomb shelters. The copters were dropping grenades that threw off a thick red smoke.

Before we could reach the shelter, the copters swooped lower. I could see the pilots staring at us, and I kept wondering if they realized we were POWs. Then the copters dipped closer still, and everyone panicked. All the prisoners raced for the woods. Many of the guards ran right along with us. And I could hear Jose calling out "Hail Marys" and "Our Fathers" one after the other.

Later, after the planes had gone, leaving only a trail of red smoke behind, Anton went to Rat Face and told him how he was now certain the camp was to be attacked. The smoke, he explained, was the way in which the area was marked as a target.

Rat Face must have believed him. That same day, we moved to the emergency camp.

Not long after, they started giving us vitamins and iron shots. This had never happened before. There was no question about it —we were being gotten into shape for something!

One night, Mr. Thieu came to explain. In a matter of weeks, everyone was leaving for North Vietnam!

We were to go in two groups, six in each. Each group was to be assigned twelve guards, who were to be brought into the camp especially for the trip. The guards, now stationed in South Vietnam, were scheduled for leaves to their homes in the north.

One group of prisoners was to be led by Tuk, a new officer who had come to the camp several months before. The other group—the one I was to be in—would be taken by Mr. Thieu. Rat Face was to follow later with the South Vietnamese prisoners.

The trip north was to be made on foot up the Ho Chi Minh Trail. It was going to be a long, long walk. And that explained the vitamins and iron.

We were all plenty jittery at the idea of moving north. No one had any idea what to expect there. Still, in a way, it was exciting. Finally, something different was happening to us. And, though no one said so, we all figured there'd be a good chance of us going to Hanoi. POW life there had to be better.

Also, I was really pleased that we'd be making the trip with Mr. Thieu.

The first group of six—including Kushner, Anton and Harker —left on February 1, 1971.

Eighteen days later, at seven in the morning following breakfast, my group moved out. Fred Elbert, who had been sick for some weeks, was the only white guy among us. The rest of the group were Ike, Davis, Lewis, Jose, and myself.

We took off from the emergency camp, returning to the regular camp to pick up some supplies. All the old guards stayed behind. I stopped to say good-by to a few of them. Then I walked to the supply room to see Mama Son.

There was no regret at taking off from the camp, or from anyone in it. Whatever heaviness I felt was in leaving behind the guys I had come to know, to rap with, to share ideas with. And I thought of the times we'd joked together, and sometimes argued. It hurt that they were no longer around to make the trip north—

to make any trip, anywhere, ever again. Cannon, Ski, Williams, Burns, Bob Sherman, the others.

If there was any one person I really felt sad about leaving, it was Hannah's little boy, born right there in the mountains, and probably to be there for many, many years to come. No one to play with except the guards, slapping him so hard you could hear it, abusing him, sticking cigarettes in his mouth.

I really felt bad for that little boy. I almost wished I could take him with me.

CHAPTER 17

Ho Chi Minh Trail, March 1971

The Ho Chi Minh Trail winds its way hundreds of miles between South and North Vietnam, with branches shooting off into Laos and Cambodia. In some places it is enough of a road for trucks. But most of the way, it is not much more than stretches of jungle paths, sometimes wide, sometimes narrow, sometimes nothing at all, requiring travelers to cut their way through the underbrush with machetes.

During the long Vietnam War, the Ho Chi Minh Trail served as a major supply route for North Vietnam. It was also the only way for traveling on foot, north to south or south to north. A long, long walk.

For the first ten days, before reaching Laos, we had to do our own cooking. Food had been provided for this period, mostly rice.

Every morning we'd start at about six o'clock, walk forty-five minutes, then take our first break. Between eleven and one, we'd always stop for lunch and a long rest period. Usually, we'd reach our stop point for the night by three or four in the afternoon.

In the beginning, I had a really tough time of it—a weakness very much like malaria hitting me the first day out. I could hardly eat, and it was impossible for me to carry any supplies, so my load was divided up among the others. I carried a stick to help along the trail. But between the heat and the constant climbing from lowlands up a mountain then down again, I was really slow.

At first, Mr. Thieu tried to set the pace of the group to my ability to walk, but this brought us into the overnight camp long after the other civilians or military who were traveling the trail had been there. During the first ten days, the camps were really nothing more than shelters for us to spend the night, and there were always enough men, women and children on the trail to fill them. We'd either pass by or move along with these travelers every day, depending on which way they were going, north or south. There were people from every walk of life: women taking their children north to school, families going to visit relatives, military personnel on orders, troops, scatterings of civilians. And after a while, we'd often get to meet up with the same travelers again, either on the trail or at one of the camps.

With few exceptions, the people were friendly, even though they knew we were Americans. It helped that our guards often told them we were on our way north to study, that even though we were American we were sympathetic to the North Vietnamese. Jose learned of this when he overheard some guards discussing us with a group of civilians. We asked Mr. Thieu about it, and he explained that this was done to minimize any chance of trouble with the people along the way.

Soon, we got to know some of the civilians well because they continued to travel with us each day and stay at the same camp with us at night. Like the one we called Hat Man, a funny, pleasant little guy who wore a different hat every day, and sometimes would switch several times along the trail.

Most times, we'd start off in the morning with a special guard who acted as a guide. It was his job to get us about halfway to the next camp. Then, another guard would meet us there to lead the way to the stopping-off place for that night. Each morning, many different groups of travelers would take off at the same time. As the day went on, the groups would spread out along the trail, depending on how fast or slow they walked.

Because of me, our group was always far behind the others. After a while, it was decided to allow me to fall back on my own. No one was worried about my taking off, since there was really no place else to go except along the trail. So, many times, I'd end up walking by myself for hours. In a way, I liked it. I could set my own pace and rest whenever I felt the need. And it made it possible for the guys to arrive at a camp hours earlier than before.

Sometimes the trail would follow close to the truck route,

open roads that carried a steady stream of trucks with people and supplies. Most of the supply trucks were moving north to south, taking materials to supply points for the North Vietnamese troops.

Quite often we'd pass these NVA soldiers on the trail, hundreds at a time, officially volunteers on their way south. As soon as we spotted them, we'd stand to the side of the trail to let them pass. The minute those up front got a glimpse of us, they'd pass back the word to the others— "*Mỹ, Mỹ, Mỹ*"—Americans. Then, by the way they'd stare at us, most of them really young, we could tell they'd never seen any Americans before.

Many showed their hate, spitting down at the ground as they moved past. And often, those who carried walking sticks struck out with them, hitting us on the legs. One time, the sting really caught me by surprise, and, without thinking, I swung my own stick, catching the passing soldier square on the arm. He stopped, his face twisted in anger. Then, the men behind pushed him along, and he continued on down the trail.

When it came to getting whacked this way, Fred Elbert really got the worst of it. Since he was the only white guy among us, there was no mistaking him as an American GI. We hardly ever passed any NVA troops without a number of them taking a swipe at him. Being weak as he was, it was plenty rough on him—and he had few kind words for any Vietnamese.

Several times, we met companies of women troops on their way south, hundreds of them together. You always knew when they were coming. Walking in the intense heat, carrying packs and weapons, the sweat just poured off them—and they smelled like polecats. But that didn't stop the excitement any. As soon as someone spotted them, everyone started jabbering away: "Women, women, women!"

They'd pass by in single file, and sometimes it took twenty minutes or more. We'd grin across at them and many would smile back and blush. Whenever we stopped at the same camp with women troops, a number would always come over to us to feel our hair or skin. Then, giggling, they'd chatter away in Vietnamese like we understood every word they were saying. They'd always ask if we understood—and of course we'd nod, smile, and say we did.

We reached the border of Laos on the tenth day, walking all the way, never once using the truck route. Mr. Thieu explained that the truck route was faster, but many stretches were unsafe. Many nights, when our camp was near the road, we could hear U.S. planes dropping bombs and firing at trucks. Sometimes they were so close we were amazed they didn't spot us.

A number of things were different as soon as we crossed into Laos. The change in terrain was immediate. In South Vietnam, it had always been jungle-like—many trees, a wetness to everything. Now the land was mostly flat and open, and there was no protection from the sun, which covered us every day like a steaming, hot blanket. So from early morning on, we were drenched in sweat from our hair right on down to our Ho Chi Minh sandals.

Now, all the camps were under the control of the Democratic Republic of Vietnam, and they were very well organized. Each camp knew exactly how many were in and out. Our guards needed passes for every prisoner. Medical teams were available to us if we wanted to report on sick call. And, happily, there was no more cooking for ourselves. Now, meals were prepared for us. Sometimes we ate meat and were given rations of sugar and milk. The guards were given ration tickets for each man, and there was always plenty of food.

The meals were first come, first served, so the guys were perfectly satisfied to let me fall behind when I found the pace too fast. My sickness was completely gone; still, like always, it was a problem for me to walk at a steady, fast pace. Before long, I'd just run out of energy.

As before, we'd spend the night in hootches, only now they were larger and sturdier than the ones in the south. Should all the hootches fill up with travelers, latecomers would sleep in hammocks.

When we saw the very first camp in Laos, we were all very surprised at how out in the open it was. It seemed like the perfect target. We asked Mr. Thieu about it.

"Do not worry," Mr. Thieu reassured us. "This camp has been here a very long time and has never been bombed. Come—I will show you why."

He then pointed out how all the hootches were built down into the ground so that each roof was at the same level as the surrounding bushes. The tops of the hootches were covered with green leaves, and this camouflaged the camp so well that, from the air, a pilot couldn't see it at all. Every few days, the leaves on the roofs were changed to make sure the color was always right.

As we continued to meet different people on the trail in Laos and at the camps each night, we'd hear more and more often how lucky we were to be going to Hanoi. It was the same story from everyone—civilians, army personnel, even our own guards. We were constantly being congratulated, and the guards told us many times how in Hanoi there would be *"beaucoup"* bread, fish and meat. As far as they were concerned, not only did nothing in South Vietnam compare with Hanoi, but nothing did anywhere. To them, it had to be the greatest place on earth. And, after a while, we were just about convinced we were heading for some paradise.

As before, all the people were friendly to us. Only some of the younger kids would give us a hard time now and then, calling us names. However, even though most everyone was not hostile, we were told never to go anywhere without a guard. As Mr. Thieu explained, "We can never know what some people might do. Many have suffered greatly in the war."

According to Mr. Thieu, they were taking no chances with us. We had been given a medical when we left the south, and they meant to see to it that we arrived in the north in exactly the same condition of health, with no extra scars or cuts.

The more people from North Vietnam I got to meet, the more I was struck by the fact that they were healthier-looking than most Vietnamese from the south. They just didn't have that undernourished look we'd seen so often in the southern hamlets. Especially the women. Many of those from the north were on the heavier side. If you ever saw a heavy woman in the south, you could be sure she wasn't poor and that she came from some well-to-do family.

As we moved deeper into Laos, evidence of the war was all around. American bombs had left their marks, and the Ho Chi Minh Trail area was heavily spotted with them. And now, almost as common, it seemed, were wreckages of U.S. helicopters that had been hit by North Vietnamese anti-aircraft fire.

Mr. Thieu told us how American planes were bombing in Laos to try to help the South Vietnamese troops. "But it will not help," he said. "South Vietnamese soldiers are being killed by the hundreds. Many are running away. Did you hear on radio how thousands have been trapped by NVA troops?"

If we had any reason to doubt Mr. Thieu, or some of the radio reports we'd heard, we soon learned first-hand just how true it was. After we left the camp one morning, we came upon hundreds of South Vietnamese prisoners resting by the trail. We could hardly believe how many there were—five hundred or more—scattered all around. They looked filthy, their uniforms, or what was left of them, in rags. Many were wounded.

At the next station that night we saw them again, and we were to travel with them, on and off, during the rest of the trip through Laos. At each camp, they were made to work, mostly carrying wood supplies.

During the following days we heard the story of what had happened from the South Vietnamese themselves. It had been in an area right near the Ho Chi Minh Trail that 1,500 South Vietnamese troops had been surrounded for days by the NVA. American planes provided air support, pounding at the enemy. This kept the NVA from getting to them, but it also prevented the South Vietnamese from getting out. They had no food or water and were depending on the American planes to bring in supplies. It got so bad, some had to drink their own urine to stay alive.

Jose spoke to a number of the prisoners, and the story they told, in great anger, was that just when it looked as if the Americans could fly in food and supplies, a number of U.S. planes were shot down. Immediately, the remaining helicopters in the area concentrated completely on rescuing the American pilots, forgetting about the Vietnamese completely. And then, when the Americans left, the NVA troops moved in.

Thinking back again to the many times I'd faced the military philosophy that one American life was worth more than a thousand others, no matter who they were, the story was not hard to believe.

As we came to know some of the South Vietnamese prisoners, we learned that many had crossed over on their own, that they had no real concern for winning the war. Some were friendly. Others cursed and spit at us, shouting, "Number ten, number ten!"

"If it wasn't for them"—Jose understood them to say—"we wouldn't be here!"

It was hard not to feel angry at these South Vietnamese, supposedly our allies, spitting and calling us names.

As to whether there really were 1,500 South Vietnamese captured, that seemed to be the truth, also. When we finally met up with Harker again, he told us how his group had come across the other half of the prisoners—about seven or eight hundred. The entire Laos campaign, it seemed, was bad news for the South Vietnamese. Mr. Thieu kept telling us how their troops were retreating everywhere, but of course we were never really sure that we were getting the straight facts. He also made a point of how there were more American planes coming to their aid than ever before.

A long time later, looking over accounts of the war, I read how a thousand U.S. planes had gone into action that March of 1971. And how South Vietnamese forces had retreated with heavy casualties.

At one station, all of us staged a protest and refused to eat. Our food rations were always more than what the guards received, and we realized that some of the guards had switched tickets on us. Also, we noticed how others were given a sugar ration at this camp and we hadn't received one.

The camp was crowded with civilians and military. Groups of people stood by, watching how we refused to get in the chow line. Some came over to ask why, and Jose explained in Vietnamese. Many shook their heads sympathetically. When Hat Man, who was still traveling with us, heard what was wrong, he ran off to report it to the camp commander.

First, Mr. Thieu came over, furious with us for staging the scene while everyone watched. "You cannot protest!" he raged. Davis and Ike said nothing, but I started to argue with him. "Buffalo Head, be quiet!" he shouted. That's what he called me when he was angry.

Then he pulled out a booklet and read a regulation to us. "Do you not realize," he said, "if you do not obey, the army has the authority to kill you?"

As angry as he was, we didn't take Mr. Thieu's threat too seriously.

Then the camp commander came charging over. When we explained what had happened, he said immediately, "Yes, you are supposed to receive a sugar ration at this camp." He ordered the guards to give us all the sugar they had, and he straightened out the food rations.

Later, a number of people offered us cigarettes. I'd found that the Vietnamese often enjoyed watching us try to smoke *Thôc Laò,* a tobacco that made you temporarily high with the first couple of drags. They'd laugh at how we'd react. It was never a problem for me, because no way could I smoke the stuff. It was really harsh and burned like crazy when you inhaled it.

Before leaving the camp, Fred Elbert, who'd been getting steadily weaker with edema, turned worse. He couldn't continue and we had to leave him at the camp's medical station for treatment.

With only a couple of days to go before we reached the border of Laos and crossed back into Vietnam, Mr. Thieu announced that soon we were to travel by truck. Under normal circumstances, all of us would have been very happy at the idea of riding instead of walking, but not here. The entire area, especially the truck route, had been under heavy bombing attacks for days.

"We'd rather walk, Mr. Thieu," I said. "We've been prisoners for three years, you know—too long to die now!"

Mr. Thieu stared at me in annoyance. "I have been here over twenty years," he said.

"Yes, Mr. Thieu—but it is just that we would rather go the safe way."

"It will be safe." Then he laughed and said, "Anyway, why should you be afraid? They are American planes."

"Mr. Thieu, that high up, they don't know if we're Vietnamese or American. And bullets do not know faces."

Mr. Thieu smiled. But I could tell he was angry with us for complaining.

As it turned out, the truck route, while we traveled on it, was very peaceful. One area that took several hours to ride through was more than peaceful. It had been destroyed so completely, we called it "no man's land." Once it had been a string of small hamlets and villages. Now, it was leveled as far as the eye could see. The land was flat and the damage from the bombs was everywhere—houses burned to the ground, the few standing trees charred black, no leaves, no animals . . . nothing. It made me think of the old Smokey the Bear ads asking us to prevent forest fires.

Here was an example, Mr. Thieu told us, of the American plan to force people living in the country to relocate in the hamlets built by the U.S. Army. "But, of course, it changes nothing," Mr. Thieu said. "It is only moving those who fight the United States from one place to another. The people are told it is done to improve how they live, but they know it is just an attempt to place them where they can be controlled."

"If everyone is moved out, then why is the area bombed?" I asked.

"So that no one can move back," Mr. Thieu said.

And I again recalled how we'd been trained to destroy all means of survival in an enemy village. Kushner and Anton, the only two without infantry training, had always disbelieved that the army taught this. Maybe now, when they rode hour after hour through this barren, desolate land, they'd change their minds.

As I looked out at where houses, hootches and farm land used to be, I wondered how many people must have been killed there under American bombs. Even if they had been warned to move.

We unexpectedly received a very special treat at one of the last camps in Laos. Three beautiful Vietnamese singers and their accordionist entertained all of us, and our guards, with a private show.

The musical group traveled from one camp to the other, performing for civilians and soldiers who were there for the night. Their performance at this camp was to take place the following day, only we were set to leave early in the morning. When the girls learned this, they insisted on coming over to sing for us.

It was a clear, quiet night, and we all gathered around at one hootch. The girls stood in front of us, singing softly, the accordion providing the accompaniment. Their high-pitched voices were so lovely, it wasn't even needed.

At times like this, it was almost possible to forget for a few minutes that we were POWs, and that the Vietnamese were our captors.

The very first day after we crossed back into North Vietnam, I did the fastest running of my life. We were at a camp in the province of Quang Binh, just off the truck route. From this point on, we'd been told, there was to be no more walking—and right then, we were waiting for trucks to take us to Vinh Linh.

It was raining heavily and just starting to get dark. Suddenly, one of the guards ran up and shouted for us to "run fast" to the bomb shelters. I couldn't figure why and thought maybe it was some kind of practice.

Then I heard the planes rolling in—a sky-full of them. Within minutes bombs were exploding nearby, and we thought it must be an attack on the road. We jumped up and tore for the shelters.

With each blast, it seemed as if the whole area shook. I was really scared, my mouth so dry I couldn't even swallow my own saliva. Never, ever, did I run so fast.

Then, as the attack continued, we realized that the planes were bombing a fuel dump that was close by, and, with luck, we'd be okay.

A short while after it quieted down, the trucks came in for us. The backs were open and we climbed up, sitting on the floor. Just before we left, I asked Mr. Thieu, "What are we gonna do if they come back?"

Sometimes Mr. Thieu could be funny. He looked at me very seriously and said, "Just like the Vietnamese do, Daly. Run like hell!"

As we rode past the fuel dump, flames and smoke still gushed up into the blackness. The sky was clear, the air very fresh. We sat together, wrapped in blankets. I remember it as a very beautiful night.

We pulled into the outskirts of Vinh Linh about two o'clock the next afternoon. There, in a sparsely settled area, we were assigned hootches. It was explained that we were to stay here until the following day. Then, we were to leave by train for a final destination.

That night, before we went to sleep, Mr. Thieu came into our hootch to say good-by. He spoke slowly, looking from one to the other, and we could tell he was really sad.

Mr. Thieu said he hoped we'd soon all be going home, that the war would be ended. "You must all learn a lot," he said. "You must all become very progressive in how you think."

Then he turned to me. "Especially you, Daly. You are sometimes a hothead. You must change."

Before he left, Mr. Thieu paused, looked back at us again, and said, "I will miss all of you very much. I wish you good luck."

For a few minutes, no one said anything. All of us liked Mr. Thieu. His farewell speech had touched each of us.

The following day, we were turned over to a new group of guards. Now we were under the orders of the North Vietnamese Army. Our old guards from the Provisional Revolutionary Government no longer had any authority. Finally, we were ready for the final leg of our trip to the north—forty-eight days after we had started out.

The railroad station was only a short walk from the hootch area. Just before we were to go, Jose overhead Mr. Thieu asking the new guard commander if he could continue on with us. He was told it could not be permitted.

We had always known that Mr. Thieu liked us a lot, but we never really realized just how much affection he had. It was then we decided that, before we left, we'd sing the patriotic song *Giâi Phòng Mien Nam!* for him.

The train station in Vinh Linh was crowded with civilians and military. Our train was waiting; it looked like something out of a Western movie, smokestack and everything. Many of the South Vietnamese prisoners were being led onto the boxcars, in which all of us were to travel.

Minutes after we arrived at the station, our new guards handcuffed us one to the other. "I am sorry," Mr. Thieu said. "I ask that they not use handcuffs—but I no longer have authority." He then went around to each of us, feeling to see that the handcuffs were not too tight, asking if they hurt. You would have thought we were his kids.

Then I said, "Mr. Thieu, we would like to sing a song for you."

We stood together in a line, and Jose started us off, "One, two, three . . ."

When Mr. Thieu heard the first notes, he could hardly hold back his emotion. As we sang, little by little, people in the station moved around us, joining in, singing the familiar patriotic words.

Mr. Thieu stood motionless. You could see how all he had to do was blink and the tears would come falling down his face. It was in our eyes like that, too. We had been with Mr. Thieu for a long time.

CHAPTER 18

Plantation Gardens, Hanoi, Spring 1971

We climbed down from the boxcar and almost thought we were celebrities or something instead of POWs. The big brass was out in force to meet us—twenty high-ranking officers in uniform, men and women.

The train had stopped a good distance outside the Hanoi railroad station to avoid the crowds. We'd been in the boxcar for almost twelve hours, handcuffed, sleeping that way on the car floor. It was great to get on my feet again and move around.

As soon as the guards took off the handcuffs, we were blindfolded and led to several waiting jeeps. The ride to the camp couldn't have taken more than ten minutes. When the blindfolds were removed, we found ourselves in a large cement courtyard.

From end to end, the yard was almost the size of a city block, and it was divided into two sections by a brick wall that stretched about halfway across it. We stood in front of a long one-story structure containing a row of about fifteen rooms, each with a door opening onto the yard, like a motel. At the other side of the courtyard, near the gate through which we had just been driven, was another similar building. Just beyond it, I sensed, was a city street. The camp, it seemed, was right smack in the middle of Hanoi!

More buildings, smaller ones, were scattered around the yard, one of them two stories high with a front porch. Guard towers were set back in the corners of the yard, and another brick wall, like the one that divided the area in the center, bordered it on three sides, separating the camp from the city outside. The wall was only about six feet high, and, looking over its top, we could actually see the tops of houses on the Hanoi street just beyond it.

In the center of the entire area, there was a dirt hill filled with flowers, and it was because of this, I learned later, that the camp was called "Plantation Gardens."

All of us just stood there, looking from one spot to the other, hardly believing. It was like no other POW camp I'd ever seen. And probably what surprised me more than anything else—right there in the middle of the open area, as big as life, was an honest-to-goodness basketball court!

The room at the very end of the long building was ours. A real room to live in! And, on top of that, electricity! No more kerosene lamps that hardly ever had any kerosene to keep them lit.

The guard who had followed us inside spoke English. He took our names. Then he said, "We eat second meal of day now. Are you hungry?"

We all answered yes, and the guard told us that food would be sent. Afterward, we would be given time to rest.

When lunch arrived, delivered to the room, we all thought we were dreaming. We had rice soup, noodles, canned pork, and a small loaf of bread for each of us. We ate like we were starving, all of us exclaiming between mouthfuls, "Man, this is living!"

During the meal, we talked very little. We had noticed a speaker on the wall and imagined that the room was bugged, that anything we said could be heard through the speaker. Actually, we soon found out, it was only a radio.

After eating, a guard came to the door to collect the dishes. When he opened it, I spotted Harker just outside our room in the courtyard. We grinned at one another. "Hey, you guys, how you doin'?" he called out.

"Hey, Harker, where you at?"

"We're right in the room next door. How come you guys so quiet? You all scared to knock on the wall?"

The guard left and we all crowded around the window. Outside, in the courtyard, we caught sight of Harker, Kushner, and the others.

Well, how about that, I thought, here we were, all back together again. Except for Elbert. And they'd told us he'd be coming as soon as he was well enough to travel.

Later that day, another officer came in to see us. He was the one North Vietnamese at the camp we'd get to know best during the months ahead. He was a political officer, and it was his job to work closely with all of us—to give us our political indoctrination. Next to the camp commander, this officer was the big cheese at Plantation Gardens. And so, to all the POWs, he became known as "Cheese."

"Do you know what tomorrow is?" Cheese asked us.

We all said no.

"Tomorrow is your holiday," he said. "It is Easter, and you will have a special meal."

It came as news to us. Not one of us had even realized that the following day was Easter.

Then Cheese said, "You must now be given your Vietnamese names. This will help the guards who speak no English."

Then, based on our English names, each of us was given a name in Vietnamese. My name was "Da." Jose, whose last name was Anzodua, was called "Dua." Lewis was the only one whose Vietnamese name didn't sound like part of his English name. He was named "Wi."

The next day, our Easter dinner turned out to be a feast! Noodle soup, goose, pork, potatoes and bread. Everyone was given a bottle of beer and a shot glass of wine.

That afternoon, one of the guards came to visit us. His name was Fung, but after a while one of the guys began to call him "Cool Jerk," the title of a recording that had come out in the sixties. The nickname stuck, and from then on, Fung was always Cool Jerk.

Of all the guards, he was just about the friendliest. Cool Jerk loved to talk. That first time we met him, he started out asking us all kinds of questions. How did we like the camp? Where were we from in America? How big were our families? Within a few days, the questions turned more and more personal. Soon, Cool Jerk wanted to know if I had a girl friend and if I planned on getting married.

That was one question I'd been asking myself. Many times I'd thought back to that last evening with Renee, when I'd asked her to marry me. Remembering our on-again, off-again relationship, I knew for sure that Renee hadn't just sat around waiting for me. And I also considered something else. In many ways, I wasn't the same guy I had been then. And just as my ideas about things seemed to be changing, maybe my feelings for Renee were different, too.

The only way I could ever describe how different Plantation Gardens was from all those POW camps in the south would be to say that it was like going from hell to heaven. Aside from the room with electricity, there was much more. We'd each been issued two blankets, a clean set of clothes, another set of work clothes, a toothbrush, soap and a cup. After South Vietnam, you couldn't put a price on things like these.

We took a bath every day in a room that was set up with a huge tub and buckets. We bathed two at a time, dumping water on one another after soaping down.

Probably the only thing about Plantation Gardens that wasn't as good as in the south was that now we had less freedom. In a way it was understandable, considering how much larger the camp was, with over a hundred prisoners, ten officers and about seventy-five guards. Still, we missed being allowed outside all day.

Here, we had only one twenty-minute free period. The rest of the day we were stuck inside together, just sitting around, reading, or playing cards. Before long, we were right back into the daily arguments again. We were always fighting and teasing each other over something. Jose and I were at it all the time, arguing over everything from sex to religion. And now we were back to six guys again. Julius Long, one of the men who'd made the trip with Harker's group, was moved in with us.

Each day followed a routine. In the morning, first thing, a guard came around with cigarettes. Then, a short while later, we were given half a loaf of bread and hot tea for breakfast.

When we first arrived, we were told we could have as much bread as we wanted. Not having had any for so long, we just couldn't stop eating it. But then, after a time, we never finished eating what we'd asked for. We were then each limited to one and a half small loaves a day.

Our first real meal was at eleven—a bowl of soup, a vegetable plate of some kind with meat in it, and bread. The dinner meal, at about four o'clock, was always some variation of the same food we'd had for lunch. We soon came to realize that all our meals, for weeks at a time, would consist only of the food that was plentiful during that period. Like when pumpkins were accessible, everything was pumpkin. Pumpkin soup; stewed pumpkins with onions, pepper and meat; and so forth. Then, when the season for pumpkins was over, we'd be switched to potatoes—potato soup and stewed potatoes. At first, it was such a great change from the food in the south, we all went crazy over it.

On Sundays the guards were off, so there was no noontime meal. Breakfast was bread and a bowl of rice soup sweetened with sugar. This carried us till about two-thirty, when we received our last meal of the day, usually soup and some kind of fruit, mostly oranges and bananas.

The times of our twenty-minute free period varied from day to day, but once out we could do whatever we liked—get books, walk around, play basketball, or just stay inside. The reason the period had to be limited to twenty minutes was that only one room in the camp was permitted out at a time. While these groups were being given their turns at the twenty-minute free period, other rooms were taken out for baths, or a visit to the Club Room to take out games or books. The rule of the camp was that no two groups were to be at the same place during the same time; contact was forbidden. That meant sometimes a guard would have to get a group of POWs out of the courtyard quickly if another was about to pass by.

We asked Cheese if the camp couldn't make an exception to the rule and allow our room to take its free period with Harker and the others, since we'd all lived together for three years in the south. At first he refused, acting as if he didn't believe we all knew one another. He asked us to give him the name, age and rank of each man in the next room. Finally, convinced we were all friends, he gave permission for the two rooms to go out together. It was the only arrangement of its kind in the camp.

Our first political course lasted an entire week—classes every day from right after breakfast at seven-thirty until lunch at eleven. The other group took their classes in the afternoon. No activities were ever scheduled between eleven and one.

The classes were taught by an officer we soon came to call Roly-Poly because he always rolled his eyes, like he was reading words off the ceiling. As before, each class was a lecture, followed by a question period. And with all of it mostly just a repeat of what we'd covered in South Vietnam, we couldn't wait for the class to end.

Roly-Poly reviewed the history of Vietnam once again—the

same outline of four thousand years, period by period, right up to the war. Then, he got into an analysis of United States war policies, such as the "search-and-destroy" phase. Though I found listening to all of this again more boring than ever before, I also realized that I had come to understand a good part of it, and to accept much of what was said. Maybe half, I figured, wasn't exactly the truth, the way it was presented—still, the other half was. And those very same questions we'd been asked before, like why had we come to Vietnam, were getting still harder to answer now.

When one of the guys came back with a standard reply, such as we'd come to Vietnam to help the South Vietnamese stay free, Roly-Poly pointed to the four blacks in the room, one to the other, and asked the now familiar questions: "How can any of you say you came here to fight for freedom? Does freedom exist in your own country? Did any of you, or your families, have freedom at home?"

Of course even I, coming out of a Brooklyn ghetto, couldn't honestly say yes to that one. As for the others—Davis from Alabama, Lewis from Texas, Ike from Florida—Roly-Poly knew what their answers had to be. And even Long, white and from the mountains of Virginia, or Jose, Mexican, would have to go along. The truth of it was there'd been no *real* freedom for any of us back in the good ol' U.S.A.

I soon realized how injustice against minorities in America was something the North Vietnamese were very ready to make work for them. Not only in Roly-Poly's classes, but in the more personal indoctrinations conducted by Cheese.

Every few weeks, each of us was called in for a private meeting with Cheese, whose job it was to regularly sit down with every POW in the camp. Usually, a guard would come to our room and inform one of us that he was wanted at the officers' building, the two-story house with a porch. We'd always put on a long-sleeved shirt for the occasion.

Cheese would be sitting at his table, ready to share a pot of tea and cigarettes. He tried to keep everything as informal and relaxed as possible to make it easier for us to talk openly. It worked.

At first, Cheese encouraged me to talk about myself at random. What was it like growing up? What did my father and mother work at? What conflicts did I have at home, in school, as a youngster?

I found myself telling Cheese the truth—describing my home life, my childhood years, my interest in the church and the Jehovah's Witnesses.

"Yes, I understand you have had great interest in religion," Cheese said. "This is something we will have to talk about soon."

Somehow, I felt it would be possible for me to learn from these sessions, that maybe they could help me to gain an understanding about myself I'd never had before. From the beginning, Cheese stressed how he hoped the talks with him would help the men to better themselves, to grow, to learn. In order to help a man, he'd claim, it was important for him to know and understand his background.

After a meeting with Cheese, we'd often go back and talk about it with the others in the room. By making comparisons, we soon learned that whenever any of us had discussed personal problems and backgrounds—unhappy parents, bad living conditions, sad childhood—Cheese would always relate these problems, one way or another, to the system we lived under: capitalism.

"What causes any person to be unhappy?" he'd ask. "It is the conditions under which he lives, especially the poor family in a capitalistic country, unable to find rewarding work, unable to enjoy life, never getting the things they want, no matter how hard they work."

And just as Cheese hit hard at the difficulties facing poor people in the United States, he made a point of covering the special racial problems of the blacks. He even had newspaper clippings showing such things as race riots, murders, and what some groups like the Black Panthers were doing.

"Do you not have feelings for your people?" he asked. "Do you not want to help them? Well, to do so, you must have a method, Daly. You must learn and study."

"Study what?" I asked.

"The truth," he answered. "In order to solve the problems of your people, you must come to understand that under capitalism you can never do away with racism, never achieve social justice. Whenever there are very rich and very poor, and the very rich are the ruling class, the system can never be just."

Of course, it didn't take much to figure out that Cheese was into selling communism with just about every word—and he was doing okay at it. The one belief I had always had about communism that bugged me the most was that it was supposed to be anti-religion. I asked Cheese about this many times. Finally, he agreed to talk about it.

First he traced the history of man, as he saw it, and tried to tie it into religion. What he said was true enough, I thought, but it just didn't make his point.

"It is important to understand why man does wrong—that it is not because of some devil at all," Cheese said. "It is because of how man became the way he now is; how when he first began to take possessions, trouble started."

Cheese then talked of primitive times. How, at first, one man wanted to take away what belonged to another. Then, how one tribe wanted to possess what another tribe owned. Finally, how nations did the same thing, the stronger trying to take the weaker's possessions, so that it could become stronger still, and richer and more powerful. "This is what created wars," Cheese said. "And it is so today."

"Okay, so forget about the devil making man bad," I said. "But what about religion itself? What about the teachings of the church?"

"Religion is made for the poor," Cheese said. "It is a tool of the ruling class."

I asked Cheese to explain this theory, and he tried. I soon realized that Cheese wasn't up to answering many of my questions properly. It was to be months later, when another political officer arrived at the camp, that I would be able to really get into the discussion of religion.

Meanwhile, the sessions with Cheese were good. The talks made me think very differently about many things, and were responsible for introducing me to ideas I'd never really considered before. And the books and magazines we now read played a big part in this.

We were never forced to read the books, and at first we took them out of the Club Room just because going through them was better than doing nothing, or sitting around the room playing cards and checkers, or arguing away the day. At least, reading was a way of keeping your mind occupied.

But then, little by little, I started getting involved. So did some of the others. Now we found ourselves discussing the books back in the room, or asking Cheese questions about them.

One set of volumes was called *Vietnamese Studies*, and it was used in the schools of North Vietnam. A new edition came out each month. I remember the first one I read, *New Colonialism*. It described how Great Britain came to get all her colonies, and how the United States would "colonialize" a country, even one that was supposed to be independent. An example of this was the Philippines, which, according to the book, was still struggling to rid itself of American domination, twenty-five years after becoming an independent country.

The more books I read, the more they spurred my interest in others. And the more information I came across about the United States's involvement in Vietnam, the more I wanted to know, even though I questioned whether it was completely accurate.

Often, I'd ask Cheese questions about certain "facts" concerning U.S. policies. Sometimes, he'd answer me. Very often, he'd simply encourage me to find the answer for myself.

It was about then that Kush and Anton were moved out of the room next door into another with POW officers. In addition to separating the officers from the enlisted men, all of the older Regular-Army prisoners in the camp, we learned, lived apart from the younger ones like us. The idea was not to mix men with different backgrounds and different values, if they could help it. No one was allowed to try to influence anyone else as to political opinions or attitude about the war, and this was less likely to happen if prisoners with different opinions on things were kept apart.

We'd never been told they planned on moving Kushner and Anton. The way we found out was when Cool Jerk let both rooms out for a bath one morning. The room next door went off first, and as we stood watching, one of the guys realized that Kushner and Anton were not among them. I asked Cool Jerk where they were.

As friendly as he was most of the time, every now and then Cool Jerk would get into a surly mood. That morning, he refused to answer me and just kept saying, "Go take bath!"

All of the guys crowded around him. One shouted out, "We ain't goin' till we know what happened to them!" Then all of us were yelling at him, demanding to be told why Kushner and Anton were not with the group.

Just then, Cheese was crossing the courtyard. When he heard the commotion, he came charging over.

"You will not be disrespectful to a guard!" he roared.

"We're not being disrespectful!" Jose said. He explained the problem.

"Do not argue!" Cheese demanded. "I am an officer. You must show me respect."

"In order to get respect, you must give respect," I said angrily. "We lived with those men for three years—now why are they gone all of a sudden?"

"Da!" Cheese shouted my Vietnamese name. "You must remember you are a prisoner!" Just by the way he spoke, we realized that Cheese was on the verge of really blowing his top, that he had all he could do to control himself. Everyone stood quietly.

"If you do not want to take bath, you do not have to," Cheese said, calmer now. "We do not make you take bath. But you cannot demand anything here. You are prisoners!"

This was a very touchy point with the Vietnamese guards and officers. If there was any one thing they really resented, it was American prisoners who acted like they had something coming to them, or could make special demands, just because they were Americans. Many of the guys came on like that, and I really couldn't blame the North Vietnamese for getting worked up about it.

It was hard for some of the POWs to see anything at all from the North Vietnamese point of view. Harker's group was like that pretty much, ready to write off just about anything as Communist propaganda. The one possible exception was Fred Elbert, who'd finally arrived at the camp and was put in the room next door with another guy, Bay, to replace Kush and Anton. Fred could often fluctuate from one opinion to another —and it was hard to figure just how he might evaluate a thing.

I could understand why the guys in Hark's room were down on communism. Everything in their backgrounds and upbringing acted to make them resist what Cheese and Roly-Poly taught. And, of course, the North Vietnamese were not able to appeal to them on the basis of being both poor and black. That was a tough combination to beat when it came to hard times and hard living in the United States.

And the funny part of it was, as much as our backgrounds, as

Negroes, might have made it easier to be sympathetic to the Vietnamese at times, I sensed, as I often had, an understanding and sympathy for us on their part. Maybe that awareness helped to play a role in my going it like I did.

CHAPTER 19

The Peace Committee

Even though prisoners in the different rooms were forbidden to communicate, every group of POWs in the camp knew just about everything that was going on with all the other groups. The rooms talked up and down the line by using tin cups. Whoever did the talking covered his head with a blanket and pressed his mouth to the wall. On the other side, with a tin cup to the wall and to his ear, the guy listening could hear every word. Two raps on the wall meant you were ready to talk, three that you were finished.

Most of the talk was nonsense. To me, it seemed crazy to risk punishment for asking questions of new POWs like who won big sports events, or what were the new cars like?

One topic went on for days when a new prisoner told the others about what he called "flavored dishes," a new kind of treatment a woman used in her vagina to give it different flavors. This started a whole survey in the camp on how many of the guys "ate a woman" when they had sex. When the results were tabulated, they showed most did.

Not long after we'd arrived at Plantation Gardens, we'd heard about a group in the camp called the "Peace Committee." None of us really knew much about them except how they were supposed to be sympathetic to the North Vietnamese. One of the rumors that passed from room to room was that when some prisoners had been caught passing messages through the walls, it was the PC who had turned them in.

The first time we found out anything definite about the Peace Committee was when Cheese brought in the magazine they wrote called *New Life.*

"All of you seem interested in learning," Cheese said. "You read books and ask questions. That is good. I will leave this with you. The men who wrote it are prisoners like you. They believe the war is wrong and are helping to bring it to an end."

There was only one copy of the magazine, which was made up of hand-printed articles written by the six members of the Peace Committee. Each man wrote telling why he was against the war, and some of the articles described U.S. fighting strategy in Vietnam—search and destroy, destruction of "enemy" villages, bombings of cities. The six were so completely against everything the United States was doing in Vietnam, it was hard not to believe that each of them had been brainwashed.

After we all read the magazine, Jose reacted to it by saying he'd like to find out more about the group. Long immediately put them down.

Whenever it came to real differences of opinion in the room, things generally followed the same pattern. Most often, Davis would go along with whatever Long thought. Then, Lewis and Ike followed Davis. It was like that this time, too.

As for me, I thought a lot in the magazine made sense. As time went on, I even began to accept some of the things I'd doubted, especially after seeing films of American bombing raids.

One of the buildings on the far side of the courtyard was a movie house. One side of it faced the camp, the other opened onto a Hanoi street, accessible to Vietnamese civilians. Every few weeks we were shown films of Vietnamese neighborhoods, schools and hospitals that had been bombed by U.S. planes.

We didn't know if it really meant anything, but the members of the Peace Committee were moved in as our next-door neighbors. Up until then, we'd been in the last room of the building. Now we were shifted over one room, as was Harker's group. Our old room, on the end, was given to the PC. With one new member, Alwine, we were seven now.

Even though we were right next to the Peace Committee, we still never met them. And they seemed reluctant to break the rules by talking through the walls. However, little by little, we discovered more about them, and who was who. Now and then we'd catch a glimpse of them through the window.

As in all the other POW camps, day-to-day living was completely routine. There was very little to break it up, except the constant quarrels among us. Jose, who always looked to represent the room, and who had the advantage of speaking Vietnamese, was always in the middle of every discussion or question that came up. And just as often, he was in the middle of every squabble.

The two of us continued to argue regularly. As far as religion went, I'd pretty much given up the idea of getting any of the guys to hear the truth about God, as I would have liked to have told it. That was a lost cause. Especially with a mixed-up guy like Jose, who put down religion every chance he got—and was the first to start praying when things got rough.

Often, we'd all sit around talking sex, or arguing about it. Jose always insisted you could hardly find a fourteen-year-old girl in the U.S. who was still a virgin. We'd argue about things like that.

Most of the guys had always put me down when I'd criticize their attitudes on sex or religion, or the cursing that went on all the time. I'd never gone along with them on these things, knocking them right from the start, in South Vietnam. But I'd noticed how, as time passed, I was becoming like the others. More and more, I'd catch myself cursing like crazy, or even making up a sex story just to be able to join in the talk. Or I'd laugh with the rest of them when they played at being queer. Not that they really ever did anything, just talked or kidded around. Like one of the guys yelling out after we'd gone to bed that he was going to hop over on so and so and give it to him, and the answer coming back, "C'mon, man, I'll show you somethin' you'll never forget!"

But the crazy thing about it all was that the more I tried to act like the rest of them, the more often I'd run up against one of them asking something like, "Hey, Daly, how can you talk about preachin' when you don't do the very things you preachin' about, man?"

So, either way, I'd come to understand there was just no way I could make it with these guys. When I didn't talk or act like they did, I was put down. And when I did, I was condemned as a hypocrite.

Sometimes the arguments got so heated that even Jose couldn't take it, and he'd ask Cheese to put him in solitary for a few days, a small room that could sleep two. When a prisoner was placed in solitary as punishment, he wasn't allowed outside that room at all, except to take a bath. But actually it wasn't all that bad. And it sure was a good way to get away from it all.

I'd always imagined the guards in a North Vietnamese POW camp to be really tough, hard-core honchos. As it turned out, plenty weren't the friendliest, but most of them treated us okay.

One guard we called Sergeant Sook couldn't have been mean if he'd wanted to. He just never got angry and was always laughing. Like many of the others, he'd always want to learn English words, especially the slang ones, and he'd carry around a small notebook to write them down.

We always came up with appropriate nicknames for the guards and never even tried to remember their Vietnamese names. The one who was in charge of opening the door every morning, we called Turn Key. The officer in charge of the guards, who was really well built and knew judo, was Judo Joe. One of the funnier guards, always clowning around, was named Monkey Man.

I got along with most of the guards, and it always bugged me how the guys put them down or cursed them out behind their backs. Sometimes, if a guard didn't understand English, they'd curse right at him. You could often tell by the expression on his face that he realized something bad was being said to him. Very often I'd hear things like, "I hope those B-52s blast every one of them—destroy the whole damn country!"

I could understand what made POWs act and talk this way, or sometimes, when they were really upset over something, threaten a hunger strike or purposely waste food. They did it out of the bitterness and depression they felt, having been captives for years, wanting to be home, tired of sitting around every day. Still, I hated to see it.

One day, when I was alone with Cool Jerk, he asked me about the way some of the prisoners behaved. "Da, why do your comrades act as they do? Why do they think they should demand things? Look how they waste bread. People outside on the streets do not even get bread. Da, your comrades are never satisfied!"

During one of our sessions together, when Cheese said he wanted me to write a letter that could help to end the war, I realized that the objections I'd had to signing letters in the south didn't seem important anymore. It was hard to know why my personal concerns of the past didn't matter now, why I felt differently. Probably there were a number of reasons—the films, the books, my talks with Cheese.

As it turned out, all the guys in the room agreed to write letters, and, probably most everyone in the camp did, also. But before the decision was made, there was plenty of discussion about it in our room, and with Harker's group, too. Again, I heard many of the same doubts and arguments that had come up in South Vietnam. As before, most of the guys agreed that they could always claim, if they had to, that they'd been forced to write letters, or tortured into it. After all, the Code of Conduct was written by men who had never had to face these decisions, or had never had any understanding of them.

Actually, most of the letters written by POWs in the camp were never made public by the North Vietnamese. I realized, months later, why they wanted them on file, available to be used against a POW if needed, even after he returned to the United States. What was really behind it was that the North Vietnamese never really trusted any POW completely. Something Cheese said made me very aware of this. He told me how some prisoners had been released in the past, only to claim, as soon as they were free, that they'd been tortured by the North Vietnamese. While in captivity, they'd always spoken out against the war.

"The U.S. military wants to use prisoners to give the American people the impression that all of you are tortured here, that life for the prisoner is horrible," Cheese said. "Those released were ready to say anything once they returned home. That is why we release no more POWs."

Cheese hesitated for a minute, then slowly stated his way of thinking of such things. It was a notion I was to hear again: "It takes many years to know a friend, Daly—but only minutes to learn an enemy!"

During the weeks following that session with Cheese, I wrote two letters, one addressed to the American people and one addressed to the Mayor of New York City. Although Cheese suggested the approach to the letters, the content of each was left entirely up to me. The main points Cheese made was that the letters should evoke sympathy, that they should make the American people want to do something to try and bring the war to an end. That made sense to me.

I wrote of my hopes for returning home soon. I denounced the war and questioned why millions were being spent to bomb the Indochinese people, and how this money was needed so desperately at home. While profits were being made on the war, I said, American GIs were dying every day, and the lives of American POWs were in danger, too.

What I put down in my letters was really not very different from what Americans were saying at that time all over the United States, including members of Congress. And I believed every word of it. Somehow, I hoped, these letters might help to save some lives, both American and Vietnamese.

The very first incident that involved me in any way with Air Force Colonel Theodore Guy, the commander of the American POWs in the camp, was a letter to him—one I didn't write and didn't even want to sign.

It came about when Harker told us that the camp grapevine had our room labeled as sympathetic to the Peace Committee. Nobody understood just why, maybe because we lived right next to them. Whatever the reason, when the guys heard about this, it really shook them up. Jose called a meeting.

What bothered everybody most was what might happen after being released if it was reported that they had been pro-Communist, or had helped the North Vietnamese.

"We should write a letter to Colonel Guy," Jose suggested. "Let's let him know exactly where we stand—that there are no reds in this room."

"We could get into plenty of trouble by doin' that," I said. "I think it's a bad idea."

The guys discussed it for a few minutes. The fear of being thought pro-Communist proved greater than that of the consequences of being caught getting a note to Colonel Guy. It was agreed to send it, and everyone in the room was to sign. I made it clear that if the letter was discovered, I'd deny writing it and claim I only signed because I had to.

Jose wrote the note. It denied any involvement with the Peace Committee and ended with the line, printed in big letters, "Better dead than red!" We left it in an area where each group emptied its latrine can, stuck behind a nearby roof shutter. On the way back, as we passed Colonel Guy's room, Jose called out, "Look behind the roof shutter near the latrine pit!"

Then, nearby, we spotted a guard watching us. We didn't know for sure whether he'd overheard.

Back in the room, we kept watch out the window. A short while later, we saw a group of guards and the camp commander head for the latrine pit area. For twenty minutes, they continued to tear up the place, looking everywhere. Then a guard came for Colonel Guy and took him out to the main building. We were really sweating it.

Finally, it all quieted down. Nothing happened.

We learned much later that another group found the note. Our declaration of loyalty never even reached its destination.

And that ended my first incident concerning Colonel Guy. Unfortunately, it was not to be my last.

In early November, we were told that any of us who wanted to could write a Christmas letter home. The messages were to be taped and played over the "Voice of Vietnam" radio program.

I was happy at the chance to get word to my family that I was okay. And I was perfectly satisfied to make certain that the letter contained the kind of statements that would ensure its being sent and used on radio. I wrote:

Dear Mom and Family,

I hope all of you are well.

I'm in good health and miss everyone very much.

Tell my friends I said hello and maybe I'll see them all soon.

We read many books here, and I've been able to learn a lot about the Vietnamese people.

Mom, if I knew before what I know now, I'd probably be a minister today and not here.

I wish all of you a very Merry Christmas.

God bless you all,

Your son, Bubby

CHAPTER 20

Plantation Gardens, Hanoi, Christmas 1971

As the petty arguments in the room continued day after day, I considered the idea of moving in with the Peace Committee more and more. Despite all the gossip and rumors, the one thing I knew for certain about them was that they were against the war and had the courage to say so. As for the rest of it, I decided I'd just have to learn for myself.

I remembered how when I'd first read their magazine, I'd wondered, like the others, if maybe they'd been brainwashed. But now, a lot of what they'd written about kept popping back into my head. And when I put it together with many of the points made by Cheese, somehow much of it began to fall into place for me.

Of course, I never forgot that, as a political officer, Cheese had a selling job to do, and that there was good reason to question some of what he said. I did. And many times, I'd argue a point with him or just let him know that I didn't buy it.

Still, for the most part, I believed Cheese was telling it like it was. If my accepting his ideas meant I was being brainwashed, then I guess I was. Only I didn't see it that way.

Then, other things kept nagging at me. Like the lies the army had pounded into our heads. How as prisoners of the Vietnamese we'd be tortured or killed. Instead, it seemed to me they'd always treated us the best they could. Even in the south with the VC, our food was as good—or as bad—as what the guards ate. And now in North Vietnam, we had clean rooms with electricity. We took baths regularly. We had beds and blankets. At Easter, we'd even been given that great goose dinner. All that was far from torture.

The honest truth was, the Vietnamese just weren't the monsters we'd been told they were. In the four years I'd been in Vietnam, since I first saw those poor tattered kids in Chu Lai staring up at me and begging, I'd come across a good number of the Vietnamese people. I'd seen or talked with them in the villages of the south, traveling the Ho Chi Minh Trail, as a POW, on the battlefield. They'd been peasants, Viet Cong, NVA soldiers, workers, professors, Montagnards. And the more Vietnamese I came in contact with, the more I knew in my gut what I had believed before in my head—that the war was wrong and we had no right to be there tearing this country to pieces.

Still, joining the Peace Committee was something else again. Sometimes, I'd hate the war so much I'd be ready right then and there to make the move. But I really preferred to meet them first. And I kept wondering how I could work that out. What I didn't realize was that in a very short time I was to be given that very opportunity.

Sometimes I tried to figure what had influenced my thinking most since coming to Plantation Gardens. One thing, certainly, was the books. Especially *Vietnamese Studies*, and the chronology of the war. Reading them, I not only learned about the struggles Vietnam had faced for over four thousand years, but I also came to see how the United States—which as a kid I had always thought of as the greatest and most humane country in the world—had really been helping to destroy this little nation.

Like how Eisenhower and his Secretary of State, John Foster Dulles, poured in over a billion dollars to aid the French fight the Vietnamese. And that was back in the early fifties!

Or how U.S. Congressmen actually admitted that the main reason we were interested in Indochina was because it was immensely wealthy in rice, rubber, coal and iron ore.

Or how, in 1954, Ngo Dinh Diem, the president of South Vietnam, refused free elections to determine the government of the country—and even turned down North Vietnam's invitation to plan them, as had been called for by the Geneva agreement. And then how the United States, instead of demanding that free elections be held, increased its aid to the Diem dictatorship.

Or how President Johnson kept talking peace in 1965 and held up the bait of a billion dollars for the development of North and South Vietnam—but while he talked, ordered the U.S. Air Force to batter the north with round-the-clock heavy bombing.

Or three years before, while I was a prisoner in the south, how General Westmoreland, in Saigon as head of all U.S. forces in Indochina, finally confessed that the war could not be won. He had waited until his farewell press conference to admit it.

So facts like these—and many more just like them—helped make clear to me just what the United States had been doing in Vietnam all these years. And then, sometimes, I'd remember other things. Like being in high school, with no real interest in Vietnam then, and hearing the Secretary of Defense, Robert McNamara, tell Americans how the war was almost over. How many years ago that was! And now I'd have to question: Did the U.S. government really believe it then, or was it just another way to deceive the American people?

Also, what really got to me was hearing the casualty reports on the camp radio every day, and regularly seeing the films of bombings, of the suffering of the Vietnamese people. No matter how much you didn't want to, when you saw those films, you just had to believe that the United States was bombing hospitals and schools and neighborhoods where people lived, not just military targets like they said. And when I'd ask myself why my country would do such things, I'd hear Cheese telling us, "The only way one country can force another to surrender is when the majority of the population is made to suffer. But here, this plan will not work, because all the Vietnamese people are determined to fight. No suffering, no matter how great, will stop them from rising up together to save their country."

Somehow, when Cheese said it, you knew it was so—that nothing could make the Vietnamese give up their fight. Their unity could even be seen right in the camp, in the attitudes of the North Vietnamese Army guards, who never fought, never argued, and who were always ready to share with one another. Like eating together out of one large bowl. "No need to divide food," Cheese would say. "Men should be able to eat community style. If there is one bowl of rice, each man knows how much is for him to eat, and he must be considerate of the next man."

And so, the more I saw, the more I heard, the more I read—the more I questioned.

A short time after Thanksgiving, we began to see preparations for Christmas going on when we'd look out the window, or during the daily twenty-minute period outside in the courtyard. Every once in a while, we'd catch a glimpse of the Peace Committee, busy fixing up decorations. They were not restricted to a twenty-minute free period each day, and could come and go as they wanted to.

One day, a few weeks before Christmas, Cheese came into our room and asked how we'd like to celebrate Christmas with the Peace Committee. He called them that, just like everyone else.

"This is your first Christmas in North Vietnam, and you are not familiar with how we celebrate," Cheese said. "We will have a party in the big room of the main building. Each room will come to celebrate, one at a time. Since the Peace Committee is your neighbor, perhaps you would like to celebrate together."

"What about our neighbors on the other side?" Jose asked. "Will Harker and the others be celebrating with the Peace Committee too?"

"That is up to them," Cheese said. "We will permit it if they wish."

"Well, we'd like to talk it over," Jose said. "Can we give you an answer tomorrow?"

Cheese nodded and left the room. Then, the seven of us sat around to discuss it.

"Hell, not me," Long said. "You all can do what you want, but I ain't lookin' to be pegged Commie. An' you can bet your ass that's just how Colonel Guy will have us down."

"Yeah, it's bad enough they got us livin' next to them," Davis said.

The others started yelling out their opinions, mostly against, when Jose held up his hands. "Hold on," he shouted above the voices, "let's think all this through. Now just what if they're getting ready to release some prisoners? The Peace Committee would be the first to go, right? How about if they're lookin' for others to let go with them?"

"You just never know," Ike said. " 'Specially the way all those Christmas decorations are bein' fixed up."

"Not only that, have you noticed all the cleaning up, even whitewashing the walls?" Jose asked.

It kept going around and around. I just sat back and listened.

As far as I was concerned, this was my perfect chance to meet the PC and judge for myself if all the rumors about them were true or just a pack of lies.

As for the possibility that they were looking to release us along with the Peace Committee, Jose had a point. For one thing, we'd been kept right near them when they could have moved us anywhere after taking us out of the end room. Instead, they just shifted us next door. Also, with Long the only white among us, and with only one black in the Peace Committee, together we'd make up a good mixed group to release.

Finally, someone suggested that we talk to the guys in Harker's group next door and get their opinion.

Jose knocked to let them know he was ready, covered his head with a blanket, pressed up against the wall and explained what had happened. "What do you guys think?" he asked, then rapped the signal for them to talk. We stood around waiting as he placed a tin cup against the wall and put his ear to it. A minute later, he turned to us.

"Hark says he wouldn't have a thing to do with those Communist bastards. And he thinks we shouldn't go, either."

So on and on it went, like everybody's life depended on who we celebrated Christmas with. Finally, it was agreed we'd go. Maybe Jose's bait that it could help to get us released had made the difference.

When Cheese returned the next morning, we gave him our verdict.

Just after breakfast on the morning of Christmas Eve, Cheese came to our room and left the door open.

"Today we will not lock your door," he said. "You will not be restricted to twenty minutes outside. Those of you who wish to associate with your neighbors in the Peace Committee may do so. It will be for you to decide."

After Cheese left, we just sat there staring at the open door, hardly believing it. Right then, the six members of the Peace Committee came marching into our room, all smiles. "Hey, how y'all doin'?" one called out. They introduced themselves and we all shook hands. For the next ten minutes or so, all thirteen of us sat around shooting the bull, joking about what a great time we were going to have at the party that night. Then the slight fellow called Chenoweth stood up. "Maybe some of you guys would like to visit over at our room for a while," he said.

Jose and I took off with three of them—Chenoweth, Riati and Young. The other three stayed on and started a card game.

I hardly recognized our old room. The Peace Committee had changed everything around, and now it was all decorated for Christmas. A small Christmas tree stood in the corner.

"It looks great," I said.

"We've still got more to do," Chenoweth said. "Maybe all of you can give us a hand this afternoon. A few of the guards are coming in to shoot some film."

Then, for the next four hours, the five of us sat around and talked. Each of them took a turn explaining why he was in the Peace Committee and the reasons he believed in what he was doing—and why he was convinced the war was wrong. Riati, who was part Indian and could have been taken for a Vietnamese himself, rambled along, slow and intense. Chenoweth, from Portland, Oregon, and very well educated, went on easily in a smooth flow of words. Young, quiet and serious, talked nonstop on the Vietnamese way of life.

By the time they'd finished, I knew I wanted to move in with them. I told them how I agreed with their feelings about the war.

"Why do you feel the war is unjust?" Riati asked.

"For many reasons," I said. "For one thing, I buy the argument that I was not really sent here to fight communism, or to fight for freedom either. Communism exists in many parts of the world, even right in the United States. No need to come to Vietnam to try and stop it. As for freedom, we all know well enough that no such thing exists back home."

Riati nodded. "Hell, I've known that all my life," he said. He jumped up, crossed the room, then returned with a thick packet of papers. "This is a book I wrote," he said. "It's the story of my life with no punches pulled. Maybe you'd like to read it."

When I finished Riati's book a few days later, I almost cried. I could hardly believe the horrible time Riati's family had experienced, the kind of life his mother had been forced into. And I thought how it really takes a good person to be able to tell personal things like that, to try and make others understand.

What Riati explained to me later was that it had been possible for him to write about his life and his family without embarrassment because he really didn't blame his family for what had happened, or for how they had brought him up. Instead, he blamed the conditions they lived under, and he blamed society.

"Why do you think the United States is in this war?" Chenoweth asked me.

"As long as the war and the bombing go on," I said, "a lot of people profit by it. Big business benefits. Corporations make money. But it's all at the expense of the American people. The more money spent on the war, the less there is to help the people at home overcome poverty, or fight cancer, or get an education, or build better schools."

"Exactly," Chenoweth said. "And that's why we do what we do. Because this war is not in the interest of the American people, and it's important to help shorten it, even by a day."

And then Jose asked some questions. And they asked some of him. As I listened, I was completely convinced that if there was any way at all to help end the war as a POW, it was by being a part of the Peace Committee.

"I'd really like to move in with you guys," I said.

"Well, it's important for you to understand a few things first," Chenoweth told me. "For one, the PC is like a dirty word around this camp, and living with us might make things plenty rough on you later on. You might lose your pay, too."

"That's right," Riati said, "you'd have to be prepared for that. If the money is really important to you, it'd be better for you to forget about the PC."

"Sure, the money's important," I said. "But it must mean a lot to you guys, too."

"But we understand the risk," Riati said. "And we've all made up our minds that helping to end the war is worth whatever we sacrifice."

I thought how really different they were from any guys I'd ever met in the army; really devoted, and working for something important, not squabbling and bugging the hell out of one another. And then I had a crazy idea. Maybe, living with them, I might even be able to get across some of my religious beliefs. Maybe they'd be open to a little preaching—not like it was with my bunch.

On the way back to the room, to my surprise Jose agreed that he'd like to move in with the PC, too. Then he added quickly, "But I'd like to see what the other guys in the room think. We can kick it around at lunch."

So, just like always, Jose was not really ready to take a stand until he was sure everyone else was ready, too.

Back at the room, we described the meeting with the PC. I told everyone I was ready to make the move as soon as possible. Then Jose asked, "How about you guys?" without revealing his own opinion.

Long said no right off. Davis followed. Lewis and Ike hedged by saying that they saw nothing wrong with associating with the PC.

"That's no answer!" Jose said, annoyed. "Do you want to move in with them or not?"

"Okay, then," Ike snapped back at him, "the answer is no! I'm not just about to stick my ass out and get it burnt later. And I've got a wife and kids to think about."

"How about you all, Will Daddy?" Davis asked me in his Alabama drawl. "Ain't you afraid of losin' all that loot?"

"Well, let me try and explain how I feel," I said. "You see, no matter what might happen to me if I join the PC, I just don't have any fear about it. I feared before, and I learned my lesson. It was because I was afraid of going to prison that I ended up in the army, and that's what put me right here now. Fear did that. Being afraid —even though I knew the war was wrong, and that what I believed in was right. Well, I'm not fearin' anymore. I'm not going to fear the truth or doing what I think right. I'll just have to take my chances on losing that money."

We had just finished lunch, and everyone sat around listening. I went on. "You see, I was satisfied at first not to associate with the PC, because I really didn't know much about them. Just what I'd heard. And who knew whether to believe that or not? But now, after meeting them, it's all different. I think they're really sincere. And I feel it's important for me to speak out with them, to do something, not just sit back and leave it to the next man."

That afternoon, all of us went to the PC room to help with the remaining Christmas decorations. Two of the guards had their cameras on us when Long got a close look at one of the large drawings on the wall. It was a picture of Santa Claus carrying a huge sack of gifts over one shoulder. One of the packages jutting out of Santa's sack had a message written on its side. It read: "Nixon Sucks!"

Long blew his top and refused to be filmed anywhere near the drawing. The guards allowed him to move away.

It really didn't bother me one way or the other. I kept remembering how Nixon had told the world during the election campaign about his great secret plan to end the war.

That night—Christmas Eve—every POW group was taken, one by one, to what was now called the Christmas Room in the main building. The room was all decorated for the holiday. A large tree was dressed with tinsel and colored lights.

Each group received a personal greeting from the camp commander, drank wine and beer, and sang Christmas carols. Every man was given a small wrapped gift of candy, fruit and cigarettes, donated to the camp by the Catholic Church of the Democratic Republic of Vietnam.

Our room was the last to go, since we were to join the PC for a longer party. In addition to the camp commander, Cheese, Roly-Poly, and several guards were there. Also, a new political officer who, before long, we were all to know very well. Some of the men in the camp, we learned later, already knew him from South Vietnam and had found him to be plenty tough. They called him Mr. Bad.

So we sang, sipped wine, and talked for hours. There was a real holiday spirit, a warmth and friendliness I'd never experienced before in Vietnam.

All that evening, and again on Christmas Day, the radio speakers in each room played Christmas carols and rock and roll. Once on Christmas Eve, and three times Christmas Day, religious programs were broadcast—one for Catholics, another for Protestants. The programs had been recorded weeks before in the radio room by the officer we called Skinny, who also worked for the "Voice of Vietnam."

For the Catholic program, Skinny started out by introducing the priest, who gave a short sermon about the birth of Christ and how the symbol of Christmas was peace on earth. Skinny translated.

"Many Catholics in Hanoi have never experienced Christmas as you POWs have at home," he said. "They have never been able to enjoy a Christmas dinner with their families, or to commemorate the birth of the son of God, Jesus Christ, on Christmas Eve.

Instead, every year, they have known only war and bombs and fighting. It is the obligation of every Christian to see that Peace on Earth will soon come, so that there may be peace in Vietnam, as well as in America."

And then, a Vietnamese choir sang Christmas carols.

A short time later, a similar program for Protestants was played.

The noon meal on Christmas Day, given to every POW in the camp, matched what we would have had back home. It consisted of turkey, beef, french-fried potatoes, salad, noodle soup with clear noodles and meat cooked in, a banana, bread, a bottle of beer and a glass of wine. And to help keep the day festive, each room in the camp was given a bottle of whiskey.

Knowing that turkey was a traditional American Christmas dinner, the Vietnamese had brought them in from the Soviet Union and raised them especially for the holiday. Actually, I think, POWs in North Vietnam were just about the only people in the country eating turkey at that time.

On the day after Christmas, Cheese left our door open again. Only now, the old fears were back. Most of the guys refused to go out. Once more, they decided it was better for them not to be seen associating with the Peace Committee. And just to make sure they weren't tempted, it had been voted to ask the camp commander to keep the door closed and locked.

Lewis and Ike had disagreed. They thought it just didn't make sense to be limited to twenty minutes of freedom when they didn't have to be. They'd argued that to worry about "being seen" with the PC was foolish, since the courtyard was blocked off and couldn't be observed by other prisoners anyway. However, when Hark passed the word that now many of the POWs in the camp had decided all of us were buddy-buddy with the PC, probably because of attending the Christmas party together, that had settled it.

It really didn't matter to me what decision they made. I fully intended to visit with the Peace Committee, and told them so. I was with them that entire day, returning only for meals and to sleep.

The following day, December 27, the door of the room was locked again. After breakfast, I called to Turn Key and asked to be allowed out.

The better I got to know the PC—I had now spent time with the other three members, Kavanaugh, Rayford and Branch—the more I was convinced that living with them was the only answer for me. I wrote a letter to the camp commander and asked to be moved as quickly as possible.

Back in my own room that night, I told everyone that I expected to move very soon. They all crowded around me, shook my hand, and wished me luck. Everyone, except Long, told me how they really sympathized with what I was doing, even though they couldn't do it themselves. But they understood, they said. And when we returned to the States, if I ran into any problems, they'd do anything possible to help.

I was really touched and couldn't help feeling sad to be leaving them, despite all the arguments and bickering of the past months. After all, we'd spent a big chunk of time together, and in a way they were almost like family. For the moment I even forgot how, just a few days before, Jose and a few of the others had given me a hard time, saying how I really wanted to move only for the extra food and cigarettes it was rumored the PC received.

The next morning, December 28, while I was over at the Peace Committee's room, Cheese came in. He turned to me and smiled. "Okay, Da"—he called me by my Vietnamese name—"you can move now."

Chenoweth, Riati and Kavanaugh went back with me to help carry my belongings. None of the guys were there—all of them had been taken out for a bath. By the time they returned, I was completely moved out.

Within minutes, the shouting started. Everyone, except for Davis and Lewis, took part in it. "Hey, Will Daddy, you traitor, you really did it!" "Traitor Daly, Traitor Daly!" "You just like the Prince and the Pauper, Daly—moved from rags to riches!" "Our day will come, too, Daly, you traitor!" I wasn't surprised by it. Still, it hurt. It made me sad.

But I soon forgot it. Now, there were too many other things to think about. No more empty, wasted days. Instead, a new understanding. A new way of living—and sharing.

A whole new world of ideas.

CHAPTER 21

The Letter, North Vietnam

Each man in the Peace Committee did his own thing. It was like a library situation, in a way. Whenever we weren't involved working together on some particular project, like a new issue of the magazine, each of us was on his own. We could stay in or go out. We could exercise or play basketball. We could read, study, or write.

Cheese brought in different books and magazines. It was up to us to decide which ones, if any, we wanted to read. Bob Chenoweth, for instance, was interested in world history, so he pored over all the available foreign publications and was always making maps or taking notes.

Of all the guys, Chenoweth was really the center of the group, the best-informed, I thought, and the most involved. As I got to know him, it was surprising to me how he'd come to accept the Vietnamese point of view on so many things, considering his well-to-do background and life in Portland, Oregon. Yet he probably had a greater understanding of the war and its problems than any one of us. He even looked scholarly—slim, wearing glasses, like he might have been a student or serious businessman. Watching Chenoweth work and study, I really admired him.

After I joined the Peace Committee, one of the greatest influences on me—on all of us, I think—was the new political officer, Mr. Bad. A professor in civilian life, he had taken over for Cheese. There was just about nothing at all he couldn't talk about or explain. We had an idea that the camp commander had not been completely satisfied with indoctrination results under Cheese.

At first, Mr. Bad spent most of his time with the POW officers, so we didn't get to see him that often. Then, each of us began to be called in for private sessions with him, as we had been with Cheese. And, more and more, he'd just drop in unexpectedly to talk.

We realized immediately how different Mr. Bad was from Cheese. Where Cheese had often avoided answering a question, or couldn't really express his ideas successfully, not so with Mr. Bad. He had answers for everything.

During our first private meeting, Mr. Bad covered many of the same personal areas that I had discussed with Cheese. When he wanted to know why I had joined the Peace Committee, I explained my reasons.

Then he asked, "But do you understand the war, Daly? What do you think it's all about?"

I answered this as best I could. He nodded. "Yes, you understand much," he said. "I think you will find it very worthwhile to work with me."

One of the subjects I looked forward to discussing with Mr. Bad was religion. I'd discovered quickly after moving in with the PC that, if anything, they were less into religion than the last group, especially those who were more sympathetic to communist philosophy. Two of the guys, Kavanaugh and Branch, were quite religious, each in his own way. Sometimes we'd get into it. But for the most part, I never really had the chance to spell out my thinking to the members of the PC, and I never was completely satisfied with what some of them argued as the nonbeliever's point of view, either.

In one of the earlier sessions with Mr. Bad, I asked him, "Why does communism reject religion?"

Before replying, he said, "Well, why do you believe in it, Daly? Why is it, do you think, that those who are religious have hopes for some kind of everlasting, happy afterlife? Have you thought why? Have you ever considered what kind of people are drawn to such beliefs?"

"Yes, I think I have. I studied with the Jehovah's Witnesses."

"Then you will agree that it has always been the poor, the lowest economic class, that has turned to religion, starting back in

Biblical times, when it was the slaves. Organized religion is directed to the poor; it tells them that the rich can never enter into what is called the Kingdom of Heaven, because money is the root of all evil. Religion tells the poor man that he has more of God's favor than the rich; it asks him to be faithful, to be obedient, to accept his suffering. Then, the poor man is told, in the afterlife he will be happy—and since he has nothing else to hope for, he accepts this. So you see, Daly, religion plays a very important role for the ruling class. It keeps the rich, rich—and the poor, poor."

As Mr. Bad spoke, I suddenly had a flash of my Brooklyn neighborhood, the slum streets of Bedford-Stuyvesant, jampacked with churches everywhere.

As if he were reading my thoughts, Mr. Bad said, "All the churches in your country—think of the great amount of money they collect. If that money were used to make life better for the poor, to give education, no tax money would be needed for such things in the United States. Instead, the church money goes into investments. Some of your churches even invest in military and make profits from the war."

Now, again, I found myself thinking back, this time to 1962, when I left the Cornerstone Church in Brooklyn, the second largest Baptist Church in New York City. And I remembered how it was because I resented the collections that were taken all the time, sometimes as many as six in one day, some asking for hundred-dollar contributions, or telling the congregation how no coins were to be given, only "greenbacks."

So in ways like that during my meetings with Mr. Bad, I'd often associate some point to personal things that had happened in the past, only now I'd think of them differently. Many times, a theory of Mr. Bad's was one that I had never seriously questioned before.

I began to see that, like most people, I had accepted many religious beliefs on faith. As much preaching, talking and arguing as I did, I'd never really been stimulated into wondering about a lot of it before.

Whenever Mr. Bad visited our room, if someone asked a question he'd always be happy to answer it. Then, liking to talk the way he did, before you knew it he'd be on to something else. Sometimes he'd just go on talking for an hour or more. But we liked it. That's the way we learned, just listening to Mr. Bad talk.

As a member of the PC, none of us were forced or pushed into doing any writing or studying, not by the camp or the others in the group. And, as with any bunch of guys, each one of us was different and had different ideas about things. Still, there'd be few arguments and it was easy to talk together, except maybe on the touchier subjects, politics and religion. We even practiced self-criticism, honestly, telling both the good and the bad—and it worked, not like in South Vietnam.

Right from the start, I'd wanted to be involved doing things. I wrote two letters in protest of the war and two articles for the magazine. If a letter was considered really good, it was taped and played on the "Voice of Vietnam." That didn't happen with either of mine.

The articles were entitled, "A Soldier and a Christian" and "The Vietnam War Through the Eyes of a Conscientious Objector." In the first article, I wrote about the Jehovah's Witnesses teachings that a man couldn't belong to the church, to God's army, and belong to a military army at the same time. In the second, I wrote about some of the things I saw happen in Vietnam, things I saw the U.S. Army do that were contrary to my religious teachings and to what I believed.

It annoyed all of us in the PC that we never received any comments or criticism on the magazine. Mr. Bad's only reaction to my articles, or to the whole magazine, was, "We appreciate whatever you do." Personally, I thought the two articles were pretty good. Kavanaugh had helped me with them.

The youngest guy in the group, Kavanaugh was very strong on religion himself at that time. He was from Denver, was married, and had one child. Sometimes, as much as I liked Kavanaugh, I thought he was really fanatical about his religious beliefs. Some months later, as he got more into Marxism, he rejected all of them —at least for the time being.

Most of the guys, I realized, had a very open mind when it came to studying communist philosophy and went along with a good part of it. I'd kick around some of the points with them, at first, bringing out the arguments I'd always believed—how, under communism, the state controlled everything, people were forced to accept the government, there was no freedom of religion.

"You believe as you were taught to believe," they would tell me. Then they'd describe how communism worked in North Vietnam, how the country had been improved, how more schools and hospitals had been built, how every kid got an education. Not being informed, I really couldn't argue. So instead, I just listened.

Sometimes, I'd make comparisons between communism and the teachings of Jehovah's Witnesses. Surprisingly, the two weren't always that far apart. And some of the differences left me turned off to particular Jehovah's Witnesses points of view, like the teaching that it was useless to go out into the street to demonstrate, to protest the war that way. Instead, we'd been told, it was better to serve God, get others to believe, that the true answer, and happiness, would be there in the life afterward.

Yet the more I saw in Vietnam, the more I believed how really important it was for everyone to protest—for me, as a soldier and POW, to tell what was going on, to expose the wrongdoing in any way I could.

And the more I talked with Mr. Bad, the more I came to understand that there were very basic differences between many teachings of the church and of Marxism that could never be brought together, no matter how you tried. I don't know if that had any bearing on Kavanaugh getting away from his religious thinking, or on Michael Branch, who stopped praying and saying his rosary every day. I was sorry about this sudden change in Branch, because it bothered me to see someone give up his religious beliefs, even if they were ones I couldn't accept for myself. I asked Branch about it. He denied that the political indoctrination had anything to do with it.

One of the first things I was aware of after joining the PC was the different attitudes of the guards. The ones who'd been friendly before, like Cool Jerk and Sergeant Sook, were even friendlier. And now most of the others always had a greeting or a smile. Often, they'd talk about their personal lives, their homes and families. Some were very knowledgeable, like Turn Key, who'd been a schoolteacher, or another guard who had studied Russian in South Vietnam and helped Chenoweth translate the Russian magazines.

The guards had a volleyball team that played against the teams of other POW camps in the Hanoi area. When it was their turn to play a "home" game, the PC was allowed to come out and cheer them on. It was things like that, getting to know the guards as just people, that after a time almost made it possible to forget what our relationship was—that they were guards and we were prisoners. In fact, as I learned more about the Vietnamese people, their struggles and their way of life, the easier it was to think of the guards—who were really the only Vietnamese we knew—as good friends.

When I thought back to all the stories I'd heard about how rough the North Vietnamese were supposed to be on POWs, I could hardly believe the way things were. One night I brought it up, and several of the guys told me how it hadn't always been like that.

In the early years of the war, they explained, before the North Vietnamese had much experience with American POWs, they had been very strict. Men would be lined up and beaten if they broke any rules. Even several members of the PC, some years before at a different camp, had been hit for simple things like talking in the room when they weren't supposed to. Little by little, though, all that changed. As the North Vietnamese learned more about the prisoners and began to realize that all Americans weren't hard and cruel, as they'd always thought, they stopped using strong methods, changed their rules, and became more lenient.

I suppose as more Americans got to know the Vietnamese, even the Vietnamese enemy, they began to think of them differently, too. The truth is, as you get to see the human side of a man, it's hard to think of him as some kind of animal, no matter how you'd been taught before.

What really gave me a strong feeling about the Vietnamese people was the chance to get out among them, to actually see how they lived, to watch them going about their daily lives. Before I'd joined the PC, the group had been taken on two trips into Hanoi. Now, another was scheduled, this time to the circus!

Three of us went out together, accompanied by six guards and Mr. Bad. We were all dressed alike—heavy black suits, white shirts, and skinny dark ties. The suits looked like something out of the twenties.

Before going to the circus, we wound our way around the Hanoi streets in two jeeps. Mr. Bad gave us a running commentary.

When we stopped in some residential area or in a park, people crowded around or turned to look at us. It was hard to know for certain if they realized we were prisoners, but many must have known we were Americans. Somehow, the children knew right off. They'd call out to us, *"Mỹ, Mỹ"*—Americans. Never was anyone hostile, and, time and time again, people smiled at us or waved a welcome.

"Twenty years ago," Mr. Bad told us, "there were only one school and three hospitals here. Today it is very different."

To make the point, the jeep drove past several schools.

"Do you know that two million died here of starvation under the French in 1945?" Mr. Bad asked. "At that time, the French put on a campaign to get Catholics to leave the north for the south, to go to zones under French control. Otherwise, they told them, they would be persecuted here. They said to the people, 'Virgin Mary is going to Saigon.'"

As we continued to drive around the city, I was impressed by the clean streets and French-style houses, well kept, even though they were jammed one next to the other. The people, with few exceptions, were neatly dressed in plain, everyday clothes. Markets were busy. Everyone seemed active and looked to be in good spirits. If it wasn't for the many bomb shelters and the few spots that still showed scars of the old bombings, you wouldn't have thought the country was at war. I told this to Mr. Bad.

"Yes, it is true," he said. "But all of the people are very involved with the war, even though it may not look so. Every man and woman is prepared to fight, and almost all of them have their own guns."

I thought about that. If it were true that the government encouraged the North Vietnamese to arm themselves, the people must certainly be squarely behind the war. Otherwise, what better way to bring about a revolution?

I took a harder look at those we passed—mothers with children, older men, youngsters. If these were oppressed people, I decided, it surely didn't show.

At the circus, we sat in front-row seats. All around were Vietnamese families and children, and a number of foreigners were spotted among the audience. I sensed that it was known we were Americans. Yet, throughout the performance, the people simply ignored us, except for an occasional nod or smile.

On the way back to the camp, I told Mr. Bad what a great experience the day had been. He nodded, pleased.

"It is our hope to take all the prisoners in the camp on such trips before they go home," he said. "Perhaps, soon, we shall begin to do this."

As it turned out, it wasn't too long before other POWs in the camp, in addition to the PC, were taken out into Hanoi. But it wasn't the same city, then. Those trips took place after the bombings of April, 1972.

It was April 16, a bright Sunday afternoon, and we were all outside in the courtyard. Several of the guys were reading, two were tossing the basketball, a couple stood shooting the bull with one of the guards.

Many times Mr. Bad had told us how, before long, American planes would bomb Hanoi and Haiphong. It would be a tactic of the United States, he explained, in trying to drive a harder bargain at the conference table. According to Mr. Bad, Nixon would try to force North Vietnam to accept his terms by hitting at the Vietnamese people and making them suffer, destroying areas where they lived in the major cities.

"The United States tried this before when it bombed Hanoi in 1968 and is threatening it again," Mr. Bad said. "I believe it will happen. And many bombs will not be directed to military targets, but to where there are the most people. It is the same theory the United States used against Germany in World War II."

It was hard for me to believe. Even though I'd already seen films of the destruction of some residential areas, I just couldn't imagine U.S. planes intentionally leveling heavily populated areas. But the North Vietnamese believed it. And they expected it to happen any time.

Still, when the B-52 bombers came rolling in that Sunday afternoon, everyone was caught by surprise. By the time the warning was given, we could already hear the planes—and the first bombs were falling on Hanoi before the alarm went off in the city.

By standing on chairs at the window, we had a view over the six-foot wall to the street closest to the camp, one crowded with the familiar two-story houses. It was in a complete state of wild, screaming panic. The raid had been so sudden—and the alarm so late—that swarms of families and children had not made it to the bomb shelters before the first nearby strikes.

As bomb after bomb exploded, some only blocks away, we

took turns on the chairs, staring off into that street of terrified people. And even as the earth shook with the bombs' impact, we were too stunned by all of it to even think of taking cover. All I could picture was some man or woman or little kid being shattered to pieces by an American bomb.

As the raid went on I was suddenly, for the first time in my life, filled with a real hate. I hated every plane and every pilot who flew them. And I felt so sick at what was happening outside that window—so sick and ashamed and sad at what my country was doing to these Vietnamese people—that I started to cry.

A couple of the others cried, too. Until, just like that, all of us were yelling and shouting out our hate for those B–52s, and for the madman who would order them to do this.

After about twenty minutes, the raid ended. During the bombing, Riati had gone over to the bed and started writing. He was still at it, and we crowded around him. After a few minutes, he handed us the written pages to read.

It was a letter to the camp commander, and at first I found it shocking. Riati explained that after watching the bombs fall on Hanoi, he wanted to do anything possible to help end the war. It was not enough, he wrote, just to send letters or make broadcasts. He wanted to do more than that, and he was even ready to consider joining the North Vietnamese army, if that was the only way he could help!

For a minute we all just stood there, thinking over Riati's words. Then Chenoweth and Young asked Riati if they could sign the letter also.

"Well, that's up to you," Riati said. "I wrote it as being only from me since I didn't know if all the rest of you had the same feelings."

Then, one by one, each of us spoke out on how he felt the same and wanted to sign. My going along didn't come easily. My emotions were all for it—but it was like a double-edged knife. I think we all found it hard to believe we would even consider bearing arms against the United States.

CHAPTER 22

Studying the War

The Peace Committee was spreading out and growing. We now had twelve members and had taken over the last four rooms in the building, three for sleeping, one as a study room where we also ate. The study was set up with a desk, book shelves and two tables.

Before getting in the new members of the PC, when there'd only been the seven of us, it had been really fine, everything going along smoothly. We were always friendly toward one another. Despite differences now and then, there was never a quarrel worth remembering.

At that time, Chenoweth was the leader, if you were to think of anyone that way. All of us looked up to him, and there was never any question about his sincerity, involvement, or understanding of the PC goals.

Riati, in his own way, came across the strongest. Half Indian, half Filipino, he was a very emotional guy who really took a strong stand on things when he had a mind to, like with the letter during the bombing.

The most studious of the group, next to Chenoweth, were John Young and Michael Branch. Even though they were both always into a book and scribbling notes like crazy, you could have easily taken either one for an athlete. Young was tall and lanky but heavier than he looked, and Branch was well built and muscular, too. Young took his studies very seriously and was teaching himself two languages. Whenever he gave an opinion on something political, he sounded like an authority, like his theory was the only way it could possibly be. Branch was still into his religion at that time.

Rayford, whose whole name was King David Rayford, the other black in the group, was the one guy with a different background as far as family ties went. Everyone else had still been with his family right up to the army: Chenoweth, fairly well off, from Portland; Riati from a large poor family in California; Young, living a middle-class family life in Illinois; Kavanaugh, from Denver, married and a father himself; and Branch, brought up in a religious family in the small town of Allen Heights, Kentucky. But Rayford, who was originally from Mississippi and then moved to Chicago, had left his home at an early age. He'd made his own way ever since, often a free and wild kind of life that might have been the envy of some of the guys, but wouldn't have gone over too big back at my church in Brooklyn.

One of my early run-ins after joining the PC was with Rayford when he defended some POWs who went around demanding more privileges and calling the guards "gooks." I told him how none of us were in a position to demand anything. The way I saw it, we should consider it a blessing we were alive and being treated as good as we were.

"But we're *Americans*," Rayford argued.

"That's no big deal here," I said. "And it don't entitle us to put down the Vietnamese. We're no better!"

But squabbles like that seldom happened, though things might get a little hot sometimes when we argued politics or religion, the two touchy subjects. Aside from that, we just about never blew up at one another. We pooled our cigarettes and ate community style, like the Vietnamese. We always enjoyed sitting around together at the end of the day, just talking, or listening to the "Voice of Vietnam" play American recordings, like Frank Sinatra or Bob Dylan. And we refrained from cursing—at least, most of the time.

It continued like this, easygoing and friendly, even after Fred Elbert came in, the first of the new members. Since I'd known Fred in South Vietnam, I filled the guys in about him, how he was from a well-to-do family on Long Island, and whatever else I could remember.

In order to get to know someone before he moved in with us,

we'd been allowed to put him on a three-day trial, then to take a vote. Elbert passed with no trouble.

There was a short period of time before the next four POWs joined the PC, first one, then three right together, one after the other. During those weeks while we were still only seven, the routine of the camp went along with no fuss. Mr. Bad or Cheese held classes regularly, and every once in a while the camp brought in a special political officer to bring us up to date on the antiwar movement in the United States. It was important for us to understand the strength of the antiwar sentiment back home because this could influence how we might appeal to the American public in our letters.

When there were no regular classes, we ran our own on various subjects. Chenoweth taught us English. We gave ourselves history lessons, working our way through the countries. Africa was the first continent we covered, and before long we'd made great progress. Our main limitation was the few books available to us, so we'd dig out information from any source we could find: foreign magazines, Vietnamese study books, or copies of the *Daily World*, the Communist newspaper published in the United States.

We always kept up on the news over the radio, and we were aware of most things as they happened or at least, what news was broadcast: the U.S. Senate debate on the resumption of bombing in North Vietnam, how the South Vietnam Third Division fled in Quang Tri, the charge by the North Vietnamese delegation in Paris that the United States bombed dikes in Vietnam.

Also, surprisingly, the books made available to us began to change. We were given the *Pentagon Papers* to read; some antiwar plays performed in the United States; the autobiography of Malcolm X; a book by George E. Smith, a prisoner of the VC who had been released; *The Enemy* by Felix Greene; a number of others; and then, though we could hardly believe it, *The Godfather.*

The *Pentagon Papers* were read over the in-camp radio show that was put on every day. Kushner read them. Each day, the POWs put a program together which was broadcast into the rooms by different prisoners, reading from a script. War news was read —the U.S. casualty figures and how many planes were lost. Then sports, like baseball results. At one time, Colonel Guy had passed along the order that no POWs should agree to present any of the programs. A couple of days later, he did one himself.

During this period, there were more trips into Hanoi—visits to an army museum, to the Vietnamese National Theater. We were also taken into the bombed areas, shown the destruction of houses and schools, the damage to Universal Park.

One stop I'll never ever forget was at a hospital in Hanoi. We were led inside and shown a group of deformed babies, born like that because their mothers had eaten crops sprayed with poison from American planes.

My sessions with Mr. Bad took us deeper and deeper into things. The further along I went with my readings—I was well into Marx and Lenin now—the more we were able to discuss the nitty-gritty of communist and socialist philosophy. Learning was exciting, just knowing what these political and economic teachings were, even if I didn't buy all of them. And one thing was for sure, there was a heck of a lot more to communism than I had always thought, not just the simple ideas about it I'd always had—that it was a system where all the workers worked for the state, where everybody was supposed to own and share together one day in the future (but meanwhile were miserable), where the system was forced upon all the people at first, where there was no freedom of religion.

During one of my talks with Mr. Bad, I told him how I'd always believed that the Communists outlawed religion.

"That is not so," he said. "We permit religion. It is the people themselves who turn away from it as they become educated."

As time went on, I was aware more than ever how the teachings of both the Jehovah's Witnesses and communism had many common goals, like peace and happy lives for the people. But where communism fought and struggled against what it believed to be wrong, the Jehovah's Witnesses saw the pain and suffering and corruption of today's world as signs that its end was near and the day of reckoning was coming. They found justification for this belief in the Bible.

When I brought up the subject of the Bible with Mr. Bad, he asked, "Daly, who wrote the King James version of the Bible, the one used by so many Americans? Who was King James?—the King of England in the 1600s, right? And King James was the head of a great power, much like the United States today. And under the rule of King James, many people suffered, many were killed. Then how could such a man translate God's works? How could he claim to be a man of God? If he was, how is it possible he could put thousands to death?"

He went on for some time about the Bible and King James, talking nonstop like he did whenever he became involved in what he was saying. Then he repeated, "But you must understand, Daly, that here we do not prevent the people from practicing any religion. As they learn, as they become educated, they give it up. And with this education, other important changes happen. The people improve the way they live. North Vietnam is now greatly changed from how it was before 1945, when we were a backward country. Without education this could not have happened. Just as in your country, a man born in the ghetto will never be able to improve himself as long as he is denied the opportunity of an education. He will continue to live in dirt and filth, a way of life forced upon him by society."

And as Mr. Bad said this, I thought how back in Bed-Stuy I'd known families who were really good people and who tried as best they could to keep a clean house, without being able to.

Mr. Bad always taught and made his points like that. He'd be certain to base at least part of what he said on things we knew to be the truth. Then all the rest was much easier to accept.

And the surprising thing was, Mr. Bad would be the first to admit that his indoctrination was a kind of brainwashing. Only the word had a different meaning for him.

"When you brainwash a person, you tell him the truth," he said.

And whenever Mr. Bad asked a really important question, one that was supposed to make you think, he'd always time it perfectly. Like once, after a long discussion on religion, one that had me going on about the teachings of the Jehovah's Witnesses, he said, "Daly, do you think you lived according to the moral beliefs of the Jehovah's Witnesses?"

I didn't answer right away. Then I admitted, "The truth is, though I felt I believed, I often did not put the teachings into practice. Maybe that's why I always held off on joining. I think if one *really* believes, he will do. That if you do not have the good works, you cannot be a believer!"

After that, more than ever, I had to question just where I stood.

At last, I received a letter from home. It was great to hear that everyone was okay, and to learn that my mother had received my Christmas letter and a tape of my voice. I wrote back immediately, asking her to send me more news of everyone and photos.

Within a short time of each other, four more joined the PC following Fred Elbert: Don MacPhail, Jon Caviani, John Sparks and Dennis Tellier. Branch had been dead set against admitting any of them. We should have listened to him.

After the trial period and interviews, Branch was not at all convinced that the four were sincere in why they wanted in—and, actually, we all had our doubts. We wondered if they'd understand our studying books by Marx and Lenin. We even considered the crazy possibility that maybe they were put up to joining the Peace Committee as spies for Colonel Guy.

I had my own theory. For weeks, Mr. Bad had been talking to us about the importance of unity, stressing over and over that if it wasn't for the unity of North Vietnam, where thirty-three minority groups had been united as one, the country could never successfully defend itself against such a powerful enemy as the United States.

"It took me years to fully understand the importance of this," he said. "Now tell me, do you think you have unity in your group?"

We told him yes. He asked, "Then nobody can divide you, right?"

Remembering these talks, I couldn't help wondering if Mr. Bad was encouraging the bringing in of the new men as a test, if he knew all the time that as soon as they started to live with us our peaceful times would soon be over.

Whether planned or not, it didn't take long for the trouble to start.

The way I figured it, each of the four had his own reasons for wanting to get in with us. John Sparks had been in the PC when it first began. The end of the war looked a long way off then, and the guys had started to talk about the idea of remaining in Vietnam. That's when he'd gotten out. Now, with the peace talks in full swing, he probably thought: Why not wait it out a little more comfortably?

Tellier, who seemed a nice enough guy, was a little on the nervous side. He'd been in a room with sick POWs, and they complained to Cheese that his walking around all day disturbed them. They wanted him out and gave him a hard time about it. Tellier knew that the only way to make a move was to say he wanted to protest the war and ask to join the PC.

MacPhail was really against the war, I decided. Still, I sensed other personal reasons for wanting in. Maybe the extra privileges.

As for Caviani, he was different. Older than the rest of us, he came from a well-to-do family in California that owned land and was into a winery. As I saw it, Caviani left the room he was in because he just couldn't get along. I knew he certainly bugged the hell out of me. Especially when he got into telling his war stories, ones in which he was always the hero.

As the new men came in, we were given the extra rooms. First, we had two. Then we were spread into four, one as the study. To do this, the other groups in the building next to us had been moved into another part of the camp, and the entire small section of the courtyard became ours, set off by a specially built tar wall.

With the new rooms, some of the guys shifted around a few times, but I always lived with the same group—Chenoweth, Young, Branch and Elbert. Somehow we always stuck together. Even after the arguments started.

Thinking back on it, it's easier to understand how Caviani began to influence some of the guys the way he did. In most POW groups, there was one guy who was especially looked up to, usually because he was the brightest. In South Vietnam, it was always Kushner. In the PC, before Caviani came in, everyone turned to Chenoweth all the time. Then a guy like Caviani would come along—older, wealthy, college-educated.

One of the first things I noticed was how after Caviani started to work in the camp flower garden every day, it was no time before Riati went out with him to mess with the flowers. Then you'd always see the two of them together. Soon, Kavanaugh and Rayford began to hang around with them all the time, and, before long, Sparks and MacPhail, too. Little by little, they started to stick by themselves.

The split started without any of us realizing it, and we only found out later why it kept getting wider. What we didn't know was that Caviani was going from one guy to another, spreading rumors, like telling someone that he was being put down by someone else in the other room, things like that. Before long, half the guys were carrying grudges against somebody. The atmosphere was seldom ever friendly, the way it had been. And though there still weren't any out-and-out arguments or fights at that time, we were really split right down the middle. One room didn't visit the other, and soon we weren't even eating at the same table.

Then the idea got around that maybe all of us in the PC had really been brainwashed by the North Vietnamese after all, that they only let us believe we were making our own decisions about things. I was really surprised when I heard Riati and Kavanaugh talk like that, and my guess was that Caviani had got them thinking that way.

Next thing, fighting started. Even among guys in the same room. Stupid fights, over nothing. Like when Riati and Tellier came out of the bath punching away at one another until the guards broke it up.

Riati was screaming about how he was fed up with everything, and started up again about how he was tired of being brainwashed by the Vietnamese, how he hated them.

I called him on it. I was really angry at what he had said, and, without thinking, I blurted out, "How can you say that? How can you say you hate the North Vietnamese when you wrote that letter April 16th? You were willing to consider never going home again for the NVA then!"

Suddenly there was dead silence. All of us had agreed to say nothing about the letter to the new members of the PC because we figured they just wouldn't understand. And we just never knew whether they might make trouble over it. Now, the four of them stared at us in surprise. Immediately I realized I'd made a bad mistake.

At last, Riati spoke. He was calmer now and explained that he had been angry before—how he really hadn't meant what he'd said about the Vietnamese. He'd just been blowing off steam.

Remembering how many times I'd heard Riati speak sympathetically about the Vietnamese, how he even spent most afternoons with one of the guards so he could learn Vietnamese songs, I believed him. But then I wondered what had gotten into him. What was it that was bugging all of us, pulling us apart?

After several more silly fistfights, Mr. Bad called all of us in. "We must get to the root of the problem," he said. "There must be a reason for all of this trouble."

We all insisted that there was nothing really wrong. Actually, none of us did understand it then. My group talked every night, wondering how we could straighten things out, get it all back to where it was.

Then, Caviani told Mr. Bad that some of the guys didn't want to study communism like the others. He claimed this was behind most of the trouble.

The next day, all literature was taken out of the sleeping rooms. We were told that there were to be no more open political discussions.

Nothing changed. In fact, the arguments and tension got so bad, several of the guys were talking about getting out of the Peace Committee. Some wrote letters to the camp commander.

Then, just around the time that the peace agreements in Paris looked like they might be on the track again, we came to understand the real source of the trouble. Rayford started it by coming over to our group one night to visit. As we talked, little by little we began to realize how rumors had been passed around, stories that had no truth to them at all. Like how several of the guys were supposed to have made remarks about Rayford, or how Riati was supposed to have gone around saying he was liked more by the Vietnamese than the rest of us because, as a mixture of Indian and Filipino, he looked more like them. Crazy things like that.

But after a while, I came to realize more and more that as a POW, as much as you're aware of the world outside and the war, and as deeply involved as you can get in talk of politics, or religion, or anything—still, your real world is right there in those few rooms. And it's like everybody in your world is just those other POWs, the guards, and the officers. After a while, living like that, things can get all out of proportion.

Every day now we kept hearing about the agreements on the "Voice of Vietnam." If anything really brought us together again, it was that. We realized how important it was for us to discuss the problems we might have to face after being released.

So we started meeting at night on flower hill. At first, it was the five from my room; then, Rayford, Riati, and Kavanaugh strayed along. Soon, the eight of us were out there every night, trying to decide what made the most sense for us to do.

There was no question that the other four could make trouble for us if they went to the army with stories, or told about the April

16th letter. No way would the military understand that. Or many other things, either. Unless all twelve guys were really together— able to explain things, if they came up, in the right way. Other- wise, anything could happen. With any members of the PC testify- ing against the others, it could mean charges, or even prison.

Night after night, we kicked it around. As far as the eight of us were concerned, we knew enough now not to count on the other four. No matter how many times they'd tried to make it seem that they thought and believed as we did, somehow, all of us had always had our doubts. Now, with it beginning to look like the peace agreements could happen any day, it was clearer than ever that MacPhail, Sparks, Tellier and Caviani were withdrawn from the rest of us.

The more we examined the situation, the more it began to seem as if there was only one choice for us, and it wasn't the greatest: not to return to the United States at all. To request asylum in Sweden. Or if that didn't work, to remain in Vietnam.

I wasn't very happy about the decision. And I wondered, if it came right down to it, whether I'd be able to stick to it. When I thought how it could mean I'd never see my family again, I began to doubt it very much.

When we told Mr. Bad of our decision to ask for asylum in Sweden, at first he didn't come right out and say he believed we shouldn't, but it was clear that's what he thought. He told us that he didn't think the army would ever bring us up on charges, and that if we really wanted to help the American people, the place to do it was back in the United States.

Using one of Mr. Bad's favorite lines, we said, "We appreciate your trying to help us, but we know the U.S. government better than you, and we think we'll end up thrown into prison."

"You lived there, it is true," Mr. Bad said, "but we can almost guarantee it will not happen. Other prisoners will think very care- fully before testifying against any of you. Remember, we have signed letters and information about them in our files, and we will not hesitate to use them. Also, the peace agreements will stipulate that neither side will take action against prisoners for any antiwar activity while in captivity."

We told Mr. Bad we'd continue to think about it, but mean- while we wanted to write a letter to the Swedish Embassy in Vietnam.

A few nights later, MacPhail and Caviani came by to talk with me. The three of us went outside, away from the others.

"We know you're not like the rest," they said. Then they tried to convince me I should return home, how important it was for me if I wanted to be active in the Jehovah's Witnesses. What they had no way of knowing, of course, was that by then I had serious doubts about joining the church.

Meanwhile, Mr. Bad saw to it that our letter was sent to the Swedish Embassy. At the same time, he started on a real campaign to try to influence us to go back to the States after being released. Every week or so, a special high-ranking Vietnamese officer came to the camp to lecture the eight of us. They showed us news stories and other reports on how strong the antiwar movement in the United States had become, pointing out, over and over, that many Americans would support us if we returned.

We continued to stick to our decision, even though some of us wavered every now and then. At least, the way the peace talks were dragging, it looked as if there was still time to change our minds if we wanted to.

Right about then, we noticed from our window how a flow of trucks and buses was moving people out of the area. We asked Mr. Bad about it.

"We are evacuating old women and children from parts of Hanoi," he explained. "We still believe, as we always have, that before the agreements are signed and the war is over, the United States will destroy Hanoi and Haiphong. It will be one last attempt to make us surrender—by bombing to the ground the cities in which we take the most pride."

"Then why does Kissinger go on negotiating?" I asked.

Mr. Bad smiled. "You must remember, your President Nixon is a very smart man. He knows how to fool the people. With your elections coming soon, it is important for Nixon to look as if he is ready to make peace. However, the capitalistic countries do not have the mentality to understand that a nation like ours will survive anything they can do to us. We will never surrender. In the end, the United States will be forced to sign the agreements."

It was hard for us to believe that the United States was getting ready to begin large-scale bombings of Hanoi with peace so close. But the NVA had no doubt of it. Large-scale models of planes were hung from the trees in the camp for the guards to practice shooting. A machine gun was mounted on the roof of our building.

As the weeks went on, the peace talks seemed to run into one snag after the other. We were beginning to think they'd never work out, when, one afternoon, the announcement came over the "Voice of Vietnam"—at last, final agreements had been reached. After many concessions by both sides, the papers were to be signed by the end of October!

The whole camp went wild! Hollering and shouting went on all that day and night. All the doors were opened and the prisoners were allowed out in their immediate areas—enlisted men, officers, and, separately, the Peace Committee.

But Mr. Bad told us, "Do not build up your hopes. It could mean a great disappointment for you."

He was right. Once again, the agreements weren't signed. Kissinger, who was supposed to come to Hanoi to initial them, never showed. And Nguyen Van Thieu denounced them as unacceptable to South Vietnam.

It was to be much later that the American people would learn what really had happened. A report in a magazine published in the States would show how, as amazing as Mr. Bad's claims had sounded, somehow he really had known exactly what he was talking about all along.

The study by Tad Szulc, a former *New York Times* correspondent, was based on unpublished documents and revealed how Kissinger had met with Nguyen Van Thieu in Saigon back in July and admitted to him that the United States had to talk peace because of the upcoming election, but that once the votes were in, America was prepared to really bombard the north. Kissinger even recommended that Thieu plan to invade the north after the election.

According to the study, on October 21, Nixon cabled North Vietnam that "the text of the agreement could be considered complete." Then, in November, he sabotaged the agreements by bringing many new changes and issues into the peace talks, knowing North Vietnam couldn't accept them. Now it was possible for the United States to bomb Hanoi—and keep Thieu happy at the same time.

The failure of the agreements in October really tore down the morale at the camp. One more time, the prisoners' hopes for freedom had been shattered. But then, when I recalled one of

Nixon's speeches, it didn't seem too surprising that he wasn't all that bothered about us. I remembered how he'd said, at a time when he was being pressured to bring the POWs home, that five hundred prisoners could not decide the policies of the United States. I suppose, had I felt the war was justified, I'd have been able to go along with that.

Then, with Christmas less than a month away, the POWs in the camp realized once again they were not to be home for the holidays. The Peace Committee started to make decorations and displays for the "Christmas Room" where, as in years past, parties were to be held for each of the rooms. Only this time, all the original members of the PC weren't very enthusiastic about it. They told Cheese how they believed the other POWs really couldn't care less about how the room looked, that as long as they got the special Christmas dinner they'd be happy.

"Why don't we just forget it this year, Cheese?" they asked. We always called him "Cheese," not like the other POWs, who only referred to him that way when he wasn't around. He never seemed to mind the name.

"No—it is your holiday," Cheese said. "The big room should be decorated as the camp commander wishes."

Late in November, the camp started to allow two and three rooms out together at the same time. This had never happened before, and it encouraged the men to think that maybe the signing of the agreements would happen soon, after all.

Then, one week before Christmas, the final preparations for the holiday stopped cold. The following twelve days and twelve nights were to be the worst period of time I'd ever experienced during my five years in captivity!

CHAPTER 23

Plantation Gardens, Hanoi, Christmas 1972

It was late in the afternoon, about six-thirty. All twelve of us were taking a bath when the siren went off.

Just hours before, one of the guards had told us, "Tonight they will bomb Hanoi with seventy-five B–52s!" No one had known just when. Now—we all knew.

We raced back to our room half-naked, still wet. The same five of us were still living together—Branch, Young, Chenoweth, Elbert and me.

Minutes after we got inside the room, it was like an earthquake. All the lights in the camp, and in the city outside, had been blacked out. And as the first bombs started to explode, I knew it was really different than it had been in April. This time it was right at us!

The building was shaking so bad I thought for sure it would come crashing down. At first, we were too scared to go near the window. We just sat down on the floor, lit cigarettes, and tried to keep talking.

Bombs hit really close. Railroad tracks and a bridge, just beyond the residential area outside the wall, probably were the targets. But the strikes, practically right in the courtyard, told us that the entire area—streets crowded with houses—was catching the worst of it.

Suddenly Cheese was pounding at our window. He yelled to us to stay under the beds until a guard came around with shovels.

Then we were to dig a long bomb shelter along one wall of the room.

We didn't bother taking cover, although the beds, each one a board covered with a straw mat, supported by wooden horses, could have served as pretty good protection. Instead, we just sat there, feeling the ground shake under us.

About ten minutes later, a guard dropped off the shovels, and, with the raid going full-blast, we started digging. First we had to break through the cement floors, and it was really hard going.

The bombing seemed to go on forever, the roar of the B–52s deafening. Right in with it, we could hear weapons being fired from the street and the automatic machine gun blasting away from our roof. It was possible to make out cries of pain and horror from the people in the Hanoi neighborhood just outside the wall.

I pictured those streets—rows of houses, all close together. I imagined them being blasted to pieces. And I could see the dead with each strike, forty, fifty, sixty. I kept asking myself, over and over, how can we do it?

Then I thought how there probably had never been any moral question involved from the military point of view. Just as long as it was the United States dropping those bombs, that made it okay. That made it morally right. And most any army chaplain would be ready to give those planes his blessing, just like the ministers in the field had blessed the soldiers and asked that they be protected— while they were out killing other men. And here I'd always believed religion was supposed to be teaching you to love your enemy, not offering special prayers to keep you protected while you murdered them. Well, maybe the Jehovah's Witnesses did teach we're not supposed to have political views, that all governments on earth are wrong, and that we can never achieve peace in the world by protesting, because peace can only come to man through God . . . but right then, I couldn't buy it. As I imagined that city of people being destroyed all around me, I knew for sure I just couldn't wait for God to do away with all wickedness. Because what was happening out there was plenty wicked, was plenty wrong, and I planned on speaking out against it every chance I got.

And now, as we dug away, wondering if the very next strike was to be on us, we cursed every plane in the sky, and we cursed the man who'd put them there.

Finally we just couldn't stand it. Shouting out our hatred, our sense of horror, we ran to the window. The scene outside was not to be believed.

The courtyard was spotted with guards, out in the open, firing away. But the really amazing sight, the one I'd never ever forget, was outside the wall, on that narrow street of two-story houses.

As fires burned, as houses came crumbling down, as the wounded cried out, the people of that street were out fighting against the swarm of B–52 bombers. They stood lined up along the street—women, old men, little kids—and everyone, just as Mr. Bad had told us, had a weapon. Some were rifles, some hand guns, but everyone had something. And they all stood there, right out in full view, pointing their weapons into the sky.

We could actually see the planes as they made passes and went back up, each zooming down with its horrifying roar, and it was hard for me to understand how these Vietnamese people had the courage to stand up against them. And as I watched the men and women and children, and knew that others of all ages just like them were fighting and dying on streets just like this one, I hated those B–52s more than ever. I understood what these people were fighting for, and I knew what they'd had to undergo for so many, many years. And I just couldn't think of them as enemies at all, but more like brothers and sisters. And I felt so tremendously sorry for them, it was all I had to do to keep from crying again, as I had the last time.

Then, suddenly, there was a huge explosion in the sky as a B–52 caught a missile. It was like an enormous searchlight had been thrown on the entire area.

Even worse than seeing that American plane get hit was the way I felt about it. One of the guys shouted out, "Great! That's one less!" And the horrible truth was, I couldn't help, in a strange kind of way, but think like that, too. I thought how every plane that completed its mission would just mean one more plane that would be back again with more bombs. And for every plane that was shot down, hundreds of people who'd otherwise have been killed would still be alive. And if enough planes were lost, if enough millions of American tax dollars were blown up, then maybe the American people would get angry enough to force a stop to this senseless war.

After thirty-five minutes, the raid stopped. Now there was

quiet, except for the wail of an ambulance siren and the cries and moans of the wounded.

At eleven that night, it started all over again. And a couple of hours later, the B–52s returned for a third time. We made it to bed that night at two-thirty.

The bombings went on, night after night, following the same pattern. Three different raids, always about the same times. We finally finished digging our bomb shelter on the third day.

Just sitting around during those raids, waiting for them to end or for the roof to cave in on us, was driving all of us crazy. Finally, we met with Mr. Bad and asked him if there wasn't something we could do. We wanted to help in any way we could. We offered to do anything, even go out into the streets and carry the wounded.

"We appreciate that you want to help," Mr. Bad said, "but we cannot allow that. It would surely be claimed that we were forcing you to do this, should it become known."

We were so angry at being refused, we actually considered a hunger strike to protest. Once again, we went to Mr. Bad and Cheese about it.

"What you are doing now is very important," Cheese told us. "Your letters are of great value and will surely help to end the war. We highly appreciate your offer, but you must remember that we are here to protect you."

One day, they took us into Hanoi. We were driven in jeeps from one section to the other. Damage was everywhere, rubbish piled high on the sides of the streets. One neighborhood had been completely knocked out. In some areas, we saw factories that had been hit. We also saw wrecked schools, a large market place—and a hospital.

Our jeep turned down the block where the foreign embassies were, and Mr. Bad pointed out where the French mission had been hit in October and the French delegate-general killed. Wherever we drove, we saw people moving things. Children carried baskets loaded with bricks from caved-in buildings, oxcarts transported belongings. The Vietnamese Red Cross was everywhere.

We were slated to go to a museum that afternoon. Minutes after we arrived, the alarm went off. Unexpectedly, it was a daytime raid. We ran back to the jeeps and raced for camp. Just as we sped past the gate, the first planes came sailing in.

Later that afternoon, I had an argument with MacPhail. We had seen one of the newest American planes, an FB–111 bomber, shot down the night before—and he was going on about how terrible it was that so many American planes were being lost.

"Sure it's terrible," I said, "but what about all the thousands of people those bombers are killing?"

"But those are American pilots—American planes!" MacPhail exploded.

"You sound just like people I've heard before," I told him. "Vietnamese lives, even thousands of them, mean nothing. But one American life is a whole lot. Man, I don't want to see nobody die, but I'd rather a few than many, no matter who they are. If in some way I could save many lives by giving my own, by all means I'd do it. Because what is one life, even mine, compared to the lives of many?"

I don't know if I got across. It was that same old argument, how, to some, one American life was more important than a country full of foreigners.

And that really wasn't so different than the basic philosophy of the U.S. military. The way it trained soldiers, they were bound to think like that. That's why I often wondered, when the trial of First Lieutenant William L. Calley, Jr., made the news, why there was so much concern over whether or not he was acting under some special orders when he murdered twenty-two unarmed South Vietnamese civilians at My Lai. As if that would change the right or wrong of it—legally or morally. The truth was, as I saw it, and as I was taught by the army, it was accepted policy to go into a village like that and kill. So, as guilty as Calley was, as guilty as every pilot was who dropped a bomb on civilians, that's how guilty the U.S. Army or Air Force was. For it was often *official* policy to murder defenseless men, women and children.

It wasn't much of a Christmas. There was still no word on our request for asylum, but we were beginning to doubt that it would come through. Even if we were to decide in the end that we weren't going to live in Sweden, it would have been good to know that the choice was there, if we'd wanted it. Now, more than ever, we were really worried about what to do when peace finally came.

On Christmas Eve, each group of POWs went over to the Christmas Room—missing all of its decorations of the year before —to have a drink with the camp commander and to be wished a Merry Christmas on behalf of all the guards and everyone at the camp. They were all short get-togethers, no songs or festivities.

Our group's visit was even shorter. Just as we arrived, the air-raid alarm went off. We missed receiving the camp commander's good wishes—and the drink, too.

All the prisoners had the special Christmas dinner the following day. That morning, as all the food was being prepared on a long table in the courtyard, suddenly an American reconnaissance plane came swooping down over us. The guards ran for their weapons, but in minutes the plane had climbed again and was gone.

Cheese looked after it and laughed. "Oh, I guess they come to see what you will eat today for Christmas," he said.

That evening, we all sat around listening to Christmas carols. Mr. Bad came by to visit. Once again we discussed our conflict with him over what to do when the agreements were signed. Up until then, we hadn't mentioned our idea of staying in Vietnam. Now, with no word on Sweden, we brought it up.

"I still believe that it is best for all of you to return home," he said. "Also, the agreements will be certain to stipulate that all prisoners must be released, and we will be obligated to do this."

He thought for a minute, then said, "There is only one way possible for you to remain here, if that is what you finally decide you must do. You must each take individual action. Once we have released you, we will have carried out our obligation. Then, if you refuse to go, it will be up to you. There will probably be a formal ceremony, and newspaper reporters will be there from all over the world. It will be clear to everyone that the decision to remain was made by you, and we could not be accused of breaking the agreements."

"But who knows when all this will be?" Mr. Bad continued. "Meanwhile, you must consider this decision very carefully. And remember, it is our belief that you can do greater good at home than in another country. There, you will be able to tell the American people the truth about the war."

After Mr. Bad left, the eight of us talked about it into the night. Most of the guys were in favor of staying in Vietnam, if Sweden didn't work out. I just didn't know.

Actually, that Christmas night, the end of the war seemed a million years away. Especially when we received our Christmas present from the U.S. Air Force—an all-out bombing raid, as usual.

Two days later, we were all told to pack our belongings: we were moving to another camp. The raids had been going strong, night after night, the same horrible pounding, the same ear-splitting sound of the B–52s, like thunder. Some of the guys had gotten so edgy, they were ready to jump into the shelter at the first sound of the alarm.

We started loading on trucks about six-thirty in the evening. The back of the open truck was enclosed with canvas, making it impossible to see out. We squatted on the floor with a small group of other prisoners who were blindfolded. Among them was an air force captain—Edward W. Leonard, Jr. I didn't know him then, but I'd heard the older members of the PC talk about him. Seems that some time back, before I'd moved in, Leonard had managed to get close enough to the group in the courtyard to shout out an order that they should stop all antiwar activities. As I'd heard it, the only reply from the guys was to jab a middle finger up into the air.

No sooner had we settled into the truck than the alarm went off. The bombers were right on time for their first raid of the night. We started rolling anyway.

As we bounced along one Hanoi street after the other, we could hear the planes overhead, and every now and then the nearby powerful impact of a strike. None of us were too happy about being out in the middle of it, and we wondered why they couldn't have waited until morning to make the move. Maybe they didn't want the people on the street to see that they were transferring prisoners.

Luckily, it was a short ride. About ten minutes later, we slowed up, turned, then stopped. We had arrived at the biggest POW camp of them all, known as the Hanoi Hilton.

The camp was enormous, the one huge building spread out over a number of city blocks. It had been built by the French and looked like an old castle in a way, some sections in three levels, some in two, and one part of the building one story high. All of it was connected, and one area contained a tremendous courtyard.

The twelve of us were led into a part of the single-level section. There were six rooms, each set up like a barracks, and big enough for twenty prisoners. We had one for ourselves.

As we learned the next day, all of the POWs from Plantation Gardens, plus some new ones—a total of 108—were put into this same area. Three other sections of Hanoi Hilton held different POW camps with American army prisoners, air force pilots shot down in North Vietnam, Germans, Canadians, Filipinos, and some foreign civilians. One area was for Vietnamese who had been jailed for various crimes. When the entire camp was filled, it was capable of holding over ten thousand prisoners!

Since Hanoi Hilton was situated right near North Vietnamese Army headquarters, all the personnel from that building were living there then, because it was considered safer during the bombing raids.

All of us settled into the new camp quickly. The rooms weren't set up for studying as they had been at Plantation Gardens, so most of our time was passed sitting around, reading. Now some of the books were more for enjoyment, like Dickens's *A Christmas Carol* and *Tom Sawyer* by Mark Twain. I read these, but also kept on with the others, trying my best to understand them and asking questions of Mr. Bad whenever I could corner him. As always, he was ready to take off on one subject or another. We covered a whole range of things.

He spoke about how he believed President Johnson had been a good puppet for the business interests in the United States, but how Nixon was the best puppet capitalism had ever had.

Without really getting into it, he said he believed that there was much about President Kennedy that no one knew, and that the whole truth would come out years later.

We spent hours discussing Lenin's *Imperialism, the Highest Stage of Capitalism*, but I noticed he was evasive when it came to answering my questions about the political and economic differences between the Soviet Union and China today.

When we got into religion again, Mr. Bad talked about what he claimed it did to Vietnam—how the country was invaded three thousand years ago by Catholic missionaries who were really being used by their kings as a way of getting a foothold in Vietnam.

Mr. Bad covered the theory of evolution, and tried to show me how, if I bought it, I just couldn't go along with the Biblical approach to things.

He also put down the Christian religious teaching that the man is the head of the family, and talked about how communism accepts both men and women as equals, with no special roles.

There was just about nothing that Mr. Bad wasn't ready to talk about. As always, when he told me his opinions about things, I had the feeling he was making them simple. It was as if he figured how, when you're dealing with a baby, you give him baby food at first. But it was okay with me. I enjoyed listening to him talk. Mr. Bad was very convincing, and, as he put across his ideas, it was hard not to go along with them. But I thought how I had plenty of time to think things through. Sometime in the future, I could make up my mind about what I really accepted—and what I didn't.

At one point, it almost looked as if the peace agreements would be wrecked again. The reason was that the United States continued to bomb, even though it had agreed to stop. We could actually hear the strikes from the Hanoi Hilton, although Hanoi itself wasn't being hit. Finally, when North Vietnam threatened to refuse to release any POWs, the bombings stopped.

A few days later, Mr. Bad told us how North Vietnam had received letters from all over the world congratulating the country for surviving the American bombardment. Many countries had doubted, he explained; even the Soviet Union. China had been the only country to believe they could do it.

Meanwhile, life at the Hanoi Hilton wasn't all that bad. Rather than just sit around, we volunteered to help out in the camp and were assigned to work in the kitchen, rotating two at a time. That's when Riati and I spotted Monica, the German nurse I had known in the South Vietnam prison camp.

She looked very different with her long hair, and I didn't even recognize her at first. Monica wasn't all that pretty or shapely, but as the first female we'd seen in a while, she must have come across as the most fantastic-looking woman in the world when we described her to the guys.

With the bombings stopped, we looked forward to the special New Year's dinner. One thing about the Vietnamese, they never missed a holiday, neither theirs nor ours. In North Vietnam, we always celebrated Christmas, Easter, New Year's and the Fourth of July, plus Vietnam's Independence Day and Tet. In the south, we celebrated the founding of the NLF, too.

We were still up in the air about what to do if the peace agreements were ever signed. I felt a little better about the possibility of returning home after hearing Ramsey Clark over the radio. During his visit to Hanoi, he insisted that any POWs who had made antiwar statements needn't worry about what would happen to them in the United States, how if that was all they did, no action should be taken against them. If it was, Clark said, we could look him up for help. That was good to hear from a former United States Attorney General.

Jane Fonda came right into the Hanoi Hilton around that time, too. She never met any of us, though. No American visitors were ever allowed to see POWs captured in the south—not even Gus Hall, the American Communist leader. Even then, it had never been revealed that prisoners captured in South Vietnam were being held in northern camps. The tapes we had made for broadcasting had never indicated what area we were in.

While at the camp, Jane Fonda met with some of the American pilots who'd been shot down. We listened to her interview of them over the speaker in our room. One of the men she spoke to was well known to all the POWs. I could remember having heard him denounce the war for years when I was in the south, and, since, in Hanoi. He was Captain Walter E. Wilber of the U.S. Navy, who'd been a prisoner almost five years. A short time later, I was to meet him.

Restrictions about going out of our rooms had been relaxed from what they had been when we'd arrived, like they had been those last weeks at Plantation Gardens. All POWs were allowed outside into the small courtyard in our area at the same time, except for the Peace Committee. When we took our time out in the mornings, the others went out in the afternoon. The PC was always kept separate from the other prisoners, and it stayed like that until the signing of the agreements.

Finally, on January 27, that actually happened. Every guy in the camp was really happy about it, only this time there was no celebration, no shouting and hollering. There had been too many disappointments for that. Now, there was less show of joy than there had been in October. Guys could be heard to say, "When the day comes that I'm on that plane, that's when I'll believe it!"

Immediately, with the signing, all restrictions on going out were lifted. Even the PC could mix with the others now.

As tiny as the courtyard in our area was, most of the 108 enlisted men and officers jammed into it. Caviani, Tellier, Mac-Phail and Sparks went charging outside the first day. The rest of us took our time about it.

It didn't take long for the four of them to start talking to Colonel Guy and the other officers, like Colonel Purcell, who until a few weeks before had lived with the German prisoners. After the doors were opened, they just couldn't wait to get to them. Within no time, stories and rumors about us were spreading like crazy throughout the camp. Tellier, who may not have meant to make trouble for us, probably never even realized what harm he was doing. He went around telling everyone about the books we read, saying, "These guys must all be Communists."

Most of the PC didn't go out at all that first day, and the couple who did weren't too warmly accepted by the others. When I went outside on the second day after the signing, I overheard Tellier going on about the books. Later, I took him aside and said, "Dennis, if we were Communists, we wouldn't be prisoners in this camp at all. You really should understand things before you go around talking about them."

After a while, the other prisoners stopped shying away. One by one, they came over to us to talk, but almost always it was to ask questions. The one we were asked the most was, did we plan on going home with the others? When one sergeant who had been with army intelligence wanted to know what I was going to do, I just told him that, according to the agreements, all POWs were to be released and to return home. Didn't he even know that?

Then Mr. Bad called the eight of us into his office. He told us how Caviani, MacPhail, Sparks and Tellier had requested to be moved away from the Peace Committee. Mr. Bad had observed how they'd met with Colonel Guy and the other officers, and now he decided not to allow them to separate from the PC, just like that.

Meanwhile, he told us he thought it would be a good idea if we talked directly to Colonel Guy and Colonel Purcell, too. "You should make them understand how you know about some of the things they did as prisoners," he said. He showed us letters that had been written by both Guy and Purcell, and also some of Kushner's. Among them was one which Kush had written to Congress, and which fourteen POWs, including the eight of us, had signed. What I didn't know then was that my mother had also received a tape of that letter, delivered personally by the army. It had been recorded from the "Voice of Vietnam." Then, two army men had taken it to my mother's apartment so that she could hear first-hand how her son was "helping the enemy."

Mr. Bad also let us listen to tapes that had been made by Colonel Guy and Colonel Purcell. These were antiwar messages which had been broadcast in other POW camps, but which we had never heard before.

"It's very possible that charges could be brought against any of you," Mr. Bad said. "I still believe, as before, that if any action is taken, nothing will come of it—the American people will not allow your government to punish you. However, if there are to be charges, they will probably be against you enlisted men rather than the officers—they will always choose the peons, whom they do not care about. Therefore I advise you to speak to Colonel Guy. Don't sound threatening, but let him get the idea you are aware of the letters and broadcasts."

The next day, Chenoweth and Riati did get to talk with Colonel Guy. Without naming anyone, they got across how we knew that many of the guys in the camp had written letters or made broadcasts at one time or another.

The one who spoke with Guy and Purcell more than any of us was Rayford. It seemed like they cornered him almost every day. Rayford reported back to us that he had been told he'd have nothing to worry about if he returned to the States. The officers claimed they had been told that he'd done nothing wrong.

Maybe they were trying to set up Rayford as a witness against us. Whatever, one thing was made very clear to him: charges were to be brought against the other seven of us.

CHAPTER 24

Free at Last

Later in February, just about all the talk at the camp had something to do with the coming POW release. Every day, the prisoners asked Mr. Bad and Cheese when the first men were scheduled to go.

We knew the time must be getting close. All the prisoners had been given medical check-ups and dental treatment. Those men who showed signs of being run-down or underfed received extra rations, canned goods and meat. Chenoweth, as skinny as ever, was one of these.

Just about then, word came from Sweden that as a neutral country it could not take us in. Now, once again, the eight of us were back to the problem of what to do. If we could believe what Colonel Guy told Rayford, trouble would be waiting for us.

Most of the guys were convinced that it made the most sense not to go back. To stay right there in Vietnam. Chenoweth and Riati were really strong about it. As for me, with the release just a short time off, I knew that what I wanted more than anything was to get home again. I made up my mind that, first chance, I'd tell the guys how I felt.

We were finally separated from Caviani, MacPhail, Sparks and Tellier. We were moved to new quarters in another part of the camp. Right across from us, in a row of small rooms—old cells, really—were Captain Leonard, some Canadian officers, and some missionaries. All of them had been kept apart from the rest of the camp because they'd been captured in Laos and were not to be released with the rest of us.

The prisoners had received some Red Cross packages, and some of us visited with Leonard and his group to share them. They were all very friendly. Influenced by the missionaries, they sang spirituals all the time and held religious services on Sunday. Captain Leonard came across as a really nice guy. Somehow, he reminded me of a minister.

One night, I decided to tell the guys I planned on returning home. We were sitting around talking when I sprung the news.

"I got something to tell you all," I said. "I've been thinking about it for a long time now. When I was first captured, and even before, I always prayed that I could be alive when the war was over so I could see my family again. Now that the time has come, it's something I just have to do. Even if it means going to prison."

Everyone got on me at once. "You'll be a political prisoner, man!" "It's a real stupid move, Daly!" "Nothin's better'n freedom, don't you know that?" Finally, they decided to call in Mr. Bad about it.

He came over a short while later. "Well, he can do whatever he wishes," Mr. Bad said. "It is his decision to make."

Meanwhile, as the days passed, the North Vietnamese left no doubt they preferred that all of us return. They continued calling us into special meetings where a high-ranking NVA officer briefed us on current happenings in the United States—like Watergate. "Nixon is using the POWs to gain support," he said. "None of you will be put into prison."

He explained again how if we didn't return, the United States could always use this as a pretext to break the agreements.

Mr. Bad assured all of us once more that if action was taken against us, information on the other POWs in the camp would be given out to the press.

Next, he explained the procedure for release. The 108 prisoners in our area were to be divided into three groups. The Peace Committee was to be in group number two. The reason for this was so that if there were any problems in turning over the POWs, they'd find out with the release of the first group.

Then, to our surprise, Mr. Bad offered us the chance to go over the lists of POWs and point out which men we'd prefer to have return with us in group number two.

It was announced that all the prisoners at camp were invited to attend a "farewell" show at which the leading performers of North Vietnam would entertain. The show was to be put on several times in the huge courtyard, and each night a different section of the camp was scheduled to go.

We arrived early. Immediately, as we took our seats, we noticed seven men who were not dressed in the pajama-like uniforms of the prisoners. Each wore a blue jacket, pants and a cap. We took them for Russian reporters.

As we sat waiting for the show to start, Chenoweth started talking with the men. After a minute, he turned around to us, grinning. "Hey, you guys, do you know who this is?"

They turned out to be a group of air force pilots, and the one Chen was talking to was none other than Captain Walter Wilber. After hearing his broadcasts for so many years, it was a real kick meeting him, like he was a celebrity. None of us knew then, of course, that Wilber and one other pilot were to be the only two American officers to have charges brought against them.

It was a great show—singers, dancers, the works. As a souvenir, each of us in the PC was given a tape of it.

It wasn't long after the show that the first POWs, including a group of pilots, were released. A story in a Hanoi newspaper showed a photo of Captain Wilber. At the ceremony, when he was turned over to the Americans, he had refused to salute.

About a week later, Mr. Bad asked all of us in the PC if there were any special requests we'd like to make before going home. If so, he would try to fulfill them. We asked for two things. A chance to go to the national theater again—and to be able to eat some authentic Vietnamese dishes.

A few days later, we were taken to the theater. And then, for four days in a row, we had special meals, wonderfully prepared Vietnamese food that we'd never tasted before.

March 14. In two days, we were told by Mr. Bad, the second group of prisoners would be released, including us.

"Once you are all back in the United States," he said, "you will be able to work toward your future goals. Remember, the way of the revolutionary is always to know when to take advantage of the right situation at the right time. And when you care about the masses, you must always ask yourself if what you do—if what decision you make—is best for the majority of people."

"What if we decide it is best for us to stay in Vietnam?" someone asked.

"Then you must make this move on your own, with no official help from us. At the airfield, in front of all the newsmen and cameras, you can be certain that if you refuse to walk over to the waiting Americans, no violence will take place. The United States would look very bad trying to force you on a plane."

The following night, the camp gave the eight of us a farewell party. It was held in another section, away from our area, and we spent several hours drinking beer and wine and singing songs.

All the guards were there: Cool Jerk, Turn Key, Sergeant Sook, Monkey Man, Judo Joe. Cheese, Mr. Bad, Skinny and several other officers, too. Even the camp commander attended.

At first, we just had a good time, laughing, singing the Vietnamese songs. Everyone seemed happy. But then later, as each of the Vietnamese got up to speak his farewell to us, the party turned very sad.

The camp commander spoke first. Cheese translated. He wished us good luck and success in the future. Then, one by one, each officer and guard made a short speech. They told us they hoped we would visit Vietnam again when the country was at peace. They asked us to tell the American people about their country. They said how they hoped we would speak to our friends about the Vietnamese and their struggles. Some asked if we'd send them photos of our families. And they all wished us happiness in the years ahead.

As they spoke, more than one wiped away tears.

Finally, we all exchanged addresses and said good night.

Back in our room, someone said quietly, "Well, I guess we're going back." And no one seemed to argue.

We remained up talking most of the night. Everyone agreed how important it would be for us to stay in touch once we were back in the States so that we'd all know immediately if any one of us was in trouble. Once in a while, someone mentioned how we could still change our minds, even at the last minute, and walk off to the side at the airfield instead of going over to the American delegation. But I sensed it was said mostly out of fear of what might be waiting for us on our return. At this point, I knew, we'd all be going back.

March 16. We were up at five-thirty. We washed, shaved and dressed in new blue suits that we had been fitted for several days before. After breakfast, we collected our things and whatever souvenirs we had. I was nervous and excited. It was like going away on a trip for the first time in my life.

Then we walked around the courtyard, the buildings and the kitchen to say our last good-bys. All of us gave our razor blades to the guards. When I asked Cool Jerk if I could send him anything, he asked for some good books, in English.

Later, Mr. Bad came by with final instructions. He told us to control our emotions at the airfield. "Many cameras will be there," he said. "Do not do anything foolish. Do everything that everyone else does. Salute when you are supposed to—not as Captain Wilber did. As an officer, he may be able to do such things, but you must not. When you go by the tables, do not motion to us or wave good-by. That could be bad for you."

At last, we lined up to march out of the camp. There were thirty-three of us in group number two. Buses were parked on the street, outside the prison wall. Barricades had been set up all around, and crowds of people pushed against them. Policemen held them back, as if a parade were passing by.

Photographers and reporters were everywhere. A woman newspaper photographer, wearing a very short mini-skirt, ran alongside of us, taking pictures. Some of the guys whistled at her.

We filed onto the bus, and all eight of us sat together. Young and I were side by side. Outside, the people shouted and waved, *"Mỹ, mỹ, mỹ!"* Here and there I saw an angry face, but for the most part the onlookers showed no signs of bitterness or hate. I couldn't help wonder how it would have been if all of this was happening in the United States and we were Vietnamese prisoners. How would the American people have acted toward us, especially after twelve days of bombings that had destroyed a good part of the country? My guess was that nothing could have held them back.

One of the guards said to me, "The people are happy you go. They always say that when every American has gone from Vietnam, then there will be no more trouble."

I just sat there looking out, watching, and suddenly there was a terrible, sad feeling at leaving. I just couldn't stop my eyes from filling. I looked around at the other seven—and realized that it had gotten to all of them like that, too.

The buses started moving finally. I noticed how a number of the POWs were staring at us in disgust. Colonel Guy, sitting right across from me, was one of them.

As we rode to the airfield, it was hard to know just what I was feeling. I kept thinking how it was really true, I was on my way home. And I wondered how I'd act when I first saw my mother and the family. Would I cry? How would the family act? Would I do what I sometimes had imagined—get down and kiss the ground when I arrived?

We had a long wait at the airport. They gave us sandwiches and beer. Then we lined up just inside a doorway that opened onto the field. Outside, there were two tables, one with international observers, the other with delegates representing the four participants—the United States, North Vietnam, South Vietnam, and the NLF.

Off on the sides, behind barricades, were several hundred people and reporters. After about twenty minutes, they started calling out our names. I felt everything at once—happy, sad, nervous. I remembered Mr. Bad's instructions not to show any emotion or wave good-by.

My name was called. I started through the doorway. When I saw Mr. Bad watching me, I looked across at him and gave a little wink.

An American officer was standing at the far side of the table waiting for me. As I walked up to him, the emotion just rolled right over me. Tears ran down my cheeks.

The officer said, "Welcome back," and I saluted and we shook hands. "What are you so sad about?" he asked. Then three soldiers came up to escort me to the plane.

As I boarded, one by one all the crew and a group of WACs shook my hand. "Ask for anything you want," I was told.

Each POW had a military escort, an officer, accompany him during the flight. Mine was waiting for me, and we took our seats together.

As more men came aboard, it all turned lively and happy, everyone talking at once, people moving, cookies and coffee passed around. The crew, who had photos of themselves, asked for our autographs. Still, despite all the activity and noise, it wasn't really wild or frantic. Until we left the ground. All at once, then, all the guys started to shout and cheer. At last it hit us. It was for real. We were heading home!

The flight to Clark Air Force Base in the Philippines seemed to take no time at all. Before we knew it, the plane was touching down.

Colonel Guy was first off. He made a speech praising Nixon, which I saw later on TV. Then they called the rest of us, by rank.

As we deplaned, the colors were to one side, a group of army officers to the other. We saluted, then shook hands with the officers. People were crowded at the side, watching. They waved and shouted to us as we walked to the buses. Some pushed through to run up to us, shake hands, and tell us, "Welcome home."

A motor escort whisked us to the hospital. There, the entire staff was outside waiting, all lined up to greet us—doctors, nurses, officers. As I walked along the long receiving line, it reminded me of the "right-hand fellowship" ceremony when I was baptized at the age of twelve.

Soon after arriving at the hospital, I met my next escort, Spec. 4 Richman. Every POW had another escort assigned to him. The white prisoners had a white escort; black prisoners, a black escort, Puerto Rican prisoners, a Puerto Rican escort. I suppose it was the army's way of trying to make us feel more comfortable.

Richman seemed to be a nice guy. It was his job to do whatever he could for me, and he had taken six months of training to be prepared for it. He was always ready to get me anything I'd like at the PX, or to answer any questions. Each of us had received a booklet on all of the major current events that had taken place during the past five years, like landing a man on the moon. Richman was able to fill me in on things like that.

It was during the stay at the hospital that I realized that the army had already singled us out as "special" POWs. The first sign was when the eight of us were roomed in a different part of the hospital than the others, two to a room. In addition to one escort, as all of the other men had, each of our rooms had an additional enlisted man assigned to sit outside the door every night.

Each of us was given a free call home. When it came time for mine, Richman was right there in the phone booth with me. He dialed the number and held on to the phone until he got my mother on the line. Then he stayed next to me in the phone booth for the entire call.

It was great to hear my mother's voice. Still, after all this time, and with only a couple of minutes to talk, it was hard to find the words to say what I wanted, or to ask all the questions in my head. My mother had been alerted to the call and the whole family was there. At least, most of them. Two of my brothers were out, and by the way she told me, I sensed something was wrong. If so, I'd just have to wait until I got home to find out. My mother kept insisting everything was just great.

Any doubts I might have had that I was being treated differently were gone when one of the doctors, as he was checking me over, said, "We'll give you the same treatment as the other returnees, Daly—but you should know, you're a special POW."

Still, the luxury of the two days at the hospital was hard to believe sometimes. The army went all out, and it was great. There was nothing we couldn't have. The mess hall was set up to serve anything it was possible to think of—American dishes, Mexican dishes, Chinese food, any kind of cakes or cookies, beer—you name it, they had it.

The PX was equipped to sell just about everything at cut prices, and I couldn't resist buying a ring, a watch, and a tape deck that I arranged to have sent home. I found the barber shop hard to believe, with all the new gadgets, fancy chairs and other types of equipment I'd never seen. Lying back for a haircut, manicure and head massage, it was like I was dreaming the whole thing.

After five years in Vietnam POW camps, it sure was another world.

We left on Sunday morning with nine other POWs aboard a C–141 military transport. This time, the eight of us were no longer together. Elbert and I were the only two of our group on the plane. Our first stop was Honolulu.

We were dressed in army uniforms for the first time, and I was wearing my sergeant's stripes. While a POW, I'd moved up two ranks.

It was a good flight to Hawaii. At the airfield, we repeated the arrival ceremony that had taken place at Clark—only this time, in keeping with custom, we each had a *lei* placed around our neck.

During the time before taking off again, I bought some really beautiful flowers for my mother, even though I realized it was going to be many hours before I would see her. I also sent a bunch of flowers to my aunt.

Then, before we knew it, Elbert and I—and our escorts— reboarded the plane to take off for Kelly Air Force Base in Texas. The next time we touched down, at last, I'd really be back on the U.S. mainland.

It had been a long trip.

CHAPTER 25

Back in the U.S.A.

It took twenty-seven hours of flying time—sitting, sleeping in beds, and walking around—from Hanoi to McGuire Air Force Base in New Jersey. From there, it was only a twenty-minute helicopter hop to Fort Monmouth, where my family was waiting for me.

At McGuire, I was greeted by Colonel Wilbur F. Price, Team Chief of Operation Homecoming at Fort Monmouth. In no time, we were in the air—the colonel; Richman, my escort; the pilot; and me. During the flight, Colonel Price and I spoke over the headphones in the copter, and he filled me in on what to expect in the days ahead. He was warm and friendly, seemed sincerely happy I was home. Before we landed, he told me that if I ran into any problems at Fort Monmouth, or if I needed anything at all, to call him personally.

It was about six forty-five in the evening when we put down at Greeley Field. With the difference in time, it was still Sunday, March 18.

We climbed out into a strong, freezing wind—a big drop in temperature from Hanoi, Hawaii, or even Texas. To my surprise, despite the cold, there were about a hundred people waiting to greet me, plus an official party that included Major General Hugh F. Foster, the camp's commanding general; Colonel V. C. Devan; and Sergeant Major Jesse Tolson.

After saluting and shaking hands, we pushed through the

wind toward a waiting sedan. Photographers and reporters ran up to shout out questions or take pictures. I smiled and waved to the crowd, and they whistled and cheered. It was really a strange feeling, hard to believe that, this time, all of it was happening just for me.

"How does it feel to be back?" one reporter called out, and I answered, "Just great!"

A few minutes later, the car pulled up at Patterson Army Hospital in Fort Monmouth, where I was to be quartered. As we moved into the lobby, with the reporters right behind us, two girls working behind the desk squealed, "He's here! He's here!" As I walked past them, one called out, "Can we come up and visit with you sometime?"

"Any time you want to!" I shouted back, feeling like I was some kind of celebrity or rock star.

When I stepped off the elevator, that was the moment that really got to me, the one I'd thought and dreamed about so many times. I threw my arms around my mother, and the tears were streaming down for both of us. I hugged my sisters Pam and Phyllis and my brother Dennis, who I almost didn't recognize, now twenty-four, with long hair and a beard. My brothers James and Ralph weren't there, and I wondered why.

Finally, everyone left us together in a room where we could talk. I had a million questions—about my relatives, my friends. Who was married, who had kids now? When I asked about James and Ralph, my mother said they just couldn't make it, but I sensed something was wrong. I decided to try and find out about it as soon as the family left.

After a while my mother told me about my father and my grandmother. Both had died. My grandmother had passed on three years before. And though the family didn't get to see my father very often, word of his death was gotten to them when it happened—January 27, just one day after the agreements were signed.

The news of my father and grandmother really upset me. Suddenly, with all the excitement of being home, and the many hours of traveling, I was terribly tired. One of the doctors looked in on us and suggested it would be best if I rested. The family left to stay at Blair Hall, Fort Monmouth's VIP quarters.

As soon as I was alone, I called Colonel Price. I told him that

I was sure something was wrong as far as my brothers were concerned. He realized how upset I was about it and promised to try and find out whatever he could.

A few minutes later, Colonel Price called back. Both my brothers were being held for trial. They had been arrested for holding up a man in the street. The charge—armed robbery.

The next day, I read about myself in the papers. My picture was in the *Daily News*, and the first line of the story described me as "a Brooklyn man who reportedly made a peace plea over the Hanoi radio." The article said how my broadcast had called on President Nixon to sign the Vietnam peace accord and had urged that he not be allowed to "use the pretext of Thieu's disagreement to prolong the war."

Stories in the other papers all mentioned how I was one of eight former prisoners of war who reportedly had made antiwar statements while in captivity. None of these articles came right out and said anything about how charges could be made against me. But I got the message.

Meanwhile, an hour-by-hour schedule for every day at the hospital had been worked out. Aside from receiving complete medical and dental check-ups, I was to spend a number of hours each day with two representatives of Military Intelligence. It was their job, I was told, to obtain information that might help the army locate any men still listed as missing in action. But it didn't take me very long to realize that they were more than ready to find out about other things, like the Peace Committee, or any other former POWs I wanted to talk about.

Anton was right next door, and we saw each other every day. As I sat and talked with him there in the hospital, those years we were together in South Vietnam seemed a long time back.

Each day, I spent hours with my family. Our first big meal together was exactly what I had asked for: a dinner of soul food. Chitlings, collard greens, potato salad, corn bread, and more. It had been a long time since I'd had a meal like that.

After a few days, I was interviewed by Dr. Kamm, who asked me all kinds of general questions. When we spoke about my plans for the future—and I suddenly realized how I had none—I surprised myself by telling him that I might consider staying in the army if I was assigned to food services. It was a crazy idea, considering how I felt about the army. Yet, when I thought about getting out and trying to find some kind of job, it didn't seem all that way-out. And maybe, without my even realizing it, it might have been my way of saying: See, how can I be disloyal when I may even want to stay in the service?

All this time, Military Intelligence never missed a day with me. For hours at a time, they kept digging, asking for a day-to-day account of everything that had happened from the time I was captured, what camps I'd been in, what directions we'd walked to get to them, what other POWs had been with me, who had died.

I didn't try to cover up the other things, like my relationships with the Vietnamese, or the ideas I'd come to think about, or what I'd learned. Once, one of the questioners told me that it was possible what I said might be used against me, but they never discouraged me from going on about any of it.

I told them straight out how I'd come to believe that communism had done a lot of good for the Vietnamese people in the north. But I also told them what bothered me about it. That in turning the people away from God, it was, as the Jehovah's Witnesses would say, doing the work of the devil—"making bitter taste sweet."

I suppose, right then, all these different ideas and conflicts I went on about was really my way of saying how mixed up about things I was feeling. And I just went on talking freely, never really knowing how much harm I could be doing myself by saying the things I did.

Right then, there was someone who was really concerned about that very thing, but I knew nothing about it. Captain Harry D. Hoskins, an army attorney and member of the Judge Advocates General Court, had been trying for days to get permission to see me. The day after I'd arrived at Fort Monmouth, he had been assigned to represent me by Colonel Ross M. Goddard, Jr., the Staff Judge Advocate.

When Captain Hoskins had found out I was being interrogated by Military Intelligence, he realized that what I said during these sessions could be very damaging and used to build a case against me. He immediately wrote to the commanding general, Major General Foster, demanding to be allowed to see me so that he could offer legal advice.

Colonel Goddard received a copy of Captain Hoskins's memo, and answered it by writing to the commanding general himself. He claimed that my interrogation had "nothing to do with a criminal investigation," and recommended that Captain Hoskins not be allowed to meet with me at that time.

Captain Hoskins also talked with Colonel Price. Finally, both Colonel Goddard and Colonel Price agreed to schedule a meeting. Captain Hoskins was set to see me on March 26.

But then the Department of Defense got into it. The idea that Captain Hoskins had originally "demanded" to see me must have bugged someone at DOD. The appointment was canceled.

Of course, I had no idea at the time that all of this was happening. I just went along following my daily schedules—medical check-ups, consultations with doctors, hours of talking into a tape recorder.

Then, I had a personal problem that, compared to everything else, may not have been the most important thing in the world, but to me, at the time, it just about seemed like it. My family and neighbors on Madison Street in Brooklyn had planned a welcome-home party for me on the weekend, and I found it impossible to get a definite okay to leave the post. Colonel Price kept telling me how he was sure it wouldn't be a problem; however, he needed a final approval from Washington. The party was set for Sunday, April 1. Colonel Price promised to let me know by noon the day before at the very latest.

That Saturday morning, I stayed in my room, sweating it out. I had three men with me all the time now—Richman, a Sergeant Bland, and a guy from the military police. It was pretty clear that what the army called my "escorts" were really my guards.

At noon, I still hadn't heard from Colonel Price. I didn't bother calling him. Instead, I placed a call to the Department of the Army in Washington.

When I told the operator that I was a POW and had a problem I wanted to straighten out, she immediately connected me to "Operation Homecoming." In minutes, I was speaking to one of the generals.

I explained how I hadn't been home in two weeks and that I had to know right then if I could leave the hospital, since a party was being planned to celebrate my return. The general said he'd look right into it.

Ten minutes later, he called me back. My going home for the weekend was cleared.

What he didn't tell me was that I was going to have to take my "escorts" along with me. My mother was asked to put up Richman, Sergeant Bland and the MP for the night. In addition, two other MPs were sent along.

And still, at this time, there had been no charges of any kind brought against me.

When I arrived home, I found five threatening letters. I wasn't really surprised at getting them—still, it made me feel pretty bad, aside from being more than a little nervous at what some people might like to do.

The party got going about one o'clock, and it was great to see all my relatives and friends. There were so many things to talk about, so much catching up to do.

My old girl friend, Renee, wasn't there, and now I found out why. A friend told me she had married some time ago. The news really didn't bother me at all. I guess I had decided a long while back that nothing was ever going to come of it.

During the afternoon, my brother James called from prison. It was wonderful to talk to him, but all the time I kept thinking how, as soon as he hung up, he'd have to return to a prison cell. The call really upset me.

It was a fine party, all right, but after a while I felt like I just had to get away. I couldn't stand all the noise. Rock music was blasting like crazy. People kept coming and going. Before long, I had a very bad headache.

I stuck it out until about seven o'clock, then decided to go upstairs. A short time later, the party broke up.

Now that Military Intelligence, after eleven days of questioning, was finished with me, I finally got together with Captain Hoskins. Right from the start, he made it very plain what he thought I should do: get out of the army immediately!

He showed me copies of letters he had written, one a week before, requesting transcripts of the broadcasts allegedly made by me. He pointed out in the letter that the government had made a broadcast tape available to my family, so it couldn't be considered "privileged."

"There are no charges against you yet," Captain Hoskins explained, "but in my opinion it certainly looks like there will be. That's why I think you should be separated from the service now."

"But wouldn't that make it look like I'd done something wrong, like I was trying to hide something?" I asked. "Wouldn't it be better if I got my discharge when the other POWs did?"

Captain Hoskins considered my question, then told me, "Well, if you're going to stay in, even for a while, I think you will need a civilian lawyer." He wrote down the names of four attorneys. "I can't recommend which one you should use, but any one of these lawyers will be able to help you."

And that's how I became the client of attorney Elliott H. Vernon.

Many different things happened during the month of April, 1973—some good, some bad, and some that I myself brought about, completely mixed-up and hard to really understand.

The army must have decided I wasn't about to skip out, because it approved a ninety-day convalescent leave. My "escorts" brought me home—and left.

Even though I was officially on leave, I still spent a lot of time at Fort Monmouth, going back and forth many times each week. My medical examinations and dental clinic visits were still going on, and I was due to have an ear operation for a wart that had developed while I was in Vietnam. Also, at a later date, I was to have an eye operation to correct an affliction. I'd had it for many years, but it had become worse while I was a POW.

My first contact with Elliott Vernon was on April 6—and, from then on, we saw each other regularly, almost daily in the beginning. My main concern when I met Mr. Vernon was to ask him to help me get out of the army as quickly as possible. When Captain Hoskins had learned what I did a few days before, he had convinced me that it was more important than ever to try for separation. I had followed a crazy impulse. Without discussing it with anybody, I had signed papers requesting reenlistment for six years!

It's hard to know just why I did that. For one thing, I knew it would guarantee me the kind of medical treatment I might need. But the real reason, I think, was that I suddenly felt I'd never be able to make it as a civilian. I thought how a guy like me, without much of an education, with no training or skills, would really have a hard time getting along. The kind of job I'd end up with—if I could find one—would pay nothing at all. At least in the service, I figured, I could get a base pay of $537 a month, and many benefits besides. If I lived off post, I'd receive $150 a month for rent. While in the army, I could go to school, and for the first three years I'd be able to pick where I wanted to serve. Also, the really tempting bait the army held over your head was the $10,000 that came with reenlistment.

My religious beliefs, even though they'd changed some, were still in conflict with military service. But I managed to talk myself out of being bothered about that. Instead, I considered how I'd have plenty of chances to get across the teachings and ideas I believed in while in the army, and how I'd be sure to meet many guys who'd be able to use some preaching to.

Captain Hoskins thought my signing the reenlistment papers was a big mistake. On April 6, the first day I met with Elliott Vernon, he talked me into sending in a request demanding immediate release from active duty, withdrawing my previous reenlistment application, and, as was necessary, waiving any eligibility for medical treatment.

Elliott Vernon was bothered about the waiver and the loss of benefits. As a former Vietnam paratrooper with the 173rd Airborne Brigade who had been released with a disability, he had seen cases where men turned up with latent diseases years later, like malaria or nervous conditions.

After listening to me go over all the details of my experiences as a POW, and how I was treated after returning home, Mr. Vernon was convinced that the important step to take at that time was for him to try to learn if the army really planned to press charges against me. If they did, he explained, chances were that my request to get out would be flagged, anyway. And even though I was taking a risk by staying in for the ninety-day convalescent-leave period, following it I'd be able to get discharged without losing any benefits. That is, of course, if I hadn't been court-martialed and jailed by then.

"You were right to take Captain Hoskins's advice and get a civilian attorney," he said. "A military lawyer can't help too much from here on in. He's not allowed to represent any individual against the United States government, and he can't go into Federal District Court.

"In your situation," Mr. Vernon continued, "I think you've been deprived of certain constitutional guarantees—namely, the right to counsel while you were being questioned by MI. You know, I really believe that the military justice system is fairer than the civilian in serious offenses; it goes out of its way to give safeguards provided by the Supreme Court. But in your case, it seems they were trying to find out certain information under the guise of obtaining background on the men missing in action. You were a suspect while this questioning was going on; therefore you had the right to remain silent and not to be questioned without the benefit of an attorney. I think the entire procedure was tainted."

As I listened to Mr. Vernon, as sincere as he sounded, I found myself wondering, knowing his service background, if maybe he was working with the army—if I could really trust him. It was a heck of a thing to think, especially when he'd jumped right in and even told me not to worry about the fee, that we'd work all that out another time. Still, the way things had been going, I just couldn't help it.

It didn't take long, though, for me to feel better about it. As soon as I saw Mr. Vernon go into action, really begin to get after everybody, right on up to the top, I knew I could trust him.

Immediately, he started writing letters demanding to know if the army planned on bringing charges against me, and insisting on transcripts of any statements or broadcasts I was supposed to have made.

Right about then, the whole question of how the POWs had been treated by the Vietnamese was getting plenty of space in the newspapers. A story about Kushner ran in the *New York Times.* He told about the rough times in the south and how many of us had died. He also admitted that he had made radio broadcasts against the war, and said straight out that even now he refused to repudiate them.

In another *Times* story, Captain Walter Wilber told how he had given statements and taped broadcasts. He pointed out that he had never been tortured by the Vietnamese, and said that his remarks had been given voluntarily from the "pressure of conscience."

Of course, there were plenty of articles taking the other point of view. Captain James A. Mulligan, Jr., who'd been a prisoner for seven years, gave an interview telling of all the tortures he claimed POWs had endured. As for the guys who had made broadcasts and had cooperated with the Vietnamese, he said, "Those guys will get what's coming to them. Any guy who goes to Hanoi and gets religion about the war after he's shot down is a pure phony."

Within a short time after taking my case, Elliott Vernon had a long telephone talk with Brigadier General Laurence H. Williams, Assistant Judge Advocate General for Military Law with the Department of the Army in Washington. General Williams was completely familiar with my situation because he had spoken with Captain Hoskins.

I listened while Mr. Vernon told the general how I'd been treated since my arrival home. He also brought up all the newspaper stories about me.

"There is no intention on the part of the Department of the Army to let any charges be pressed," General Williams claimed. "We are attempting—and so far successfully—to prevent anyone from bringing such charges."

When Mr. Vernon pressed him further, General Williams said, "There is no intention—and I have this on the highest authority—to press any such charges. If he wishes a discharge, and we're not talking about anything but a good discharge, we're prepared to go ahead with that. It will take a week or two."

Then the general indicated he thought it really might be best for me to stay in the army for now and continue my check-ups. "We're concerned—and I say this sincerely—for his health. We want to make sure that he's not getting out because he fears something that is not going to happen, and possibly to his detriment."

Mr. Vernon then asked General Williams if he would be willing to put a guarantee in writing that there'd be no charges brought if I was to remain in the service for my medical check-ups. The general replied that he couldn't do that.

"But I'm an officer," he said, "and if he were court-martialed, you could call me and I would have to state that I told you that charges were not going to be pressed, and that this was the basis on which he remained in."

"You're speaking for the Commander and Chief of Staff in this regard?" Mr. Vernon asked.

"That's right," the general said.

With all of this going on, I still managed to have some fun. A few days after the start of my leave, I received two tickets for a Saturday night American Legion dance. Ever since I'd been back, my brother Dennis had been telling me about Ira Jean Worthy, a girl from South Carolina he said I just had to meet next time she visited New York. Ira Jean was in town the night of the dance, and I asked her to go.

We had a fine time that night. I immediately felt that Ira Jean was someone I wanted to know much better. She was soft, quiet and friendly. It was easy being with her, like we'd really known each other a long time, instead of this being our first date.

A funny thing happened when we arrived at the dance. They announced us as "Mr. and Mrs. James Daly." We just laughed about it.

On April 16, Elliott Vernon wrote a letter to Colonel Price and included a copy of an Associated Press story which indicated that officials in Washington were getting ready to bring forward charges against some former POWs. In the letter, he recalled that both Colonel Price and General Williams had assured him that no charges were being planned. He asked Colonel Price to determine if the news story accurately stated the official Pentagon policy.

Three days later, Colonel Price replied that, based on questions he'd put to the Department of the Army, he was able to determine that no charges were to be made. He also enclosed a transcript of a press conference on the subject of POWs that had been held April 12 by Dr. Roger Shields, Special Assistant to the Secretary of Defense on Prisoner of War matters. During the press conference, Dr. Shields had been questioned over and over again on what was being done about POWs who were supposed to have been helpful to the Vietnamese. One reporter asked specifically about Robert Garwood, and Dr. Shields said he had no information on him. Regarding possible charges to be filed against any of the former prisoners, he would only say that none were pending. He wouldn't answer positively about the future. "What might happen, I really don't care to comment on," he said.

One thing he did say, though. "We are not going to prefer charges, for example, against any man on the basis of any statement he may have made, simply on that basis."

But when a reporter asked if investigations were underway then against any former POW, Dr. Shields again refused to comment.

On April 20, Mr. Vernon decided that since he still had not received copies of the documents he had asked for, he would write directly to the Secretary of Defense, Elliot H. Richardson. He sent copies of his letter to Secretary of the Army Robert F. Froehlke; Major General Verne L. Bowers, the Adjutant General; Colonel Price; Captain Hoskins—and me.

So as April came to an end, we were still trying to find out just where we were at. Mr. Vernon remained confident that if ever charges were brought by someone, we'd come out okay. In making antiwar statements, he assured me, I had done nothing more than some officers, government officials, political leaders and show-business celebrities. Besides, he honestly believed that the army was trying its best to adhere to the "forgive and honor" policy regarding POWs established by Melvin Laird when he had been Secretary of Defense.

Then, with the start of May, I began making plans to go to Washington to attend the POW dinner to be given at the White House by President Nixon. I had spoken to most of the other guys, and they were planning to go, too.

In a way, I thought it was crazy for me to want to attend an event like this. But the truth was, I wouldn't have missed it for anything.

CHAPTER 26

The Real Enemy

With Ira Jean stuck in South Carolina, I wasn't sure who to take to the White House dinner. Finally, I made arrangements to bring my friend's sister-in-law, Marie.

Right up until the end of May, a few days before the event, there was still a mixup over our invitations. I was beginning to think maybe the White House wasn't all that anxious to have me there. Finally, though, it was agreed that we should come, and then straighten everything out after our arrival.

Just before the day of the dinner, Chenoweth called from Portland to tell me that he'd learned how Colonel Guy was in Washington looking to stir things up. I called Elliott Vernon to tell him about it. He already knew. It was true, he said. But there was nothing to be done at this point but wait.

All the guys who'd been in the Peace Committee, except Rayford, came to Washington. It was the first time since Hawaii that we were all together again. Everyone really looked different, all sharped up for the affair. Especially me.

I had decided I wanted to look very outstanding, so I went out and bought an army dress blue uniform. Some of the enlisted men I saw had on tux, but there were very few formal blues around.

During the afternoon, each state had its own POW get-together. Then, before the dinner, all of us were asked to attend an address by President Nixon in an auditorium at the Department of Defense. While this was going on, the women went to a reception given by Mrs. Nixon.

Over five hundred former POWs filled the room. Familar faces were all around me, guys I'd known, or seen, in all those Vietnam prison camps, north and south.

The President was given a tremendous reception. At one point during his talk, he made reference to the *Pentagon Papers*, saying how every country had its secrets, and that anyone who'd steal these documents should get the punishment deserved. When he asked the men if they agreed, everyone jumped to his feet. The applause lasted almost fifteen minutes.

All seven of us were standing, too, applauding like the rest. At that minute, it seemed just about impossible not to. Especially with Colonel Guy and others looking over at us.

Then President Nixon spoke about how while all of us were in prison, other citizens were out protesting the war, demonstrating in the streets, burning flags. But we remained patriotic, he said. And now, the proof of how wrong those others were was that he had gotten us home again.

Once more everyone stood and applauded. Among them, clapping like crazy, were many of the same guys who'd called Nixon every name imaginable on December 18, 1972, during the Christmas bombings.

Finally, the President offered to shake every man's hand. One by one, we filed up to him.

Bay, one of the guys who'd been in Harker's group before I'd joined the Peace Committee, was right in front of me. When he reached the President, I heard him ask, "Sir, why did you order that bombing in December? Did you realize how horrible it was?"

Nixon looked really shocked, like he couldn't believe anyone could have the nerve to ask him a question like that. He said something about what a difficult decision it had been, one of the most important he'd ever made. How it needed to be done to get the POWs home.

Then it was my turn. There I was, face to face with the President of the United States, a man I had no respect for, who I'd really hated while watching Vietnamese women and children fighting back against the bombers he'd sent to destroy them. Yet, when he shook my hand, I lied right in his face. I said, "Sir, it was an honor to serve. If I had to do it again, I'd give my life any time for my country."

Who knows why I had to say those words? Why I just hadn't been silent. Maybe it was the pressure of knowing that I'd soon be accused of collaborating with the enemy, and somehow I just had to prove I was as much a loyal American as anyone. Maybe it was hearing my mother say, "Now don't you go and say anything to get yourself in trouble!" Maybe it was because I felt as patriotic as any man in the room. That I knew how if my country was fighting a cause for freedom and justice, a cause I believed to be true and right, I really would be willing to give my life for it.

Sometimes, I guess, it's just not that easy to understand what makes us do the things we do.

The dinner was held in a tent on the White House lawn, with dancing inside. Sammy Davis, Jr., and Phyllis Diller entertained. It was really a beautiful affair.

When I came across Colonel Guy, he was very friendly and introduced me to his wife.

Later, the White House was opened to everyone, and we were permitted to tour inside on our own. I went in to look around with Chenoweth, Young, McMillon—and my old buddy, the smoke fiend, Pheister.

The following day, Friday, we all flew home.

On Tuesday, May 29, just a few days after the trip to Washington, I received a call from NBC Television.

"Would you like to give us a statement concerning the charges brought against you?" I was asked.

"What charges?"

"Oh, I see you haven't been informed that Colonel Guy has brought charges against you and seven other former POWs?"

"Sure I'll make a statement!" I said.

In no time flat, the TV crew was at my house. They told me what the charges were, a whole string of them that included aiding the enemy.

In answer to the interviewer's questions, I said how I thought that any prisoner bringing such charges was probably looking to cover up for himself. "How come Colonel Guy was the only prisoner in my camp that I knew of who received packages from home?" I asked.

"The statements I made were antiwar statements," I said. "I'm quite sure Colonel Guy made the same statements that I made. I think it's stupid for him to bring charges against another prisoner!"

That night, minutes after the interview was on the news, I received a call from Elliott Vernon. He had often told me not to make any statements about anything. Now, after watching me on television, he was very upset.

"Those comments can have an adverse effect," he told me. "Then there's the other things you must have said that they didn't use on the air but that are now a matter of record on the TV tape in the NBC files."

I agreed not to give any more interviews. That night and the next day were spent dodging the carloads of reporters that collected around the house.

The following afternoon, May 30, I appeared with Mr. Vernon before Colonel V. C. Devan at Fort Monmouth to officially hear the charges. Representatives of the Office of the Staff Judge Advocate were also there.

All eight members of the Peace Committee had been charged by Colonel Guy with failure to adhere to the Code of Conduct for prisoners of war. Aside from promoting disloyalty, undermining discipline and aiding the enemy, we were all accused of failure to obey a lawful order and disrespect toward a superior officer.

As Colonel Devan continued to read all the details of these charges, despite all of Mr. Vernon's warnings, I started to speak out against them. Mr. Vernon interrupted and asked me to remain silent. "This is not the proper forum," he said. "We will have our day in court."

When he'd finished, Colonel Devan seemed really sympathetic. He placed no restrictions on me, although he believed it would be in my best interests not to roam around the post and mix with the other soldiers.

"I really didn't expect this!" he said. And to make it easier for me to get around and take care of some personal errands, he offered me his private car and driver.

Later, back in Elliott Vernon's office, we went over each charge, one at a time. He told me he really doubted that a trial would be held, considering public opinion and the present political atmosphere. Any officer or enlisted man, he explained, can file court-martial charges against a military colleague. But now, under the Uniform Code of Military Justice, the Secretaries of the Army and the Navy (five of us were army men, three marines) must convene an investigative board to determine whether the charges warranted a court-martial.

In the opinion of Mr. Vernon, they didn't. But even if a trial did happen, he insisted, he was confident that we would win it.

Several days later, he received a brief reply to his letter to the Secretary of the Army from Major General Harold Parker of the Office of the Judge Advocate General. It simply stated that the "matters raised are being carefully considered." Now, Mr. Vernon wrote another letter insisting that he be sent all information regarding the planned Board of Inquiry—and, once again, asking for the documents and transcripts he needed to conduct my defense.

As we got into June, it was pretty clear that the army was in no hurry to make any decision, one way or the other. All eight of us were flagged, of course—no getting out now. And no one seemed to care how much of a strain we were under sweating it out.

It wasn't until July 3, 1974, that the army and the navy finally made a decision. On that day, all charges brought by Colonel Guy were dismissed for insufficient evidence.

But that was a little late for Abel Kavanaugh. On June 27, he had killed himself by shooting a bullet into his head.

On the very next day, he had been scheduled to return to his marine camp after a convalescent leave. With the charges hanging over him, he just couldn't make it.

The funeral was in Denver. Sandra Kavanaugh, Abel's wife, wanted all of us who had lived with him to serve as pallbearers. Everyone but Branch was able to get there.

It was a military funeral at a Catholic church. Marines carried the casket, and the six of us lined up along both sides of the aisle.

It was a tough, terribly sad day for all of us. Just watching Sandra, who was pregnant again, and their lovely five-year-old daughter, really shook us up.

Riati tried to talk about it on television. Halfway through the interview, he burst out crying and shouted, "Why don't they leave us alone?"

Sandra Kavanaugh made it very clear how she felt when the

reporters questioned her. "The North Vietnamese kept him alive for five years, and then his own country killed him," she said. "I blame Colonel Guy and the Pentagon for his death."

Back in New York, after the charges were dropped, I read some newspaper editorials about Kavanaugh's death.

The *New York Post* said: "Rather too late for Marine Sgt. Abel Larry Kavanaugh, 24, who had shot himself to death six days earlier, the Army and Navy recently decided to drop all charges of aid-to-the-enemy and other misconduct brought against Kavanaugh and seven other enlisted former PWs by Air Force Col. Theodore W. Guy, head of their compound in North Vietnam. Though it was a merciful, commendable decision, sparing his fellows the ordeal Sgt. Kavanaugh did not choose to face, it can hardly console his young, pregnant widow . . ."

The editorial then stated that Abel's wife was considering filing a suit against his accuser. It printed Colonel Guy's response to this: " 'I am not afraid of anything. If they do sue, I think it would be very unfortunate for the people I charged. I think they are better off shutting up right now. They should quit while they are ahead.' "

"That's quite a thought," the editorial concluded, "for the long nights of Sandra Kavanaugh."

The *New York Times* also saw fit to editorialize on Kavanaugh's death. It said, in part: "The decision of the Army and the Navy to dismiss misconduct charges against seven former prisoners of war is a wise and compassionate act, although tragically too late for an eighth accused enlisted man who took his life while awaiting the outcome of the Pentagon review. . . . The Pentagon's policy of forgiveness follows an American tradition of amnesty after wars that goes back to President Washington. In that tradition, it is time to move on to a wider amnesty, not only for the two officers who still live under the shadow of charges arising from their conduct as war prisoners but to the thousands of other Americans who have suffered in their own way, in jail or in exile, because of their opposition to a war that the American people are now trying to put behind them. President Nixon, who has vowed no forgiveness for these tormented young men, could help to heal a wounded nation by following the compassionate example set by his service secretaries."

CHAPTER 27

The End of the Ordeal

I suppose it might have made good sense for me to get out of the army fast like Rayford, Branch and Chenoweth did. Right after the charges were dismissed, all three put in for their discharge.

But a couple of things still bothered me, and I wanted to clear them up. At this point, I really didn't think I was ready to consider the six-year reenlistment that I had thought about before. Still, with the job situation as rough as it was, sometimes I wasn't all that sure.

Another important consideration was that if I stayed in the army, even for a while, I could take on-the-job training under the "Project Transition" program. This allowed a soldier, as long as he was still in the service, to take rehabilitation training in preparation for a civilian job.

And just the idea that I was not allowed to reenlist, even if I wanted to, really bugged me. Somehow, that didn't sound much like an honorable discharge. As I saw it, the decision to stay in or get out should have been mine.

The one other thing I was disturbed about was never having received my Purple Heart. Elliott Vernon had inquired about it and had been assured I'd get it. It was important—not only because I was entitled to it, but because if I should take an examination for a civil service job, it would allow me extra points.

Since I was scheduled to report to Walter Reed Hospital in Washington during July for an examination in connection with my eye operation, I decided this would be a good time to personally find out, from the top army brass, just where I was at as far as reenlistment—and the Purple Heart. I made an appointment to see Major General Verne L. Bowers, the Adjutant General at the Department of the Army.

General Bowers was very pleasant. After I explained why I had come to see him, he suggested that even though under present policy none of the army men who had been charged were eligible for reenlistment, in my case my history as a conscientious objector was also a factor.

"You know, regardless of where you are stationed, there's no guarantee that you won't have to bear arms again some time," General Bowers said. "Be truthful—are you prepared to do that?"

I considered his question carefully before answering. Then I said, "If you want a truthful answer, I don't think I can say 'yes.' "

"Well, we also took that into account when we stopped you from being able to reenlist," the general told me.

Before I left, he assured me that I'd receive the Purple Heart.

A few days later, July 24, I was back in my room at Fort Monmouth when I heard the news on the radio. At first, I just couldn't believe it.

The Pentagon announced that Edward W. Leonard, now a major in the air force, had filed charges of mutiny against seven former prisoners of war—the same group of enlisted men who had recently been cleared of misconduct charges! Major Leonard accused the army of having failed to investigate the earlier charges filed by Air Force Colonel Theodore W. Guy.

So, unbelievably, it was starting all over again, and I had to wonder how come General Bowers seemed to know nothing about it. At least, now that they were out, Chenoweth, Rayford and Branch couldn't be tried.

Elliott Vernon was reassuring. He explained that in his opinion "mutiny" required the existence of a military hierarchy that one could overthrow, or attempt to overthrow. At the camp, with officers and enlisted men separated, there was never any control by officers who could be mutinied against.

Most of the other charges were similar to the last ones. Mr. Vernon believed there was insufficient evidence to substantiate them. Still, reading them over, they sounded pretty bad.

I was accused of refusing to obey Leonard's order to "stop all forms of cooperation and collaboration with the enemy." (When this was shouted out in the courtyard, I hadn't even joined the PC yet.)

As a member of the Peace Committee, I was charged with a whole list of offenses, even including how on Christmas Eve in 1971 we all joined in the singing of the anthem of the National Liberation Front.

All of us were accused of trying to "impair and influence the loyalty, morale and discipline of Sergeant Don A. MacPhail." The truth was, we told MacPhail everything the charges claimed—and I wouldn't change one word of it today—"that the United States should not be in Vietnam, that the United States was committing atrocities against the Vietnamese people, that the money to keep the war going was going to rich Americans and that American soldiers were being killed for no reason."

Just like before, the army and navy were dragging their feet —no rush at all to make a decision on the charges. I couldn't help but think how, with all this stuff in the news about us, it wouldn't be surprising if somebody who considered himself a patriotic American decided it was his duty to catch up with us and blow our brains out.

In August, with the charges still hanging over the four of us, Chenoweth held a press conference outside the White House. The syndicated columnist Mary McGrory quoted him as saying, "I hope it won't take another death to get the charges dropped." And then she pointed out how the war still wasn't over for a lot of other Americans, aside from us. She wrote, "The Pentagon, frightened by the shattering spectacle of [Kavanaugh's] funeral on national television, hurriedly announced there would be no prosecutions. But amnesty eludes the returned prisoners, as it does all other Americans who dramatized their resistance to the war . . ."

By the end of September, 1973, the Department of the Army still had not completed its investigation or determined whether there was enough evidence to substantiate a court-martial. Elliott Vernon then decided to take the matter into the courts.

It wasn't necessary. On October 5, I was told to report to

Colonel Charles M. Milam, Deputy Commander at Fort Monmouth. Mr. Vernon appeared with me.

The statement read to us was brief: "The Secretary of the Army has dismissed charges of misconduct during captivity brought against you by Major Edward W. Leonard, USAF. You will be separated from the service as soon as medical and administrative processing is completed. No Administrative Board action will be taken."

That same day, the office of the Assistant Secretary of Defense put out a news release stating that sixty-five of sixty-seven witnesses listed by Major Leonard had been interviewed, and it was found that "much of the expected testimony would be hearsay and inadmissible as evidence in a judicial proceeding." The last line of the press release stated that we would "not be eligible for reenlistment under the current qualitative standards for the Volunteer Army."

Before the day was over, I was officially out of the army. As long as I remained in the service, there was nothing to prevent other ex-POWs from bringing charges against me. This time, I agreed—the faster I split, the better. And now, at least, I was eligible for a disability pension, and medical facilities for a five-year period.

Almost seven years had passed since that January morning at Fort Hamilton in Brooklyn. I knew it was going to take a while to really get the feeling of civilian life again. And I had a lot to think about, memories to relive, ideas to work through, to understand.

I had returned to a very different society. During the time I was away, blacks had made progress—but I saw this more as a token, ways of pacifying, like the whole Black Capitalism Program, or the gains in politics.

I remembered how Mr. Bad had always said, "If enough people get dissatisfied, a capitalistic country must do something to ease them down." Now, the rioting I remembered in 1965 had quieted, but conditions weren't that much better. Corruption was everywhere. Not only in the United States, but all over the world, including the socialistic countries. The Jehovah's Witnesses saw it as one of the first signs that the Armageddon was not far off. And often, it seemed to me that they were right—that the end was near.

Even so, I still had to find my way in the society I'd come back to. Somehow, to get beyond some low-paying job that would force me to live in a ghetto, just getting by, just existing.

And I thought, maybe in a way I was lucky I went to Vietnam. So many of those who stayed at home in my neighborhood had gotten caught up in crime, like my brothers, or hooked on dope. It could have happened to me like that.

More and more, I found myself looking toward religion again. In a strange kind of way, the entire experience of Vietnam, even the Communist teachings, had helped me to remember a good deal of what I'd been taught long before by the Jehovah's Witnesses, and to give me a clearer idea about it, too.

In many ways, the differences between them weren't that great. "Each man will rejoice from his own labor." "No man will build and another man inhabit."

The big difference, of course, was that the Jehovah's Witnesses believed that no man can bring peace to the world—except the Son of God. As for the Communist state, which didn't allow the Jehovah's Witnesses the same freedom as other religions because they openly denounced the government, they saw communism as a tool of the devil, helping the people to live better, but turning them away from God.

For a long time after my discharge from the army I was very angry. It disturbed me to see how people accepted the war as being over, while Vietnamese were still being killed every day, almost 50,000 of them by the end of 1973.

I deeply wished that one day soon that tormented country would finally be at peace. That after the thousands of years of war and suffering, its people could find happiness and contentment.

And I looked forward to the time when I could return there for a visit. As Cheese had often said, it takes a long time to know a friend. And that is how, I know, I would be welcomed.

In the meantime, though, I'd have to get busy. Finding a place for myself was going to be a full-time job.

In December of 1973, I knew for sure I was officially back again. That's when I received a "welcome home" letter from the Governor of New York State, Nelson Rockefeller. Nine months after my return.

An Afterword
Lee Bergman

After almost seven years in the army, five lived as a prisoner of war, assimilating into a competitive civilian society proved an arduous, often disconcerting task for James Daly.

During the months following his separation from the service, he found employment as a clerk, as a department store trainee, as a nighttime factory worker at $2.25 an hour.

James's dual objectives made this an especially difficult period of adjustment. He hoped not only to involve himself in a work situation that offered a promising and hopeful future—but also to gain a sense of personal understanding, to find priorities among the maze of values, to learn who he was and what he was to become.

Along the way, he experienced periods of frustration, disillusionment and, at times, an unshakable sense of depression.

The years in Vietnam, the memories and the friendships, were never set aside. With regularity, the former members of the Peace Committee called and wrote to one another, and on several occasions converged on some selected spot for a weekend of camaraderie—Louisville, New York City, Chicago, Washington.

One most significant aspect of James Daly's new life was his flourishing relationship with Ira Jean Worthy.

On a rainy Saturday afternoon in April, 1974, James and Ira Jean were married in a traditional ceremony at a handsome old church in Brooklyn. Following the wedding, hundreds of friends *and relatives joined the bridal party for a gala dinner reception. Everyone danced into the night.*

Soon after, James became the owner of his own business. As the first POW to be aided by the Small Business Administration, he purchased a small automatic laundry in New Jersey.

James Daly is optimistic about his future; however, realistically, it is open to question. To what extent the experience of Vietnam will influence it is also problematical. Elliott Vernon had an interesting comment in this regard.

"Sometimes I questioned if it wouldn't have been better for James to go to trial and be vindicated before a court of law, rather than have the charges dismissed on the basis of what the Pentagon characterizes as 'compassion—and forgive and honor.' As things are, there is still some stigma remaining, and that's why I wonder if it may have been more beneficial to have tried the case. Only history will tell us, and James's future."

As James Daly looks ahead, the years behind him and the enemy he learned to know shall never be forgotten.

On his bureau in his bedroom, a large vase holds three American flags, in place of flowers. Beside it is a display of two miniature American flags and an official flag of the United States Army —gifts of his trip to Washington, D.C., for the POW White House dinner. To one side of the flags is a framed picture of Martin Luther King, Jr.

Missing from the bureau top, where it most certainly would have been proudly displayed had he ever received it, is the Purple Heart he earned on the battlefields of Vietnam.